MERELY JUDGMENT

Constitutionalism and Democracy

GREGG IVERS AND
KEVIN T. MCGUIRE,
EDITORS

Merely Judgment

IGNORING, EVADING, AND
TRUMPING THE SUPREME COURT

Martin J. Sweet

UNIVERSITY OF VIRGINIA PRESS

CHARLOTTESVILLE AND LONDON

University of Virginia Press
© 2010 by the Rector and Visitors of the University of Virginia
All rights reserved
Printed in the United States of America on acid-free paper

First published 2010

9 8 7 6 5 4 3 2 1

LIBRARY OF CONGRESS CATALOGING-IN-PUBLICATION DATA

Sweet, Martin J., 1970–
  Merely judgment : ignoring, evading, and trumping the Supreme Court /
Martin J. Sweet.
    p. cm. — (Constitutionalism and democracy)
  Includes bibliographical references and index.
  ISBN 978-0-8139-3058-9 (cloth : alk. paper) — ISBN 978-0-8139-3077-0
(e-book)
    1. Civil rights—United States. 2. Constitutional law—United States.
3. United States. Supreme Court. 4. Judgments—United States. 5. Obedience
(Law)—United States. 6. Affirmative action programs—United States. I. Title.
  KF4749.S93 2010
  342.7308'5—dc22

                                                          2010012581

To Anat

CONTENTS

TABLES AND FIGURES

ACKNOWLEDGMENTS

This project, which began in earnest more than a decade ago, could not have been accomplished without the assistance and support of many individuals and organizations. Some of the individuals were intimately involved as the work developed, reading, editing, raising questions, challenging me, and encouraging me to pursue new lines of argument and evidence. I am particularly grateful to my dissertation committee members, the 2004 and 2005 Edward S. Corwin Prize committee members, the Constitutionalism and Democracy series editors, anonymous reviewers of this work for the press, and the editorial team at the University of Virginia Press. Many other friends and not so friendly interlocutors at lectures and conferences have had a less direct but no less important effect. In fact, some of the most cogent criticism I received came in the form of offhand acerbic remarks that I did not fully appreciate at the time. With the benefit of time, I am exceptionally proud to be part of an academy that prizes the value and practice of free speech, even—perhaps especially—when such language might be slightly painful to hear.

John Witte, Don Downs, David Canon, and Ken Mayer served on my dissertation committee at the University of Wisconsin–Madison, and I benefited from their unique strengths and talents. In 1997, when this project was first formulated, I conceptualized the issue of the value of affirmative action as one ultimately grounded in political theory. I continued to explore the legal and theoretical issues under Don Downs, but I also began to pursue the institutional dimensions of this issue, in the course of which I learned a great deal from both David Canon and Ken Mayer. A critical piece to the puzzle was added when I became fully engaged in policy studies with John Witte. While I was always given guidance and helpful suggestions, these four outstanding scholars never once attempted to make the work anything different from what I envisioned or pursued. Each pushed and prodded, but in the end, they gave me the freedom to flourish or fail on my own.

The University of Wisconsin–Madison, Florida Atlantic University, Clara Penniman and the University of Wisconsin Distinguished Graduate Fellowship, the Institute for Legal Studies, the Wisconsin Policy Research Institute, Dickinson College, the Centennial Center at the American Political Science Association, the Faculty Colloquium in Public Law at Princeton University, the University of Haifa Faculty of Law, the University of Haifa School of Political Science, and the Honors College of Florida Atlantic University provided financial and other support for my work. To those institutions and the individuals who form them, I am very grateful. As well, I appreciate the assistance I received in conceptualizing ideas, tracking down sources, and refining my thought from many others, including Booth Fowler, Charles Franklin, Marc Galanter, Evan Gerstmann, Howard Gillman, Mark Graber, Roger Hartley, Tom Keck, Mark Kessler, Bert Kritzer, Susan Lawrence, Dan Lipson, Michael McCann, Terri Peretti, Mitch Pickerill, Harry Pohlman, john a. powell, John Ransom, Andy Rudalevige, Howard Schweber, Tim Steigenga, Keith Whittington, and especially Chuck Epp and Dan Farber. Both Chuck and Dan fostered my love of politics and law and have long tolerated my ideas and idiosyncrasies, traits that won them their titles of teachers and colleagues.

I would also like to thank the editorial team and series editors at the University of Virginia Press. Dick Holway, Raennah Mitchell, Mark Mones, Morgan Myers, Marjorie Pannell, Gregg Ivers, and Kevin McGuire guided me exceptionally well through the publication labyrinth.

Special mention must be made of two people, Don Downs and Anat Hakim, both of whom know they have my eternal gratitude but nevertheless deserve public accolades. Don, whom I have already mentioned, was the primary reason I entered the academy. When I was an undergraduate in the fall semester of 1989, I watched him command a rapt student audience in 165 Bascom. Returning to Madison to teach and learn formally from Downs and others largely pales in comparison with the education I received and continue to receive from Downs over a drink, during a football game, in Independence Hall, at a fancy dinner, or over the phone. And it is with great pride that I formally thank my wife, Anat. This project would not have been finished without her assistance. Her love and support have simply made all of my dreams come true. May our children, Elli, Solomon, and Leo, learn this lesson from us—*chase your dreams.*

Some material in this book previously appeared in another publication and is reproduced here with slight changes by permission of the publisher: "Minority Business Enterprise Programmes in the United States of America: An Empirical Investigation," Affirmative Action Symposium, *Journal of Law and Society* 33, no. 1 (2006): 160–80.

MERELY JUDGMENT

INTRODUCTION

The judiciary . . . may truly be said to have neither FORCE nor WILL,
but merely judgment.
Alexander Hamilton, Federalist 78.

In 1983, a dispute over a fairly small contract to install fixtures in
a city jail began that would end years later by placing the U.S. Supreme Court at the center of the nation's affirmative action policies.[1]
The city of Richmond, Virginia, had passed a law requiring construction firms bidding on government work to subcontract at least
30 percent of the dollars at stake in the contract to minority-owned
businesses. The contract in question, which called for a bidder to
supply and install plumbing supplies in the Richmond jail, received
only a single bid. J. A. Croson Company, an Ohio-based mechani-
cal, plumbing, and heating contractor with a local office in Richmond, entered a bid that did not provide for subcontracting to any
minority-owned firms. The City of Richmond rejected Croson's bid
as noncompliant with the bid specifications and opted to rebid the
contract. In response to the rebidding of the contract, Croson filed
a federal lawsuit against the city. After almost six years of circuitous
litigation and appeals, in January 1989 the U.S. Supreme Court
ruled in *City of Richmond v. J.A. Croson Co.* that the equal protection clause of the Fourteenth Amendment forbids governments
from operating race-based programs like Richmond's.[2]

This book explores the question of what happens *after* the Supreme Court decides a case. After the legislation, litigation, and judicial decisions have settled, what then? How are these judicial decisions interpreted and implemented? What is the concrete impact of these sometimes abstract legal decisions? The lessons learned from exposing the contingent nature of the effects of judicial decision making then serve as the basis for constructing a normative view of constitutional interpretation and the relationship between the courts and the elected branches of government. As I find that political institutions enjoy considerable discretion in deciding whether and how to follow judicial decisions, largely because of their ability to defang would-be plaintiffs, I argue for a concept of judicial primacy that would better protect individuals in their enjoyment of constitutional rights.

Promise and Reality

Following the Supreme Court's ruling in *Croson,* Richmond would abandon its affirmative action program and the J. A. Croson Company would no longer be subject to the minority set-aside requirement in competing for government contracts.[3] Croson's right to equal protection under the law had been vindicated by the Court. Yet throughout the 1990s and the first decade of the twenty-first century, this one decision about fixtures in a Richmond jail played out in cities and states across the United States that had never been party to the litigation.[4] Many American cities had affirmative action programming similar to Richmond's in place at the time of the Court's *Croson* decision, and many more cities were in the process of creating, or would create over the ensuing years, entirely new affirmative action programs—all of which, if challenged in court, would be analyzed under the same stringent legal rubric delineated in *Croson.* The Supreme Court specified that these kinds of affirmative action programs, designed to assist minority contractors, would be subject to the same legal analysis as would programs designed to hurt minorities.[5] This legal standard is known as "strict scrutiny."

Because strict scrutiny has long been thought to be "strict in theory, and fatal in fact,"[6] in the immediate aftermath of *Croson* many assumed that the decision ultimately meant the end of affirmative action, or at the very least the end of affirmative action in government contracting. All of the affirmative action programs similar to Richmond's would likely meet the same dire legal fate as had Richmond's program. Once the courts decide to apply strict scrutiny, they seemingly always have found legislation unconstitutional.[7] Thus, many who reviewed the decision believed the end had come for affirmative action, eyeing the decision as the "virtual death knell for set-aside programs."[8] Ed Koch, former mayor of New York City, called the decision a "fatal blow to local minority set-aside programs."[9] One former Reagan department official succinctly summed up the end result of *Croson:* "[These programs] are gone." Even some affirmative action supporters, such as League of Cities executive director Alan Beals, maintained a pessimistic view. According to Beals, after the Supreme Court's ruling, "City leaders have to wonder about the extent to which they can design and implement local [affirmative action] policies." Facing such a daunting standard of review, it was natural to think that governments would have no recourse but to abandon race-based programming.[10]

Indeed, in response to the Court's decision in *Croson,* a small number of cities and counties around the country, knowing their programs did not meet the extraordinarily high legal standard articulated by the Court, voluntarily relinquished their affirmative action programs, or dismantled them as part of a legal settlement,[11] or relented in the face of an anti–affirmative action litigation campaign led by an interest group, Associated General Contractors, and its members.[12] Dismantling affirmative action programs during the 1990s, however, was not the typical response to the Court's anti–affirmative action ruling. Despite the belief by many that *Croson* rang the death knell for affirmative action in government contracting, at least 150 local governments enacted (or attempted to enact) revised or entirely new affirmative action programs in the ensuing decade. During the same period, when various plaintiffs challenged about thirty of these programs in court, almost without exception, trial courts did not deviate from the judicial anti–affirmative action stance adopted by the Supreme Court. But rather than affirmative action withering on the vine in reaction to a uniformly hostile judiciary, the 1990s instead became the high-water mark for affirmative action in the legislative arena.[13]

How do we reconcile the anti–affirmative action judicial pronouncement with the pro–affirmative action legislative response? Why did affirmative action grow and flourish when the judiciary was so clearly opposed to the practice of affirmative action? And in light of the constitutionally dubious status of these programs, why were there not more lawsuits against governments to stop these practices? Where were the lawsuits? I argue in this book that unconstitutional affirmative action programs, like many other unconstitutional laws, persisted and persist in part because of the actions of elected officials and bureaucrats who react to the Supreme Court's rulings and doctrinal rules not by figuring out how to survive litigation by changing legislation to comply with judicial decrees but instead by trying to avoid litigation that could challenge these programs, through blocking the lawsuits. In this way, governments are able to maintain unconstitutional laws and actions by insulating themselves from the quintessential connection between constitutional impropriety and constitutional remedy, the lawsuit. And this is true not just in the realm of affirmative action but for a host of other issue areas as well, including hate speech, flag burning, school prayer, and legislative vetoes. When the Supreme Court exercises its power of judicial review, striking down laws and acts of government,[14] the Court ruling does not neatly clear the underbrush of unconstitutional laws from around the country but rather ignites a firestorm of policy reactions to the decision, many of which successfully strike at the heart of the Court's greatest power. Elected branches of government employ what I call "checkmate" moves in responding to the Court's use of judicial review.[15] These moves steel in place unconstitutional laws by attacking the litigation nexus between the elected branches and the courts.

As Justice Robert H. Jackson once said, "Courts lack a self-starter."[16] That is to say, the judiciary is only empowered to respond to a lawsuit, with the result that governments seeking to maintain or create unconstitutional laws may do so free of judicial peril until a plaintiff files a lawsuit. Staving off litigation vitiates the judiciary's most potent power and lets unconstitutional laws persist. Avoiding litigation, however, is not necessarily an easy course of action for governments. The United States is seemingly awash in lawyers, and the news is often filled with stories of lawsuits filed over trivial events that result in huge jury awards, creating the false perception that Americans too easily turn to the courts for improper reasons.[17] Even when money does not seem to be the chief motivation behind litigation, specialized interest groups from across the political spectrum are primed to seek policy advances via litigation.[18] Yet as I demonstrate in this book, there are barriers to litigation that can be capitalized upon by governments intent on maintaining unconstitutional laws. These barriers to litigation range from traditional legal obstacles, such as jurisdiction and justiciability, to generalized social mores against litigation, but they also include political barriers that are erected when the government, through elected officials, is able to exert its unique powers of persuasion. Checkmate occurs when these social, legal, or political impediments to litigation thwart the judiciary from eradicating laws and acts repugnant to the Constitution.[19]

That governments and society sometimes contest the courts is not necessarily problematic. There may be circumstances in which either the judiciary itself has so stepped outside its prescribed judicial function or the courts have ruled in a manner so completely contrary to any reasonable interpretation of the law as to effectively require political and social resistance. Even in the more typical realm of judicial decision making, legislative responses that focus on ambiguous areas of judicial doctrine or executive responses that prod the judiciary to rethink a vexing legal issue may be warranted. The judiciary is neither infallible nor omniscient. That the judiciary is fallible and has only limited knowledge, however, does not mean it should be feckless. We need not expect governments or society to blindly succumb to an extreme version of judicial supremacy, but we should recognize the dangers of the failure to give primacy to the judicial interpretation of constitutional rights. In this book I seek to make the case that we ought to prioritize judicial determinations about the nature of constitutional rights above those of the elected branches of government. Although political resistance or social contestation can be useful challenges to a problematic notion of judicial supremacy, checkmate, in which the judiciary is thwarted from voicing its own constitutional view, threatens to imperil the role of the judiciary in our political system, challenging the concepts of separation of powers and equal protection of the law.

Dialogues and Impact

The argument of this book is located at the crossroads of two separate yet distinctly related genres of public law scholarship. The first has to do with the relationship between the courts and the elected branches of government. The literature on court–elected branch interaction posits that the courts and the elected branches, while separate institutions, share lawmaking functions.[20] Many scholars thus refer to an ongoing colloquy[21] or dialogue[22] between the various branches of government in which each branch iteratively contributes to our understanding of the Constitution. The second genre of scholarship is concerned with the difference between what the Supreme Court declares and the impact of the decision on the ground. The scholarship in this area, often termed gap or impact literature, notes the sometimes vast chasm between Court decisions and the stark reality of society. Despite the sometimes earth-shattering rhetoric of Supreme Court opinions, scholars, or pundits,[23] much of this literature explains why court decisions generally have little effect on society.

The well-trod case of abortion serves as an example of both the dialogue and the impact literatures.[24] When Jane Roe challenged a Texas abortion restriction in court, and eventually in the U.S. Supreme Court, the conversation over the constitutional place of abortion began in earnest. Once the Court decided *Roe v. Wade*,[25] dozens of state legislatures around the country considered whether to abandon existing state laws limiting a woman's access to abortion, and abortion rights groups instigated a series of lawsuits seeking to stamp out other abortion-related limitations.[26] But as pro-choice activists and politicians reacted, so did their opponents. States modified their abortion laws, sometimes in line with the Supreme Court ruling and sometimes in direct challenge to it. The Court itself continued to rule on the topic of abortion, sometimes on new issues and at other times clarifying ambiguities in earlier cases. Legislation begets judicial rulings and judicial rulings beget legislation. Thus, the ongoing colloquy analogy seems apropos.

The results on the ground, however, are sometimes another story. Although the official policy in much of the United States changed when the Supreme Court ruled that a woman's choice to have an

abortion is protected by the Constitution, the impact of the decision is slightly more questionable. How this legal right translated
into changing the lives of Americans is a difficult process to capture.
As one partial measure of the aggregate effects of the decision, in the
years immediately following *Roe,* the rate of increase in abortions
per year actually went down.[27] One reason for the slowed rate of increase in number of abortions, despite the constitutional limitations
of abortion legislation, was that the vast majority of private hospitals and health institutions were unaffected by the decision and still
routinely refused to perform abortions.[28] The Court's declaration
of the right affected only public behavior and left many women to
fend for themselves. Moreover, the ruling did not particularly touch
rural areas of the United States, because only 7 percent of rural
counties had even a single abortion provider. And when women
could find a provider, the providers and ancillary medical personnel
often found themselves performing under what one constitutional
scholar called "siege conditions."[29] Providers often found themselves
facing jeering protesters while entering and leaving their workplace,
vandalism, and physical threats. These less than ideal working conditions, combined with personal opposition to the practice, limited
the number of abortions that could be performed. Thus, while the
Court dramatically declared a right, the lives of women across the
country did not dramatically change, underscoring the gap between
what the Court decides and what actually occurs in practice.

    While the abortion example places private actors at the crucial
juncture of individuals and their exercise of their constitutional
rights, in other issue areas the government itself may be to blame.
For example, despite the Supreme Court's ruling in *Brown v. Board
of Education*[30] that "separate is inherently unequal," segregation
rates in U.S. public schools remained nearly unchanged for more
than a decade after the decision, largely owing to the actions and
inactions of public officials.[31] Following the Supreme Court's banning of school-led prayer in two cases in the early 1960s,[32] public
school officials nevertheless continued the practice for more than
forty years throughout wide segments of the United States.[33] After
the Supreme Court declared legislative vetoes unconstitutional, the
congressional practice of including legislative vetoes in legislation
persisted.[34] When the Supreme Court declared that regulating flag

burning amounted to an unconstitutional infringement on protected speech, Congress enacted its own unconstitutional flag burning statute, and to this day almost every state has similar laws.[35] And
despite the Supreme Court's ruling in *R.A.V. v. City of St. Paul*[36] that
governments may not engage in viewpoint discrimination, even in
proscribable areas of speech, hundreds of colleges and universities,
including public schools, maintained or created new hate speech
codes within five years of the decision.[37] Therefore it is not simply a
matter of Supreme Court decisions failing to change the hearts and
minds of society but of governments themselves becoming deeply
involved in evading judicial review.

The dialogic literature typically conceives of an ongoing conversation between the branches of government. In light of the instances
of dissonance between the elected branches and the courts, however, the question arises, are the courts permitting their doctrine to
go unheeded? If the constitutional dialogue envisioned by scholars
is occurring, what explains the paucity of comments coming from
the courts? When unconstitutional policies framed in affirmative
action, public school prayer, legislative vetoes, speech codes, or flag
burning statutes come before the courts, the judiciary, at the top
and at the bottom, nearly always strikes them down. Yet these unconstitutional laws persist around the country. No matter that the
courts have expressed near-unified opposition; the legislative supply
of unconstitutional laws continually outpaces the demand for their
repeal. Thus the perplexing issue becomes, where are the lawsuits?
Given the official policies that run counter to the law as declared
by the Court, why do people not sue to stop these unconstitutional
practices?

The persistence of unconstitutional laws suggests that if there is a
dialogue between the courts and the elected branches, there must be
some "conversation stoppers" involved in this exchange. The lack of
lawsuits is evidence that the courts are stymied on their side of the
conversation. Ironically, the dialogic theory already imagines conversation stoppers in the elected branch–judiciary dialogue but envisions that it is the judiciary that stops the conversation by placing
stringent limitations on what the elected branches may do. What I
have discovered, however, is that stoppages to the judicial-legislative
dialogue may also come from the elected branches, and it is these

mechanisms that derail the typical court–elected branch interaction. I characterize elected branch efforts to stop the dialogue and evade judicial review as *checkmate*. The creation of social, legal, and political barriers to litigation limits the judiciary from reining in constitutionally suspect laws and actions.

Coordinate Construction and Judicial Supremacy

Alexander Hamilton, who along with James Madison and John Jay wrote *The Federalist Papers,* long ago suggested that the judiciary lacks both "force" and "will," and possesses "merely judgment."[38] The judiciary must wait for disputes to come before the tribunals and is powerless to enforce unilaterally its decisions. Compounding the relative weakness of the Supreme Court's mere judgment is that other branches of government also possess powers that, while not necessarily duplicative of the Court's power, at least are in competition with the Court's power of judicial review by maintaining their own forms of judgment about the constitutionality of laws. This idea of "coordinate construction" or "departmentalism" is historically associated with Thomas Jefferson. Jefferson and the anti-Federalist regime came into power opposed to the dominant Federalist ideas of nationalization and judicial supremacy. The Jeffersonians bristled at the centralization efforts of the Federalists, instead favoring a series of competing power centers, including the states, to combat a strong centralized national government. The anti-Federalists also favored giving each branch of government "an equal right to decide for itself the meaning of the Constitution"[39] so as to combat a judiciary "corrupted by faction."[40] In many ways, then, the origins of coordinate construction intimate that supplying the president or Congress with the ability to fashion their own view of the Constitution is not a per se indictment of a judicial role in judicial review but instead is a functional check on the monopolistic powers of a government institution.

Scholars differentiate between a mild and a strong form of coordinate construction. The mild form is the "'dialogue' that naturally occurs between the branches . . . as they work together to come to a common understanding of what the Constitution requires."[41] The strong form suggests "if two branches come into conflict, the judiciary's interpretation does not necessarily trump the president's."

Both formulations characterize the dialogic nature of the relationship between and among the branches of government. For example, when one branch of government asserts the constitutionality of a policy, another branch has the opportunity to assist or thwart those efforts. In conflictual settings, the Supreme Court may rule that a federal statute is unconstitutional, or the president may fail to enforce a Supreme Court ruling. In the end, coordinate construction is the "process by which governmental and nongovernmental actors seek to realize their interpretation of the constitutionality of legislation and law."[42]

Judicial supremacy, on the other hand, suggests that the Supreme Court has, in effect, the supreme view of the Constitution. The Supreme Court's view of the Constitution, according to the judicial supremacy school of thought, is the single authoritative interpretation of constitutional meaning. Although one branch of legal scholarship argues that the Court *should* be the single authoritative arbiter of the Constitution,[43] it is largely Supreme Court opinions that have fueled the sense that our system is accurately described as one of "judicial supremacy." From the language in *Marbury v. Madison* that "it is emphatically the duty and the province of the judiciary to say what the law is" to *Cooper v. Aaron*'s "the federal judiciary is supreme in the exposition of the law of the Constitution" to *City of Boerne v. Flores*'s "the power to interpret the Constitution in a case or controversy remains in the Judiciary," the Supreme Court has consistently articulated the judicial supremacy line. Dworkin surmises that "the most straightforward interpretation of American constitutional practice shows that our judges have final interpretive authority."[44] The Court's assertion of judicial supremacy has been so complete as to make the issue seem "moot," according to Meernik and Ignagni. They argue that "most public law scholars either believe themselves that judicial review is typically the final stage in the struggle to interpret the Constitution, or acknowledge that while this may not be true, it is widely believed to be so by the public, the media, and government officials."

Despite the dominance of the belief in judicial supremacy, the coordinate construction view has recently been enjoying a bit of a renaissance among legal scholars describing and advocating for "the everyday process of constitutional interpretation [that] integrates all three branches of government: executive, legislative, and judicial."[45] Constitutional and political development scholars such as Bruce Ackerman, Louis Fisher, Barry Friedman, Mark Tushnet, and Keith Whittington each subscribe to a coordinate construction vantage point to varying degrees.[46] According to these proponents, constitutional interpretation among the branches of government can be thought as a "conversation" (Ackerman), "dialogue" (Tushnet), or an "ongoing colloquy" (Burt). Judicial decision making is "in the form of a continuous and rather tentative dialogue with other political elements" (Friedman).[47] The coordinate construction theorists see a process of recurrent interaction among the branches of government such that constitutional interpretation is not preordained or static but rather the subject of ongoing dialogue until "an interpretive consensus on the text" is reached.[48]

The new coordinate construction literature has largely emerged in response to notions of judicial exclusivity or judicial supremacy.[49] Larry Alexander and Frederick Schauer, who, along with Ronald Dworkin, Robert Bork, Laurence Tribe, and John Hart Ely, are the best-known judicial supremacy scholars, argue that the Constitution's true reason for being is to settle political disputes authoritatively. Without a "single authoritative decisionmaker" to interpret the Constitution, Alexander and Schauer claim, we would have "interpretive anarchy."[50] Individuals and the government would not be able to coordinate their lives under such uncertainty. The single authoritative decision maker should be the Supreme Court, largely because of the nature of judicial independence, but also because of the legal training of members of the judiciary. According to this judicial supremacy line of thought, allowing for a multiplicity of meanings of the Constitution, or even statutes, challenges both the Court's authority and governmental stability.

The debate between coordinate construction theorists and judicial supremacy proponents is often posed as oppositional. Either constitutional interpretation is a mutually constitutive affair between various components of our government and nongovernment actors, or the Court has exclusive domain over the interpretation of the Constitution. Either there is an ongoing dialogue, or the Court has spoken unilaterally, effectively ending any possible conversation.[51] Both the judicial supremacy proponents and almost all the coordinate construction scholars, however, should be opposed to the situation identified in this book. In the realm of affirmative action, hate speech, flag burning, school prayer, and legislative vetoes, it is not the Court but the elected branches that have lobbed the conversation stopper. By engaging in unconstitutional policies, the elected branches have plausibly offered their competing view of the Constitution in line with the coordinate construction school of thought. The elected branches, however, have not stopped with simply offering a different perspective on the meaning of equal protection, free speech, an establishment of religion or law, but instead have acted to forestall or avoid litigation and effectively gag the courts, thereby ending such dialogue.

Limiting the Court's function within the realm of political dialogue should be troublesome, even to the coordinate construction scholars, as the real value of "the Constitution outside of the courts" is competition against monopolistic constitutional decision making, not an inherent problem with the Court's exercise of judicial review. Thus, the coordinate construction scholars suggest that "no branch of government has the final say"[52] over constitutional meaning. This criticism should remain, regardless of the identity of the institution maintaining monopoly.

Pickerill, while sympathetic to the ongoing colloquy school of thought, finds empirically that congressional constitutional construction is limited, and suggests we ought to consider the nature of constitutional interpretation as one of "judicial primacy." Judicial primacy recognizes that policymaking is "interactive, sequential, and alternative" and that "neither institution can be *solely* responsible for either activity," but still acknowledges a special role for the courts.[53] In this book, I build on this concept of judicial primacy to suggest that this role is significantly challenged by the persistence of unconstitutional laws, and explore some ways in which the judiciary and society may be able to counteract the employment of checkmate moves. Courts need not and should not be the only voice involved in ascertaining constitutional meaning. Judicial actors are, of course, humanly fallible and susceptible to disingenuous constitutional interpretation. Yet if judicial interpretation is *not* privileged over the "constitution outside the courts," citizens will be subjected to a greater degree of losing confrontations with constitutional infirmities.

Institutions, Attitudes, and Behavior

Despite the actions, and perhaps inactions, of myriad governments in the cases of affirmative action, hate speech, school prayer, flag burning, and legislative vetoes, making it appear as if the Supreme Court were a powerless institution, unable to rein in noncompliant elected branches, this book demonstrates that Court decisions trigger actors and institutions to react by undertaking activities that would not have occurred but for the decision. Although much political science research demonstrates the inefficacy of the Supreme Court,[54] I propose that the Court can and does shape public policies. But saying that Court decisions shape public policies is not to say that Court decisions determine public policies. Rather, Court decisions are the causal mechanism for some governments to shape their policies to avoid litigation.

When researchers evaluate the impact of Supreme Court decisions, they generally focus on one of three types of impact.[55] First, they may examine the Court's role in changing *public opinion.* These studies attempt to decipher whether individual attitudes change in response to a Court decision. Most of the research to date has focused on high-salience cases, especially *Roe v. Wade,* in arguing whether judicial pronouncements affect public attitudes toward the adjudicated subject, such as abortion. Though there is little evidence that Court decisions affect the overall aggregation of public opinion—in the case of *Roe,* making society more or less tolerant of abortion—Court decisions appear to shape public opinion by helping to focus or polarize public opinion.[56] This power, however, diminishes over time as the Court revisits issues, each time decreasing the Court's ability to affect public opinion.[57] Whether one subscribes to the positive response, structural response, or conditional response theory, this literature demonstrates that Court decisions are typically mediated through an institution (the media) before filtering out to the public, and in limited circumstances the Court may have some effect on the distribution of public opinion.[58]

Perhaps more famously, many researchers examine changes in

behavior following a Court decision.[59] These studies consider whether formal legal rulings have the effect of modifying the actions of individuals. This might include what happened following judicial decisions about school desegregation, police searches and seizures, pay equity, or children's rights.[60] The individuals whose behavior might theoretically be modified in such cases include police officers faced with operating under a new constitutional right, women deciding whether to terminate a pregnancy, or judges faced with a change in interpretation of the Constitution. In each case, the ultimate test of the impact of a case is observed in how individuals modify their behavior because of a judicial ruling.

The evidence of changes in behavior because of a Court decision is somewhat limited. Schools did not desegregate following *Brown v. Board of Education* until more than ten years after the decision, and until Congress passed the Civil Rights Act of 1964 and the executive branch, via what was then the Department of Health, Education and Welfare, effectively paid school districts to desegregate.[61] But after *Mapp v. Ohio,* states that introduced the exclusionary rule for the first time (many other states had already been following a form of the exclusionary rule prior to *Mapp*) actually saw a larger increase in crime than states that did not initiate the rule.[62] In a separate study, researchers found that narcotics arrests decreased dramatically in New York City in the years following *Mapp,* but that "preventive patrols"—on which officers confiscate the illegal narcotics but do not arrest the offenders (and thus steer clear of the exclusionary rule)—increased significantly.[63] Still other researchers found by reviewing arrest and conviction rates in Cincinnati that the decision "does not seem to have had any effect whatever."[64] More recent research concludes that "the failure of the exclusionary rule to effectively deter police misconduct," combined with its costs of both police and judicial dishonesty, justifies overturning the decision.[65] Most researchers in this area have determined that the Court has at best a limited or constrained effect on behavior in society.

One area that Court decisions seem to affect to a greater degree, however, is the mobilization of activists. Supreme Court decisions may spur interest group litigation and reform efforts.[66] Following the Supreme Court's ruling regarding pay equity in *County of Washington v. Gunther,* activists used the decision to spur changes result-

ing in substantive gains for women.[67] What is particularly noteworthy is that the mobilization for pay equity reform efforts occurred as
a result of a Supreme Court decision that actually allowed different
pay schemes for men and women. Thus, even researchers who find
evidence of behavioral changes as a result of Court decisions have
determined that the effect of Court decisions is contingent. The
decision does not work as a club to command behavioral changes
in society but instead can assist in creating a rights consciousness
that takes advantage of the pairing of political opportunities with
organizational resources.

Finally, some researchers evaluate the *institutional* relationship
between the Court and the elected branches.[68] These studies explain how governments either ignore, repeal, or modify policies in
response to Court decisions. Here, too, researchers have generally
found conditional and varied responses. In examining how colleges
and universities reacted to the Supreme Court's decision in *R.A.V.
v. City of St. Paul,* one researcher found that only 2 percent of colleges and universities removed their unconstitutional speech codes,
whereas about 6 percent of colleges and universities adopted new
unconstitutional speech codes in the face of *R.A.V.*[69] The research,
however, suggests that the driving force for the policy changes had
more to do with a perceived backlash against these policies and a
sense of maintaining the college or university's national standing
rather than compliance with the Supreme Court's ruling.

One area that has seen notable policy change because of the
courts is prison reform.[70] Feeley and Rubin demonstrate that judicial decisions extended constitutional rights to prisoners and effectively ended the entire southern-style "plantation" model of penal
institutions. Rather than resulting from grassroots mobilization or
statutorily mandated change, "the entire prison reform movement
was the work of a moderate, rather traditional group of federal
judges, acting under the wary, but generally supportive scrutiny of
a conservative Supreme Court."[71]

An issue concerning the existing research, however, is that researchers typically focus on whether a particular Court decision has
had an impact.[72] Thus, we know whether *Mapp v. Ohio* changed police behavior, whether *Gunther v. County of Washington* provided an
opportunity for pay equity reform efforts, whether *Brown v. Board*

of Education integrated schools, and whether *Roe v. Wade* affected abortion rates. Yet we are largely at a loss to explain why a single Supreme Court decision may have an impact in San Francisco but not in Peoria. We do not really know why some school districts desegregated following *Brown,* or why pay equity reform efforts did not take place in the South. Thus, my work examines the idea that the impact of a single case may not be uniform across the country. After all, the Court's doctrine in *Croson* was heeded in some locations but not in others. Therefore, I focus not on the variation in impact between cases (why one case has had an impact but another case has not) but instead on the variation in impact of a single case. How can we explain why some governments, such as New York's Port Authority, voluntarily dismantled their program in light of *Croson,* other governments, such as King County, Washington, defended their program in court, and yet other cities, such as Miami, Florida, seemingly ignored the Supreme Court and maintained a program unchanged from 1989 to today? What explains the varied responses to a single judicial decision?

A traditional explanation of variance in outcomes focuses on the often convoluted and ambiguous commands within a Court decision, which may offer sufficient latitude for governments' seeming compliance with the Court's directives.[73] In other words, the Court's signals may be unclear or nonspecific, and thus may spawn a wide range of plausible interpretations. Another promising avenue for disentangling the effects of a single court case is suggested by Michael McCann. He explains that the individuals, groups, and institutions responsible for implementing Supreme Court decisions have uneven abilities to "sustain the discursive 'frame'" of judicial decisions.[74] Court decisions do not occur in a vacuum but instead are part of a series of halting conversations between the courts and the elected branches. These decisions may change in their tenor, direction, or framework, so that when policies are evaluated, individuals and institutions with different interests, knowledge, abilities, and resources may interpret and implement judicial policies, with varying results.

Although both these explanations provide plausible explanations for why the impact of a single case may vary in different jurisdictions, neither provides an adequate account of the impact of cases like *Croson*. First, many cases—like *Croson*—are remarkably clear.[75] In fact, as shown in chapter 1, the *Croson* decision presents a cogent blueprint detailing how jurisdictions can fashion constitutional affirmative action programs within government contracting in line with the announced strict scrutiny standard. Though certainly some Court decisions are vague, nebulous, and indefinite, a great many are not, including *Croson*.[76] And second, while there is a large set of possible responses to Court decisions, there appear to be dominant patterns of decision responses from different institutions. For example, almost two-thirds of the jurisdictions that maintained programs at the time of *Croson* attempted to follow the affirmative action blueprint in the ensuing years. Yet nearly every government that opted to litigate its affirmative action program was met with a stern rebuke by the courts. Therefore, instead of the Court and the implementing populations both being characterized as chaotic atomistic institutions and actors, there appear to be identifiable and predictable, if not even, categories of responses to judicial opinions. And it is these responses to judicial decisions, by the elected branches and others, that leave a wide swath of unconstitutional laws in their wake.

Social, Legal, and Political Barriers to Litigation

From the gap and impact literatures we have learned a great deal about the difficulties the judiciary faces in effecting social change. What we have learned about this impact of the Court is not terribly surprising, given the very basic precepts of our American government, dating back to Hamilton's assessment of the judiciary. What is surprising, however, is what emerges when we pair this knowledge with what we know about coordinate construction, dating back to Thomas Jefferson. Where are the courts in response to the lack of impact of Supreme Court decisions? What happened to the ongoing colloquy? School integration, affirmative action, hate speech, school prayer, flag burning, and legislative vetoes have been more of an elected branch monologue than an ongoing dialogue.

Conceptualizing the elected branch–court interaction as a dialogue is in some ways misleading. The notion of dialogue summons a concept of co-equality of the branches of government. Dialogic explanations envision the elected branches and the courts on similar footing, each asserting its own competitive views of the Constitution. What we see on the ground, however, is not equality but legislative supremacy. The branches of government are not co-equal unless one, in an Orwellian twist, proclaims that all branches are equal, but some are more equal than others. In light of the persistence of unconstitutional laws, we can ask where were and are the courts? Where were the lawsuits to enforce the idea that separate is inherently unequal? Where were and are the lawsuits to eliminate school prayer from public schools? Where were and are the lawsuits to eliminate college speech codes? Where were and are the lawsuits to attack legislative vetoes?

Judicial process scholars typically point to both formal and informal barriers to entry that hamper bringing a claim before the courts.[77] The formal barriers include both jurisdictional claims and more fungible jurisprudential limitations on judicial power, such as questions of justiciability (i.e., mootness, ripeness, advisory opinions, political questions, and standing). These informal barriers include direct costs (e.g., attorney and filing fees) and opportunity costs (e.g., settlement, time away from work). The formal and informal categorization of barriers obscures a few crucial elements of the actual litigation process. As most scholars, including the judicial process scholars who use these categorizations, realize, many of the formal barriers are quite malleable. What counts as a political question? In the end, it is simply what the Court declares. What disputes are moot? Moot disputes are those the Court declares moot. Although there is some substance to the categorization, the notion of formal barriers masks the pliability of these requirements. Similarly, informal barriers to litigation can be and often are used either to encourage or to discourage particular types of lawsuits.[78] Without quibbling that the formal and informal categorization has some explanatory force, I use a slightly different categorization of reasons why we do not have more lawsuits, and specifically lawsuits that would enforce constitutional rights. This categorization comprises legal, social, and political obstacles to litigation.

Quite plainly, there are legal obstacles to lawsuits. Only those grievances recognized by law—and law can vary from the Constitution to statutes to administrative codes to the common law—are afforded adjudication in our system of justice. Thus, legal obstacles include the jurisprudential notions of jurisdiction and justiciability, but also the procedural requirements of a lawsuit, including the need to pay filing fees and deal with fee-shifting statutes.[79] What is "legal" here is subject to revision, both by judges in terms of what is justiciable and by the elected branches in respect to how fees are allocated. Thus, legal obstacles can either be raised or lowered, sometimes by the judiciary, sometimes by the elected branches. That is to say, the government as a whole can either increase or decrease the cost of litigation using legal criteria. In this book, I demonstrate how governments use legal obstacles to fend off lawsuits, thus denying the judiciary its role in constitutional interpretation. Specifically, in discussing affirmative action in chapters 2, 3, and 4, I show how governments expend resources for disparity studies and expert witnesses in the case of affirmative action, despite their ineffectiveness in justifying affirmative action programs, and these expenditures substantially raise the cost of litigation against unconstitutional affirmative action programs. In chapter 4, discussing affirmative action in Miami, and in chapter 5, discussing hate speech regulations on campus, I also show how the concept of standing can lead to the persistence of unconstitutional laws.

Though meeting the legal requirements for a lawsuit is necessary for a lawsuit to proceed, clearing this obstacle is not sufficient for a case to proceed. Judicial process scholars estimate that less than 4 percent of individuals who believe themselves to have been illegally discriminated against actually hire an attorney, and about 1 percent commence a lawsuit.[80] Though many of the cases not brought probably did not meet the legal standards for lawsuit, the small proportion of cases that are brought suggests there may be additional hidden social aspects to litigation. Certainly this is true in the traditional meaning of "social": there may be societal pressures that either encourage or discourage litigation. But the social costs of litigation also extend to two other areas, knowledge of underlying events and knowledge of one's legal rights.

The sine qua non of a lawsuit is the knowledge of the events whereby a constitutional violation may have occurred. This is, in some respects, a tweak on the philosophical question about a tree falling in the woods with no one around to hear it. If the government violates someone's constitutional rights, and no one is around to complain, does the government action violate the Constitution? Far from being simply a philosophical exercise, this question has profound practical implications. For example, the U.S. government's efforts during the war on terror raise the very real possibility that the government has been violating the Constitution without our knowledge. Whether these government actions include the running of secret prisons throughout the world, wiretapping phones without a warrant or the use of statutorily mandated FISA (Foreign Intelligence Surveillance) courts, or imposing cruel and unusual punishment, if true, they remain effectively unknown and thus immune from litigation until they are exposed—in these cases in particular, by the media after leaks from government informants.[81] The use of examples from the war on terror is not to accuse the U.S. government of running roughshod over the Constitution; the fact is simply that we do not know whether this is true—and that is precisely the point. Knowledge of the underlying events is central to rectifying the unconstitutional aspects of government actions, and it is largely the government that controls this information.

Knowledge of the events surrounding a constitutional violation, however, is only a preliminary step toward using a lawsuit to fend off governmental encroachment on our liberties. Not only must one know the events, one must know one's rights. Such knowledge is not necessarily widespread among the public. In a well-publicized study in 2006, the McCormick Tribune Freedom Museum found that barely more than one quarter of Americans could name more than one component of the First Amendment, yet more than half of Americans could name more than one fictional character from the Fox cartoon series *The Simpsons*.[82] Eight percent of respondents could name just three First Amendment protections, while 40 percent of respondents knew all three contestant judges from the television program *American Idol*. While the discrepancy between knowledge of rights and knowledge of popular culture is somewhat amusing, the consequences of not knowing the boundaries of proper government action are profound. In a criminal case, when a defendant fails to object in a timely manner to a government violation, the defendant waives the ability to challenge that constitutional violation.[83] So, when a defendant fails to object to the racial composition of a jury or the admission of a statement tending to prove a defendant's guilt, the defendant is barred from raising those issues at a later time.[84] Research has also demonstrated that when individuals are not knowledgeable about how the system works, in order to seek representation and remedy possible wrongs, wronged individuals are unlikely to instigate litigation.[85] Knowledge of constitutional wrongs and knowledge of remedial options are both crucial to protecting constitutional rights.

These knowledge factors, however, only go so far in explaining the lack of lawsuits enforcing constitutional rights. Media reports often contain information about the backlash against lawsuits. Lawsuits, for the most part, are public proceedings, and antilawyer sentiment and antilitigation sentiment can run high. Despite the popular wisdom that the United States is a litigious society, academic scholars who have studied these issues have generally come to the opposite conclusion, namely, that given the number of legal wrongs occurring, it is remarkable there have not been more lawsuits.[86] As I discuss more fully in the chapters on affirmative action and school prayer, initiating a lawsuit imposes social costs on the litigant. Opposing social programs based on race or religion opens a litigant up to charges of racism or intolerance of religious liberty. Thus, we would expect lawsuits to occur not merely because of unconstitutional laws or acts but rather when litigants calculate that the costs of litigation are outweighed by the possible benefits to be derived from litigation. These benefits can, of course, be substantial, but the costs should at least highlight the difficulty inherent in the judiciary's role in reining in unconstitutional actions. When causes are unpopular, litigation may be impeded by social forces.[87]

Overcoming the legal and social obstacles to litigation, however, does not necessarily lead a complainant to instigate a lawsuit. Individuals must also overcome political barriers to lawsuits before pursuing legal claims against the government. Governments can both impose political costs on instigating claims and create more fruitful alternatives to challenging unconstitutional laws in court. For example, in chapter 5 I describe how unconstitutional legislative vetoes persist in federal legislation largely because of the financial power Congress holds over agencies, making it financially beneficial for agencies not to challenge these unconstitutional provisions. Congress has convinced agencies that litigation may not be in the best interest of these agencies for dispute resolution. And in chapter 3, I demonstrate how one government co-opted one of the traditional interest group opponents of affirmative action into supporting the government's adoption of unconstitutional race-based programming by assisting the interest group with its labor supply problems, resulting in a win-win solution for the government and interest group. These political barriers do not permanently block litigation, should an agency or interest group want to challenge the government, but the governments' actions have made litigation quite irrational.

The legal, social, and political barriers to litigation decrease the likelihood that unconstitutional laws will be overturned. While erecting these barriers makes some intuitive sense for institutions competing against the courts, several of the barriers are the product of the courts themselves (e.g., the prudential components of justiciability) and some are not directly under the control of the government (e.g., the social mores against litigation). Alexander Bickel, among others, lauds what he calls the "passive virtues" of the courts, manifest when the judiciary refrains from ruling on particular cases or controversies. As students of constitutional history may attest, sometimes for the Supreme Court, less is more. The Supreme Court's power arguably increased when Chief Justice Marshall refused to require President Jefferson to deliver Marbury's commission and when Chief Justice Warren refused to require specific time frames for desegregating the nation's schools. Yet these passive virtues are all too easily transformed into passive-aggressive vices. The prudential components of justiciability may be seized on by members of the judiciary substantively opposed to the direction of a Supreme Court ruling in subterfuge of the Court's democratic role. By eviscerating the Court's procedural role in reviewing the constitutionality of laws, the monopolistic tendencies of the elected branches are maximized and the threat to our system of majoritarian rule with protection of minority rights is challenged. In the next section, I expand on the concept of judicial primacy introduced earlier in this chapter to begin to discuss how a normative view of the Court's powers suggests the difficulty in accepting the current checkmate framework.

Judicial Primacy

To paraphrase the character of Gordon Gecko in the movie *Wall Street*, "Dialogue, for the lack of a better word, is good. Dialogue is right. Dialogue works." The idea of dialogue is consistent with the antimonopolistic sentiment behind our constitutional founding and is what has best served our democracy in the ensuing two-plus centuries. The different branches of government put forth their competing views of constitutional interpretation, each leaving room for the other branches to bring us closer to a consensus. Successful court–elected branch interaction occurs, then, when the process works more or less as a system of checks and balances, with a back and forth between the courts and the elected branches. Both the courts and the elected branches are free to put forth their possibly competing views of the Constitution. Unsuccessful cases of court–elected branch interactions are typified by monopolistic constitutional interpretation, in which the constitutional dialogue ends with little meaningful chance for the airing of competing viewpoints.[88] When either the judiciary or the elected branches engage in the sort of unilateral actions that stymie the other from acting, we ought to be suspect. Both judicial and elected branch monopolies are problematic for basic notions of democratic rule. In the cases of checkmate presented in this book, the judiciary is prevented from performing its part in what should be an ongoing constitutional dialogue. Yet ultimately, in some limited areas, a choice must be made between these competing interpretations. There are quite simply wrongheaded interpretations. But which interpretation of the law, or of the Constitution, should hold sway?

This book examines three different city-level responses to the Supreme Court's *Croson* decision "ending" affirmative action: Philadelphia maintained its program and unsuccessfully faced litigation, Portland created a new affirmative action program but avoided litigation by co-opting the leading opposition interest group, and Miami maintained its program on paper but avoided litigation by bureaucratically gutting the program and not creating standing for an opposed individual or group.

The Philadelphia case is one more typified by the ongoing colloquy school of thought—in other words, a case that is fairly predictable given existing theory. The Court announced one set of standards in an affirmative action case in *Fullilove,* and Philadelphia responded with a new policy; the Court announced new affirmative action standards in *Croson,* and Philadelphia responded again with a new policy. When faced with litigation, Philadelphia fought and lost—but there is very little doubt about the back-and-forth relationship between Philadelphia and the courts, much in line with existing theory and scholarship. I would thus tend to characterize the Philadelphia case as a successful court–elected branch interaction.

The case of Portland is solid evidence of a different concept of the relationship between the courts and the elected branches and demonstrates more clearly what I consider an unsuccessful court–elected branch interaction. Portland created and implemented an affirmative action program in the face of *Croson,* yet the city has never invited litigation against a plainly unconstitutional program. Portland has largely avoided litigation by coupling a new labor recruitment policy heavily favored by the leading anti–affirmative action interest group with the new affirmative action program that the mayor and city commissioners favored. The appeasement of the anti–affirmative action interest group and the particular limitations established in the enacted legislation have successfully insulated the unconstitutional program from litigation and consequently dialogue involving the courts. I would thus characterize the Portland case as an unsuccessful court–elected branch interaction.

One interesting possibility is that elected branches may engage in the sort of nefarious actions that can lead to the type of failure that I criticize, but still wind up in line with a consensus between the courts and elected branches. As I discuss in chapter 4, in the case of Miami, adducing successful and unsuccessful court–elected branch interactions can be fraught with some difficulties. The Miami case is demonstrative of a more nuanced view of court–elected branch interactions. While Miami does maintain an unconstitutional program on paper after *Croson,* because the executive branch consistently fails to implement the legislation, the unconstitutional program is only symbolic. Thus, by one accounting the interaction appears unsuccessful in that the judicial and elected branch dialogue has stopped, as in the case of Portland; in another sense, however, the interaction could also be characterized as successful in that Miami has stopped using an unconstitutional program, as in the case of Philadelphia. If one takes as a starting point that there must be faithful compliance with court directives, Miami really does appear to be successful in that one need not navigate through an unconstitutional program when attempting to contract with the City of Miami. Yet the Miami case should still be troubling to those committed to the notion of constitutional dialogue. Miami's actions, by maintaining the program on paper but failing to implement it, limit the judiciary from participating in the review of the program, because without Miami's implementation of the program no aggrieved individual has standing to assert a claim against the city—and thus there is no litigation, and the courts are shut out from the ongoing dialogue.[89]

These three very different reactions to Supreme Court decisions highlight the need for judicial primacy. Judicial supremacy finds accord only with the end result in Philadelphia, where the Court's interpretation of the equal protection clause, coupled with the violation of a plaintiff's right, ended in the elected branches in Philadelphia complying with the Supreme Court's directives. Coordinate construction, however, by positing the co-equality of constitutional interpretation, lumps together all three municipal results, including both the strategic or symbolic non-use of affirmative action in Miami and the outright side agreement to violate the Constitution struck in Portland. To suggest that in the realm of constitutional interpretation all branches of government are completely equal or to consider the Supreme Court as just another voice in interpreting the constitution is to seriously question the entire premise for having such an institution. While our system is certainly one of separate institutions sharing powers (e.g., war powers, lawmaking), each branch of government has some unique powers as well. Bills for "originating revenue" must begin in the House, the Senate has the "sole power to try all impeachments," and the president has the "power to grant reprieves and pardons." What is the Court's unique role? I suggest that the Court must be accorded a preeminent position in the interpretation of individual rights.

Judicial primacy suggests that judicial interpretation should be an omnipresent factor in constitutional interpretation but stops short of suggesting that the judiciary should have a singular or even a determinative interpretation of the law or Constitution across the board. Rather, judicial primacy points toward carving out a special role for the courts in limited circumstances. As I argue in this book, judicial primacy is especially important in the area of individual rights. Rights are, by design, different from statutory privileges, both in terms of supermajoritarian procedural requirements for amendment and in terms of their very nature. Consider just quickly the Court's standard for declaring nonenumerated rights, "implicit in the concept of ordered liberty." This is a very different standard than a statutory scheme providing for collective bargaining procedures. As such, the ongoing dialogue over these freedoms must account for such differences. Treating individual rights as one would treat other areas of law threatens the balance of our constitutional system in a way that should be troubling to the citizenry and the government alike.

The checkmate moves employed by Portland and Miami, and in the non−affirmative action context by a wide array of governments, leave in place unconstitutional policies by limiting the possibility of judicial review. As such, this elected branch attack on judicial review transforms the ongoing dialogue over constitutional meaning into an elected branch monologue. By not taking the courts' role in constitutional interpretation seriously and gearing programs toward litigation avoidance, the elected branches limit the role of the judiciary in such a fashion as to challenge the notion of judicial primacy and the meaning of equality. It would certainly be ironic to have different substantive meanings of "equal protection of the laws" that depended on where one happened to reside or conduct business.

My critique of the failure of the elected branches to abide by Supreme Court decision making should not be taken to suggest that Supreme Court decision making is flawless and ought to be taken as gospel. Expecting a formalist compliance on the part of the elected branches with the dictates of the judiciary would not be in line with the concept of co-equality of the branches of government. Rather, my critique is primarily leveled at the derailment of the process of the continual interaction between the judiciary and the elected branches. Yet presupposing full equality of constitutional interpretation among the branches of government threatens to undercut some of the central premises undergirding our Constitution, including the structural form of the Constitution and, more important, true equality under the law.

An Overview

Chapter 1 presents an in-depth look at the Supreme Court's decision in *City of Richmond v. J.A. Croson Co.*[90] After providing some context for the opinion, I provide key information contained in the decision and explain how the Supreme Court's policymaking actually triggered much of the affirmative action growth during the 1990s and the following decade. I explain the extent to which there was a judicial–elected branch dialogue, and then identify where that conversation stopped. To do so I trace both the nationwide legal and policy developments since the time of *Croson* and present evidence about the impact of the Court's decision.

Chapters 2, 3, and 4 each trace the fallout from the Court's decision in *Croson* in the three cities profiled in this book: Philadelphia, Portland, Oregon, and Miami, Florida. These in-depth case studies examine how courts, legislatures, and executives respond to judicial decisions—and how the different branches of government play the judicial–elected branch games, including how the various branches of government employ checkmate moves. Evidence of raising the cost of litigation, pay-to-play schemes, interest group co-option, bureaucratic nonimplementation, and symbolic politics—in other words, the legal, social, and political barriers—all also play a role in the elected branches' dominating the judiciary by declaring checkmate on unconstitutional laws.

Lest one believe that affirmative action is an isolated case of checkmate, chapter 5 moves beyond the realm of affirmative action to investigate cases of hate speech, flag burning, legislative vetoes, and school prayer. In these cases, we again see the same sort of patterns of unsuccessful court–elected branch interaction. The Supreme Court has declared these types of legislation unconstitutional, and the lower courts have seen fit to back up the Court, yet there are flagrant constitutional abuses all around the country in each of these areas. The elected branches of government persist in maintaining and creating new constitutional abuses and, in large part because of the legal, social, and political barriers to litigation, have been able get away with it.

Finally, in the conclusion, I summarize the key findings of my research, focusing on the central issue of the legal, social, and political facets of litigation avoidance. Both the Miami affirmative case, discussed in chapter 4, and the discussion of hate speech and flag burning in chapter 5 establish how the Court's own doctrines may limit the Court's ability to participate in the constitutional dialogue. The Philadelphia affirmative action case discussed in chapter 2 and my discussion of hate speech and school prayer in chapter 5 explain the social conditions necessary for a lawsuit. Finally, the Portland affirmative action case discussed in chapter 3 and the legislative veto case discussed in chapter 5 highlight the political obstacles to litigation. All of these cases ultimately raise the issue of the authoritative determination of law and rights, speaking to the debate between judicial supremacy and coordinate construction. I also examine how the concept of judicial primacy strengthens the judiciary's hand to enable it to compete effectively with the elected branches. It is in this regard that the idea of judicial primacy, not judicial supremacy or constitutional dialogue, best points the way toward an appropriate balance for the protection of our most cherished constitutional rights.

1

SUPREME POLICYMAKING

The Supreme Court's ruling in *City of Richmond v. J.A. Croson Co.* was neither the Court's first foray into affirmative action nor its last. In fact, the Supreme Court had ruled just nine years earlier on a federal contracting affirmative action program and would rule six years later on another separate federal contracting affirmative action program. As I detail below, there have been massive legislative responses to *Croson*, interest group activity, and executive action. Therefore it seems appropriate to think about *Croson* and its aftermath as constitutional dialogue—as the outlines of a back-and-forth examination of the meaning of the equal protection clause of the Fourteenth Amendment. Yet as I describe later in the book, government actions can derail the litigation nexus between the elected branches and the courts, leading to a checkmate situation. In this chapter I examine the setting of the *Croson* decision in terms of both the theoretical background to affirmative action and the legal context in which the case arose. I also discuss the actual opinion in *Croson,* explaining what the Court decided, the impact of the decision, and how constitutional dialogue and checkmate theories apply to the impact of the case.

The Origins and Aims of Affirmative Action

Less than a decade after the U.S. Supreme Court dismantled the "separate but equal" framework for racial segregation in *Brown v.*

Board of Education,[1] leading politicians in the United States began to come to terms with the inadequacy of formalized constitutional equality. Despite the provision for equal protection under the law in the U.S. Constitution since the middle of the nineteenth century, political practice and social views dogged race relations for much of the next century. Realizing that inaction resulted in status quo race relations, President Kennedy in 1961 issued Executive Order no. 10,925. This order mandated that federal contractors "take affirmative action" toward guaranteeing that their employees would not be discriminated against on the basis of race, color, creed, or nation origin.[2] Soon thereafter Congress, led by Hubert Humphrey and others, passed the Civil Rights Act of 1964, expanding these earlier efforts to additionally encompass private action.[3]

At the Howard University commencement address in June 1965, President Johnson illustriously aided in the transformation of the civil rights vocabulary from equality of *opportunity* to equality of *result.* Johnson exhorted, "You do not take a person who, for years, has been hobbled by chains and liberate him, bring him to the starting line of a race and then say, 'you are free to compete with all the others' and still justly believe that you have been completely fair."[4] He continued, "It is not enough just to open the gates of opportunity. All our citizens must have the ability to walk through those gates. . . . We seek . . . not just equality as a right and a theory, but equality as a fact and as a result."[5] In this way the key principle of equality, long embedded in American civil and judicial documents and rhetoric, became transformed into a more pragmatic measuring device—equal results. Within two years President Johnson had issued Executive Order no. 11,246, establishing the "Philadelphia Plan," which required federal contractors, first in Philadelphia and later in fifty-five other cities, to utilize minority employees as a precondition for the receipt of federal contract dollars.

Under the guidance of President Nixon, the United States first instituted a requirement that federal contractors have affirmative action plans with both minority and female hiring goals. Thus, by the time President Carter entered office in 1977, these programs, which at their core were designed to remedy inequities against African Americans, actually covered a majority of the U.S. population.[6] Federal efforts toward eradicating racial disparities began to take hold in state and local governments as well. Near the end of the 1980s, more than 200 separate state and local government programs existed nationwide, in addition to the more than 100 similar federal programs.[7] The impact of government contracting is extensive in the American economy. Approximately 25 percent of the entire U.S. workforce is employed by firms that contract with the federal government alone.[8] Annually, governments nationwide spend more than $450 billion in procurement contracts, with state and local governments responsible for spending more than half of this amount.[9]

As most people know it, affirmative action typically encompasses preferences by virtue of membership in a particular race or ethnicity, though women, veterans, and the disabled have also been the beneficiaries of some particular affirmative action programs. Most affirmative action programs fall into one of three areas, education, employment, or government contracting. Benefits for members of protected groups might include less stringent school admissions requirements, different standards used for hiring, promotion, and retention in the workplace, or government contracts in which members of a class receive more favorable treatment than nonmembers of the class.

Government contracting affirmative action programs—the type of claim at issue in *Croson*—are typically termed minority business enterprise (MBE) programs. MBE programs typically provide favorable treatment for minority-owned businesses in the bidding process for government contracts, which can range from the building of a new sports arena or convention center, to the purchase of office supplies or automobile parts, to the selection of accounting or legal services. Nearly anytime the government seeks to purchase a service or a good, there is an opportunity to contract with an MBE. The favorable treatment of MBEs ranges from set-asides or "sheltered markets," in which only targeted groups may compete for the government contracts, to "bid enhancements," whereby the bids submitted by MBEs are not directly compared to the otherwise lowest qualified bid, to "goals" programs, in which the government attempts to contract with MBEs without using set-asides or bid enhancements, most often by requiring primary contractors to make good-faith efforts in subcontracting with MBEs. Every level of government can, and nearly every type of government does, use MBE programs, from the federal government down to school districts and port authorities.

For nearly twenty years after the initiation of affirmative action, academics studying affirmative action have focused mainly on the legal and moral implications of such programs. There is no shortage of scholarship or commentary on affirmative action. Lino Graglia, Thomas Sowell, Linda Chavez, Richard Epstein, Dinesh D'Souza, and Shelby Steele, among others, argue against it; Ronald Dworkin, Charles Lawrence and Mari Matsuda, Kweisi Mfume, Christopher Edley, and Michel Rosenfeld, among others, argue for it.[10] The "against" and "for" arguments can be put succinctly:

> Whether you call them affirmative action or reverse discrimination, racial preferences are wrong. They are morally wrong whichever group is favored. They are also dangerous, because they reinforce the legitimacy of racial thinking and racial stereotypes. Race is simply an irrelevant personal characteristic.

Here is the counterargument:

> Color-blindness sounds good in theory but ignores social reality. Given a history going back to slavery, and the prevalence, even today, of conscious and unconscious discrimination, affirmative action is a necessity. It also ensures that the full diversity of viewpoints in our multicultural society is represented.[11]

To be sure, there are some nuances to these basic edicts, including arguments regarding possible efficiency gains from affirmative action, substituting class for race, maintaining preferences in higher education for blacks only, using affirmative action for diversity purposes, preserving affirmative action for symbolic purposes, and narrowing beneficiaries and limiting program scope duration.[12] And there are some surprising attitudes from some, including a significant change in opinion by Nathan Glazer from 1975 to 1998, and only lukewarm support for affirmative action from critical race theorists such as Adolph Reed, Derrick Bell, and Richard Delgado.[13] But in the end, we have been left with frequently repeated and simplistic arguments, mainly from two camps that indulge in caricature-like portrayals of their own and their opponents' views.

The overall reception of the affirmative action scholarship has been less than welcoming, and has included some scathing critiques. The affirmative action literature has been collectively termed "boring [and] hypocritical,"[14] "intractable,"[15] "caustic and draining,"[16] "outmoded,"[17] and a "ridiculous misallocation of scarce [academic] resources."[18] Despite the internecine academic battles over the normative basis for and the implications of affirmative action, economists and policy scholars have quietly been accumulating a fairly substantial empirical literature on the impact of affirmative action.[19]

The Legal Setting of *Croson*

The political and moral debates surrounding affirmative action can be quite complex. Yet the legal issue is, if not straightforward, at least narrow. The constitutional issue in *Croson* was simply whether the affirmative action program promulgated by the City of Richmond violated the Fourteenth Amendment's equal protection clause. The relevant components of the Fourteenth Amendment provide that "[n]o State shall . . . deny to any person within its jurisdiction the equal protection of the laws." Yet since nearly all conceivable legislation distinguishes between individuals (e.g., drunk driving statutes affect drunk drivers and sober drivers differently), courts employ varying degrees of scrutiny in determining whether challenged legislation violates the constitutional guarantee of equal treatment. Courts employ one of three standards of review in analyzing the constitutionality of disputed legislation: rational basis review, intermediate scrutiny, or strict scrutiny.[20]

The primary siphoning tool used by courts in equal protection analysis is the Constitution's demand of reasonableness. Legislation generally does not violate the equal protection guarantees of the Constitution if it "rationally furthers a legitimate state purpose."[21] As an example, we may consider a simple local drunk driving regulation. It is legitimate for a state to want to cut down on drunk driving, and legislation criminalizing driving with a 0.1 blood alcohol content would certainly be rationally related to that legitimate state interest. Or in regard to banking regulations, if state legislation permits the acquisition of in-state banks by out-of-state banks only from states with reciprocal privileges, this would merit and pass rational basis review, because the statute would be a logical law related to a permissible state interest.[22] Under this standard by which courts analyze contested legislation using equal protection analysis, nearly all examined statutes survive legal challenge.[23] There have been some exceptions, with the challenged legislation failing such a test, but such exceptions have generally occurred when the Court found a type of discrimination irrational.[24]

Beyond the constitutional demand of reasonableness, a higher level of scrutiny may be employed by courts for legislation implicating protected classes of individuals or fundamental rights. Statutes classifying on the basis of gender or illegitimacy must overcome a more difficult constitutional burden. Laws subjecting women to treatment different from that allocated to men, or laws subjecting children born out of wedlock to treatment different from that allocated to children born in wedlock, are analyzed under equal protection review with an intermediate level of scrutiny. Thus, if a state enacts a law allowing women to drink beer at the age of eighteen but does not allow men to drink beer until they reach the age of twenty-one, a court would uphold the statute on an equal protection claim only if the legislation fulfilled an "important government interest and [was] substantially related to the achievement of those objectives."[25] As a result, gender-based statutes are more likely to wither in the face of litigation than are purely economic regulations, as the government must have an important, not just legitimate, interest in the regulated subject and the legislation must be substantially, not just rationally, related to that interest.

Statutes that impinge on fundamental rights or that "suggest impermissible prejudice is afoot," whether through classification or disparate impact, are subject to the most stringent type of scrutiny used by courts. Equal protection review of legislation surrounding issues of national origin, race, alienage, and fundamental rights generally occurs under the auspices of strict scrutiny. For example, if the government sought to redraw congressional districts along racial lines, courts would uphold this legislation only if the statute was "narrowly tailored to achieving a compelling state interest."[26]

The constitutionality of affirmative action in the United States is a mixed story, ebbing and flowing across time and across areas: education, employment, and contracting. The first case to focus attention on the practice of affirmative action involved a plan by the University of California at Davis Medical School whereby the school set aside sixteen of the 100 available seats for minority students. In 1978 a plurality of the Court, in *Regents of the University of California v. Bakke,*[27] struck down this affirmative action program as violating either the Fourteenth Amendment's equal protection clause or Title VI of the Civil Rights Act. While the plurality opinion did not provide a rationale that garnered a full majority of the Supreme Court, Justice Powell's concurrence alluded to the constitutionality of race-specific affirmative action university admissions program. Such a program, modeled on a Harvard University admissions program, would allow the consideration of race not alone, but as a "plus" toward achieving the government's interest of diversity.

The Court would rule again in the realm of affirmative action just two years later, in *Fullilove v. Klutznick.* The case involved a federal contracting regulation requiring the government to spend 10 percent of federal contracts with firms owned by "citizens of the United States who are Negroes, Spanish-speaking, Orientals, Indians, Eskimos, and Aleuts." In a 6–3 decision, the Court upheld the affirmative action provision, but with varying rationales. Three justices (Marshall, Brennan, and Blackmun) only held the government program to intermediate scrutiny; one justice (Powell) found the program met the strict scrutiny standard, since Congress possessed remedial powers under Section 5 of the Fourteenth Amendment; and two justices (Chief Justice Burger and White) cryptically avoided the scrutiny discussion but instead remarked how Congress had unique equal protection enforcement powers.

In the final pre-*Croson* affirmative action case, another plurality of the Court struck down a public school teachers' union collective bargaining agreement with the school board that had a race-based component to layoff priorities. In *Wygant v. Jackson Board of Education,*[28] Justice Powell, joined by Chief Justice Burger and Justices Rehnquist and O'Connor, found that there was not "a strong basis in evidence" to justify such a remedial program. Justice White seemed to categorically reject racial balancing in regard to discharging employees and did not indicate what facts could have saved the collective bargaining agreement provision.

While *Wygant* involved an affirmative action plan surrounding employment and not government contracting, one may be tempted to believe that the ruling is not of precedential value. Even a cursory look at the procedural posture of *Croson,* however, demonstrates the relevancy. Following the lawsuit in *Croson,* the Federal District Court upheld the Richmond program (largely on the basis of *Fullilove*), as did the Fourth Circuit Court of Appeals.[29] The U.S. Supreme Court then granted certiorari to Croson, vacated the Fourth Circuit Court of Appeals decision, and remanded the case back to the lower courts to be reevaluated in light of the Court's decision in *Wygant.* Had the Supreme Court merely denied certiorari to Croson, as the Court does in close to 99 percent of the petitions it receives, it would have had the effect of freezing in place the Fourth Circuit ruling and leaving the Richmond program in place. That the Court ordered a new analysis of *Croson* in light of *Wygant* would likely prove perilous for the Richmond program.

When the Court finally ruled in *Croson* in 1989, then, opponents and supporters of the affirmative action plan at issue both had reason for optimism. The plan in *Croson* legislated on the basis of race, and therefore strict scrutiny would likely be the standard used by the Court. Not since the much maligned Japanese internment cases of *Hirabayashi* and *Korematsu* had the Supreme Court directly upheld government racial policy under the strict scrutiny standard. Combined with the vacate and remand order in light of *Wygant,* affirmative action opponents had good reason to believe that the Richmond program would be struck down. Supporters of the program, however, were emboldened by *Bakke* and *Fullilove v. Klutznick.*[30] *Fullilove* upheld a program very similar to the Richmond program, albeit with a lower standard of scrutiny, but *Bakke* seemed to indicate that in a limited fashion, affirmative action could survive even a strict scrutiny analysis.

The Opinion in *City of Richmond v. J.A. Croson Co.*

Justice O'Connor began the fractured U.S. Supreme Court opinion in *City of Richmond v. J.A. Croson Co.* by recognizing "the tension between the Fourteenth Amendment's guarantee of equal treatment to all citizens, and the use of race-based measures to ameliorate the effect of past discrimination on the opportunities enjoyed by members of minority groups in our society."[31] The City of Richmond offered a two-pronged attack to address the issue. First, the city argued that its program ought to be analyzed under an intermediate scrutiny standard, as was applied in *Fullilove,* and second, even if the Court analyzed the program under strict scrutiny, the city could meet the standard as suggested by *Bakke,* since the city's program was narrowly tailored to a compelling interest.

The premise underlying the application of intermediate scrutiny in *Fullilove* is that Congress has special constitutional powers granted to it under Section 5 of the Fourteenth Amendment, the so-called enforcement clause. This created a bit of a problem for Richmond in that a local government entity has no corresponding enforcement clause to empower the city similarly, and the City of Richmond devoted little of its brief on the merits to the issue of intermediate scrutiny.[32] This may be because the city anticipated how the Court would rule, but is likely also because of the hierarchy of scrutiny standards. If Richmond could meet the strict scrutiny standard, it necessarily would meet the intermediate scrutiny standard as well.

To make the case that Richmond's program was remedial (even beyond the specific use of the word "remedial" in the ordinance), the city pointed out that the situation on the ground at the time the ordinance was passed was dire. Between 1978 and 1983, MBEs accounted for only two-thirds of 1 percent of the city's $124 million construction contract dollars spent. This paltry spending occurred despite Richmond's 50 percent black population. Based on Congress's finding of rampant discrimination in the construction industry nationwide that came before the Court in *Fullilove,* scholarly literature on the barriers to entry for minority contractors, the lack of black membership in local trade organizations, and testimony at a public hearing from the mayor of Richmond about the pervasiveness of discrimination in Richmond's construction industry, the city argued that it had a compelling interest in eradicating the discrimination.[33]

Despite the seemingly blunt evidence offered by the city as justification for the program, the Court remained skeptical. The Court was not swayed that Richmond's legislation was actually passed for remedial reasons. The Court noted that Richmond's large black population actually cut the other way. Insofar as the Richmond City Council was more than 50 percent black, *Croson* presented the possibility that the program was the result of political strength, not political powerlessness. The Court seemed to be concerned that this program was not actually affirmative action but rather invidious discrimination against whites.

The Court rejected the City of Richmond's call for analysis of its program using intermediate scrutiny based on *Fullilove*. The Court reasoned that *Fullilove* involved a federal race-based program, and that Congress—but not the states—had broad powers to enforce the promises of the Fourteenth Amendment under Section 5 of the amendment. According to the Fourteenth Amendment text, Congress has the "power to enforce, by appropriate legislation, the provisions of this [Amendment]." According to the Court, Congress is entitled to deference in attempting to create "equal protection" under the Fourteenth Amendment, but state and local governments, the primary mechanisms that legitimated slavery, Jim Crow, and 100 years of political disenfranchisement, are not.

Without deference on par with Congress, and with an unconvincing argument regarding the remedial nature of the program, the Court struck down Richmond's ordinance as a violation of the Fourteenth Amendment. The J. A. Croson Company had been treated differently on the basis of race by the government without sufficient justification, and the city's program had come to an end. In quashing Richmond's ordinance, a full majority of the Court held for the first time that race-based legislation, no matter whether the result of purposeful discrimination or of remedial discrimination, is subject to the rigors of strict scrutiny. Finding neither a "compelling state interest" nor legislation "narrowly tailored" to that interest, the Court held that Richmond's program failed both prongs of the strict scrutiny test, and was unconstitutional.

The Meaning of *Croson*

Most observers of the Court believed that *Croson* meant the end of affirmative action. With the passage of time after the Court's January 1989 decision, however, affirmative action supporters began to change their interpretation of the case. Despite the ruling that affirmative action would be subject to strict scrutiny and the finding that Richmond's affirmative action program did not meet such a standard, affirmative action supporters did not lose hope.

In February 1989, the City of St. Louis's comptroller, Virvus Jones, urged policymakers to look beyond the Court's striking down of the program, as "the Court went further to tell cities and states how they could legally and legitimately establish race-based quotas."[34] And by March, Laurence Tribe had cautioned, "It's a mistake to read the Supreme Court's decision as a red light or command that programs prior to *Croson* be shelved."[35]

The reason for the cautious optimism stemmed from the rest of the Court's opinion in *Croson*. The Court not only disposed of Richmond's program but then, as in Justice Powell's opinion in *Bakke,* specified what a constitutional affirmative action plan would look like. The Court doctrinally specified how governments could create a constitutional affirmative action program, and thus even stirred some to think that *Croson* meant that the Court had constitutionalized affirmative action.[36] Justice Thurgood Marshall, in his dissent in *Croson,* picked up on Gerald Gunther's assessment that strict scrutiny is "strict in theory, but fatal in fact."[37] Justice Marshall had long harangued the Court for offering an illusory promise that legislation could survive the Court's most exacting scrutiny. Seeking to answer Justice Marshall, however, the majority of the Court in *Croson* proceeded to signal to courts and governments around the country how affirmative action programs could be structured in consonance with strict scrutiny. After striking down the City of Richmond's MBE program, the Court promised, "Nothing we say today precludes a state or local entity from taking action to rectify the effects of identified discrimination within its jurisdiction."

The *Croson* Court specified what actions would establish a MBE program that would be "narrowly tailored to achieving a compelling state interest" and thereby survive strict scrutiny. The Court provided both the compelling state interest for governments—"any public entity, state or federal, has a compelling interest in assuring that public dollars, drawn from the tax contributions of all citizens, do not serve to finance the evil of private prejudice"[38]—and specified five requirements of legislation "narrowly tailored" to that interest.

According to the Supreme Court, governments can demonstrate their compelling state interest with a showing of a "strong basis in evidence" of the practice of discrimination within its jurisdiction.

This evidentiary requirement, first announced in *Wygant,* means that the government does not have to be guilty itself of discrimination before enacting race-based programming—as had been urged by J. A. Croson Company—but also cannot broadly attack any and all discrimination, as had been urged by the City of Richmond. Rather, courts require that, before acting, governments must identify the practice of discrimination, with some specificity, in which the government played at least a passive role. Thus, *Croson* allows a government to correct its own prior discrimination *or* to intercede in the parts of the private market that are discriminatory and in which the government was at least a passive participant in the discrimination. For example, if the government regularly utilizes unionized contractors, and it is shown that local unions routinely discriminate against black contractors, then the government has played a passive role in the practice of discrimination. Similarly, if the government requires contractors to be bonded, and it is shown that local bonding sources routinely discriminate against Hispanic contractors, then the government has played a passive role in the practice of discrimination.

How can a government prove discrimination? In the final paragraph of Justice O'Connor's opinion in *Croson,* she spoke in the language of statistics:

> Proper findings in this regard are necessary to define both the scope of the injury and the extent of the remedy necessary to cure its effects. Such findings also serve to assure all citizens that the deviation from the norm of equal treatment of all racial and ethnic groups is a temporary matter, a measure taken in the service of the goal of equality itself. Absent such findings, there is a danger that a racial classification is merely the product of unthinking stereotypes or a form of racial politics.[39]

Thus the compelling state interest of "assuring that public dollars, drawn from the tax contributions of all citizens, do not serve to finance the evil of private prejudice" is, in the end, a statistical comparison, or more accurately a series of statistical comparisons.

The findings envisioned by the Court would be statistical disparities "between the number of qualified minority contractors willing and able to perform a particular service and the number of such contractors actually engaged by the locality or the locality's prime contractors."[40] Governments must gather data and compare the availability of separate minority group contractors (e.g., African American, Hispanic, Asian, Native American) in an industry (e.g., construction, goods, services, professional services) with the utilization of these same minority groups in a specific industry by the government in its contracting scheme before implementing an affirmative action plan or an MBE program. In defining the scope of "available" contractors, courts look to the reality of the marketplace rather than municipal geographic boundaries. Thus, the availability pool generally is considered to come from the Metropolitan Statistical Area (MSA) surrounding a municipality. Utilization is measured by the amount of contract dollars awarded to the available MBEs.

The quotient of the utilization and the availability in this regard has come to be known as a "disparity ratio."[41] When groups are vastly underutilized, the disparity ratio will be close to zero; when groups are overutilized, the disparity ratio will be greater than one. A disparity ratio of exactly 1 signifies parity between availability and utilization. No single talismanic disparity ratio exists that will trigger a favorable judicial review in analyzing the constitutionality of an MBE program. Rather, courts interpret the magnitude of discrimination on a case-by-case basis. If the number of minority contractors is sufficiently small, anecdotal evidence of discrimination may be the more useful type of information sought by a reviewing court.

The Supreme Court was somewhat less clear in its explanation of how to determine whether legislation is "narrowly tailored" to the "compelling state interest." According to the Court, one way of adducing whether legislation is narrowly tailored is to see if the legislation serves another purpose. If the legislation is a better fit with another purpose, or if other legislation is a better fit for this purpose, the legislation may not be narrowly tailored. Specifically, if the government has been attempting to rectify racial disparities for some time, it may have attempted to use race-neutral methods. If instead the government's first reaction to the discovery of racial disparities in its contracting system is to install a race-based program, this is some indication that the government's program serves another interest, such as capitulating to minority demands.[42]

A second mechanism to assess whether legislation is narrowly tailored is through analyzing the statute to see how the government arrived at the numerical goals set out in the legislation. The City of Richmond chose to set aside 30 percent of its contracting dollars for MBEs. It had arrived at 30 percent because the figure was halfway between the percentage of city contracts that had gone to minorities in 1983 (10 percent) and the Richmond black population (50 percent).[43] The city based this calculation on the method used by Congress to arrive at the 10 percent spending goal at issue in *Fullilove.*

The city also based eligibility for the Richmond MBE program on the federal categories of minority upheld in *Fullilove.* An MBE was defined in the Richmond ordinance as a "business at least fifty-one (51) percent of which is owned and controlled . . . by minority group members." The Richmond ordinance defined minority group members as "[c]itizens of the United States who are Blacks, Spanish-speaking, Orientals, Indians, Eskimos, or Aleuts." Numerical goals in affirmative action legislation must only be directed toward groups that have suffered an injury, and the response must be directed toward the availability of contractors "qualified . . . willing and able" to undertake government contracts.[44] Citing Justice Steven's dissent in *Fullilove,* the Court observed that "if there is no duty to attempt either to measure the recovery by the wrong or to distribute that recovery within the injured class in an evenhanded way, our history will adequately support a legislative preference for almost any ethnic, religious, or racial group with the political strength to negotiate 'a piece of the action' for its members."[45]

A third narrowly tailored component requires that the targeted affirmative action's numerical goals in the legislation must be flexible and cannot turn into rigid quotas. Drawing on the availability of waivers from noncompliance listed in the federal regulations in *Fullilove,* the *Croson* Court looked unfavorably on the Richmond legislation. Without the sort of adaptable legislation used by Congress, Richmond's program resembled more of an illegal spending quota than a true spending goal.

In determining whether race-based legislation is narrowly tailored, courts analyze a fourth factor: the burden shouldered by excluded groups.[46] In *Fullilove,* the Court reasoned that "to cure the effects of prior discrimination, such 'a sharing of the burden' by innocent parties is not impermissible." If the government is the dominant source of contracting for excluded groups, race-based programs will be looked on less favorably. Alternatively, if private contracting opportunities remain plentiful, the government's program imposes less of a burden on excluded groups and is more likely to be "narrowly tailored."

Finally, the Court in *Croson* spelled out the fifth narrowly tailored factor, noting that these programs should not "take on a life of their own."[47] There must be a built-in mechanism that recognizes affirmative action is a time-bound solution. After the factual predicate that gave rise to the need for the program, there must be a sunset on the policy.

The meaning of *Croson* is therefore that race-based programs may be narrowly tailored to a compelling state interest if governments demonstrate a series of statistical disparities between utilized and available minority contractors by race, ethnicity, and gender within different categories of government contracts, and then meet the five separate requirements for legislation to be considered narrowly tailored. First, the government must consider the efficacy of race-neutral alternatives to the race-based legislation. Second, the proffered statute must exhibit a relationship between the numerical goals contained in the legislation and the statistical area labor market, and ethnic groups for which no evidence of discrimination exists must not be beneficiaries of the program. Third, the legislation must be flexible and meaningfully allow for waivers from noncompliance with the goals set out in the regulations. Fourth, in determining whether the race-based legislation is narrowly tailored, courts analyze the burden shouldered by nonminority contractors. And fifth, MBE programs must contain a sunset provision, or ending date.

Some scholars claim that the Court's decision is "ambiguous"[48] or "exceptionally obscure."[49] Thus, in Cass Sunstein's view there is a "high degree of uncertainty about the law governing affirmative action." When *Croson* is placed in the context of other affirmative action decisions, Keith Bybee suggests the Court has left open political solutions and has not provided determinative guidance to the elected branches. Certainly the notion that the Court struck down

Richmond's ordinance yet specified how to set up a constitutional program seems partially incongruous. A look at the actual legal and political developments since the time of *Croson,* however, demonstrates that the only ambiguity and uncertainty are in the realm of academics. The real-world fallout of *Croson* is decidedly clear.

The Impact of *Croson*

There are typically three main avenues for assessing the impact of Supreme Court decisions: effects on institutions, on attitudes, and on behavior. In the following sections I trace the judicial and legislative legacy of *Croson,* outline the contours of public opinion surrounding affirmative action, and present some evidence about the role of the decision on individuals' behavior. Like other researchers, I find considerable evidence of legal and policy effects and limited evidence of the Court's role in changing public attitudes or individual behavior.

POST-*CROSON* LEGAL AND POLICY DEVELOPMENTS

Shortly after the *Croson* decision, the Supreme Court again revisited the issue of race-based legislation. In *Metro Broadcasting, Inc. v. FCC,*[50] the Court upheld a federal race-based program designed to increase minority ownership of radio and television stations, based on the fact that, unlike in *Croson,* Congress, and not a state or local legislature, had passed the legislation. The Court held that *Fullilove* provided for intermediate scrutiny of federal benign racial classifications and that the FCC's program was substantially related to an important government interest.[51] The FCC could permissibly seek diversity of views in distributing broadcast licenses, and minority ownership, in the opinion of the Court, was substantially related to such viewpoint diversity.

Any such hopes of affirmative action supporters produced by *Metro Broadcasting* would prove to be premature. In its 1995 decision in *Adarand Constructors, Inc. v. Peña,*[52] the Court, with the key change of Justice Thomas replacing Justice Marshall, struck down a federal contracting affirmative action program using strict scrutiny. At issue in *Adarand* was the constitutionality of a U.S. Department of Transportation program providing additional compensation to a prime contractor if it hired a disadvantaged business enterprise. Federal law provided a presumption of being "disadvantaged" based on race.[53] In remanding the case to the Tenth Circuit Court of Appeals for further decision, the Court in *Adarand* did away with the distinction between state race-based legislation and federal race-based legislation, contradicting both *Metro Broadcasting* and *Fullilove.* The Supreme Court ruled the analysis of equal protection under the Fourteenth Amendment (as applied to states or local governments) and under the Fifth Amendment (as applied to the federal government) is the same. Thus, as of 1995, "Any person, of whatever race, has the right to demand that any governmental actor subject to the Constitution justify any racial classification subjecting that person to unequal treatment under the strictest of judicial scrutiny."[54]

The Supreme Court again visited the issue of affirmative action in 2003, but this time in the realm of university admissions. Most significantly, in *Grutter v. Bollinger,*[55] the Court in a 5–4 decision upheld the University of Michigan Law School's affirmative action program using strict scrutiny. The Court reinvigorated Justice Powell's *Bakke* concurrence and found that the university had a compelling interest in achieving a diverse student body. Further, the law school's method of individually assessing each applicant's ability to contribute to that diversity was narrowly tailored to that end. For the first time in half a century, a majority of the Supreme Court justices found a race-based regulation to survive strict scrutiny.

Complicating the effect of such a ruling, however, was a companion case decided on the same day. In *Gratz v. Bollinger,*[56] the Court, again in a 5–4 decision, found an undergraduate affirmative action admissions program unconstitutional. The undergraduate scheme provided admission benefits for all minorities within favored groups (black and Hispanic applicants, but not Asian applicants) and did not involve an individualized determination of an applicant's contribution to diversity. While the Court upheld diversity as a compelling state interest, the undergraduate categorical approach was not narrowly tailored to achieving that interest.

What is particularly noteworthy about the two University of Michigan cases is that in the two 5–4 decisions, only Justice O'Connor was in the majority in both cases. In *Grutter,* Justice O'Connor was joined by the then four most liberal justices (Stevens, Ginsberg, Breyer, and Souter), and in *Gratz* the majority consisted of

O'Connor, Kennedy, Rehnquist, Scalia, and Thomas. While the ideological arrays are certainly telling, more to the point—it would be just three more years until Justice O'Connor would retire—and casting significant doubt on one of these two cases was the arrival of Justice Alito.

Justice O'Connor's replacement on the Court, Justice Alito,[57] wasted little time in demonstrating his opposition to the government's benign use of race. In two companion cases, the Supreme Court struck down two separate, voluntarily adopted student assignment programs in Seattle, Washington, and Louisville, Kentucky, that used racial criteria. In *Parents Involved in Community Schools v. Seattle School District No. 1*,[58] Justice Alito joined Chief Justice Roberts's plurality decision along with Justices Scalia and Thomas. Justice Kennedy concurred on separate grounds, while Justices Breyer, Ginsburg, Souter, and Stevens dissented. The Roberts's plurality opinion stressed that the *Grutter* opinion did not govern primary and secondary education and found that the school districts' racial balancing was unconstitutional.

The development of the Supreme Court's equal protection clause jurisprudence seems firmly in line with scholars' discursive framework notions, according to which Court decisions vary in nonlinear fashion as new disputes arise. Yet if we look not at the equal protection clause jurisprudence as a whole but instead at how the MBE jurisprudence has developed in the lower courts, a more consistent pattern emerges. The next section traces reactions to *Croson* in the lower courts, the courts that have directly implemented the Supreme Court's jurisprudence.

JUDICIAL RESPONSES

The Supreme Court, with all of the attenuated powers accorded to it by Article III, delegated to it by Congress, and accorded to it by the American people, depends on other institutions to implement its decisions. Following a Supreme Court decision, legal and political actors outside the Supreme Court are responsible for executing the Supreme Court's directives. These actors could include a school district that redraws its boundary lines to achieve an integrated school, a prison administration the opens the jailhouse doors for someone exonerated, or lower—inferior—courts that analyze a challenged federal regulation under a new standard developed by the Supreme Court. This "queen bee/drone" relationship has been labeled by some a "principal-agent" relationship, whereby the Supreme Court is the principal creating directives to be actualized by its agents.[59] How well have the Supreme Court's directives in *Croson* been meted out by the inferior courts?

The inferior courts analyzed about sixty different contracting affirmative action programs from the time the Court decided *Croson* in 1989 to August 1, 2006. The decisions included those addressing federal, state, and local programs. Judges from both state courts and federal courts have decided the fate of these programs, including laws written after the Supreme Court's ruling in *Croson*. I have divided these judicial rulings into three different time periods, based on the Court's jurisprudence. I first analyze the cases decided between the time of *Croson* and *Adarand*, followed by cases decided after *Adarand* and through *Grutter* and *Gratz*, and finally cases decided since *Grutter* and *Gratz*.

CROSON TO ADARAND. In the immediate aftermath of *Croson*, courts around the country resolved the fate of several other challenged affirmative action programs. The Supreme Court granted certiorari and vacated the judgment in light of *Croson* for an Eleventh Circuit case that would later be found unconstitutional by the Eleventh Circuit.[60] In *American Subcontractors Association v. City of Atlanta*,[61] the Georgia Supreme Court struck down Atlanta's contracting affirmative action program from 1984, overturning a trial court decision that had upheld the program pre-*Croson*. This type of ruling, in which a court analyzes an affirmative action program under strict scrutiny and promptly rules the program unconstitutional, was typical for the period. Nine other lower courts and the U.S. Supreme Court in *Adarand* all found programs unconstitutional during this time period. While occasionally a lower court upheld an affirmative action program after *Croson*,[62] in each instance those rulings were promptly reversed by an appellate court.[63]

Either the standard announced in *Croson* or the one-sided results of the lower court cases also persuaded several jurisdictions that their affirmative action programs could not withstand constitutional muster. Governments rescinded programs in New York, Connecticut, Maryland, New Jersey, and North Carolina during the course of litigation,[64] and press accounts reveal other out-of-court settlements involving the dismantling of unconstitutional programs.[65]

All told, not a single challenged contracting affirmative action program survived litigation, with a ruling on the merits. And it is that slight qualification—a ruling on the merits—that makes some difference. Courts found eleven programs unconstitutional and six cases moot because the underlying programs had been dismantled, but dismissed four cases based on standing. Standing essentially means that the parties to the lawsuit have enough of a stake in the lawsuit to receive a judicial determination of the claim.[66] Courts rejected the lawsuits of four different plaintiffs,[67] arguing that the plaintiffs in those cases did not suffer "an injury in fact." A constricted and contorted view of standing is explainable in half of these cases, as they were decided before the Supreme Court ruled expansively on this point in 1993 in *Northeastern Florida Chapter of the Associated General Contractors of America v. Jacksonville.* This case clarified that plaintiffs need not have been the lowest qualified bidder on a contract but instead must demonstrate that they competed on terms different from other bidders. A fair reading of the standing doctrine suggests that in at least three of the four cases in which courts have denied standing to plaintiffs in post-*Croson* cases since 1993, these judges attempted to circumnavigate the Court's *Croson* jurisprudence.[68] These rulings left four affirmative action programs intact, but it should be noted that dismissing a claim on the basis of standing does not preclude other parties from bringing litigation against the same challenged program. Additionally, during this period the courts decided three cases on other grounds, including on the basis of the contract,[69] or waiver.[70] In another case the court refused to issue an injunction because the plaintiff did not have a substantial likelihood of success on the merits.

We have from this period two different sets of cases. In one set are the eleven constitutional cases decided on their merits, with a lopsided 11–0 record against affirmative action. But the second set of cases involves the imposition of aconstitutional reasoning in either striking a program down, or modifying a statute, or delaying a wholesale attack against an unconstitutional program. Some of these cases may simply have been the result of poor representation,[71] but it is noteworthy that in many of these seventeen cases, the judges were able to avoid or delay striking down the challenged affirmative action programs by refusing to answer the constitutional question.

ADARAND TO *GRUTTER* AND *GRATZ.* The jurisprudence around the country from 1995 to 2003 resembled the rulings from the earlier period to a substantial degree. Courts found sixteen programs unconstitutional and one California program in violation of Proposition 209.[72] Courts blocked three challenges on the basis of standing,[73] stopped a case because of estoppel,[74] dismissed a claim for "failure to allege sufficient facts,"[75] and used statutory construction to hold that use of the word "minority" did not really imply a race-based program.[76]

Yet there is one sharp difference—at least at first blush—between the cases of this middle period and the cases of the earlier period. Three different courts upheld contracting affirmative action programs in the face of constitutional challenge. In *Ritchey Produce Co., Inc. v. Ohio Dept. of Adm. Serv.,*[77] the Ohio Supreme Court upheld a state set-aside provision; in *Adarand Constructors, Inc. v. Slater,*[78] the Tenth Circuit Court upheld part of a federal set-aside provision; and in *Concrete Works of Colorado v. City and County of Denver,*[79] the Tenth Circuit Court upheld a local government contracting program under strict scrutiny. It seems that the post-*Adarand* era demonstrates inferior court disobedience of Supreme Court doctrine.

A closer look at these cases, however, shows a different picture. In *Ritchey,* the Ohio Supreme Court found that Ohio's set-aside provision passed strict scrutiny. Yet this exact same program was then struck down by the Sixth Circuit Court of Appeals one year later in a separate challenge.[80] In *Adarand v. Slater,* the Tenth Circuit Court upheld a portion of a federal set-aside statute. When *Adarand* appealed the ruling to the U.S. Supreme Court, the United States abandoned its use by the government. Though the U.S. Supreme Court granted certiorari in the case, presumably to overturn the Tenth Circuit's maverick decision, the Court soon learned that the program had been abandoned by the government, and dismissed the writ of certiorari as improvidently granted.[81] And finally, in *Concrete Works of Colorado,* which appeared to be the only remaining case upholding a state contracting affirmative action program since *Croson,* the Tenth Circuit Court reached its conclusion because the particular plaintiff involved in the case waived his claim regarding the second strict scrutiny component of narrow tailoring. Thus, the Court found only that the government had a compelling state interest, and was able to reject the legal challenge to the program because of legal misstep without directly ruling that such a program was constitutional. In the end, just as in the earlier period, the lower courts also did not uphold affirmative action programs as constitutional.

POST-*GRUTTER* AND *GRATZ.* In the few years since the Supreme Court decided the University of Michigan cases, some may have thought that because the Court found diversity to constitute a compelling state interest, the jurisprudence laid out in *Croson* may have been modified. Justice Scalia, joined by Chief Justice Rehnquist, dissented from the Court's denial of certiorari in the *Concrete Works* case above and penned a straightforward critique of the Tenth Circuit Court's opinion. What is noteworthy, though, is that Scalia argued that "denial of certiorari in [the Tenth Circuit ruling] is important because of what it signals about this Court's ongoing commitment to exacting judicial review of race-conscious policies." He goes on to compare the Tenth Circuit's ruling to the "good-faith" deference to the University of Michigan Law School in *Grutter.* It is possible that this has occurred, but if so, only for federal cases. Since June 2003, there have been six post-*Croson* cases decided by the courts. All six have been decided on the merits. In four cases the courts struck down contracting affirmative action programs as unconstitutional, but in two cases the Eighth Circuit Court of Appeals and the Northern District of Illinois each upheld a component of a federal affirmative action program. In both *Sherbrooke Turf v. Minnesota Department of Transportation*[82] and *Northern Contracting v. State of Illinois,*[83] the courts upheld part of the Transportation Equity Act for the Twenty-first Century (TEA-21). Congress passed the TEA-21 just a few years after *Adarand.* What is interesting about these cases is that both of them are more deferential to Congress in analyzing compelling state interest. In both cases the courts found that Congress enjoys more latitude in identifying discrimination than does a component of a local government, because of Section 5 of the Fourteenth Amendment. This, of course, is inapposite to *Adarand's* evisceration of differences in analysis for affirmative action that were extant in the transition from *Fullilove* to *Croson.* This also does not change the constitutional status of state and local MBE programs under the doctrine of *Croson.*

In sum, through August 2006, I identified sixty distinct federal and state cases with reported (including both published and unpublished) decisions analyzing contracting affirmative action programs in federal or state court that should have used the *Croson* standards.[84] Of these sixty cases, thirty-six resulted in a decision on the constitutionality of the affirmative action program. In those thirty-six cases, thirty-one times a court found the legislation at issue to be unconstitutional. Three of the five cases with opposite conclusions involved a federal transportation program with a different analysis used for Congress's compelling state interest. Another case involved a ruling by the Ohio Supreme Court upholding a program that was overturned by the Sixth Circuit, and in the only federal case to allow a state affirmative action program to stand, the court ruled that the plaintiff waived the "narrow tailoring" component of the typical post-*Croson* analysis. Thus, in the seventeen years following *Croson,* not only is the overall record in the constitutional cases 31–5, a close look at those five cases reveals that no court that has dutifully analyzed an affirmative action program has upheld such a program. Tribe's contention that governments could pass constitutional muster is wrong; Justice Thurgood Marshall and his admonition of the Court for offering an illusory promise was right. Strict in theory, and indeed fatal in fact.

Yet this analysis also reveals another aspect of judicial responses. In twenty-five cases since *Croson* the courts never reached the constitutional issue. In a few of these cases the program was struck down for other reasons, and several courts dismissed claims that had become moot, but the standing cases, pleadings cases, and statutory construction cases seem to exemplify a method of at least delay, if not obfuscation. Some judges have effectively been able to maintain unconstitutional programs by avoiding the constitutional analysis. The laws challenged in the cases dismissed because of standing or insufficient pleadings could be attacked by other individuals, but by knocking out such challenges using aconstitutional reasoning, these courts are effectively raising the cost of litigation for challengers. No longer are jurisdictions simply folding in the face of litigation as they had done in the immediate aftermath of *Croson*, but governments around the country are engaging in their own form of resistance—sometimes aided by the judiciary.

LEGISLATIVE RESPONSES

Determining the legislative response to *Croson* is much more difficult than determining the judicial response. Despite three large efforts, no single comprehensive list of MBE programs in place before or after *Croson* exists. We are left with just two attempts at listing MBE programs, limited to major U.S. cities, and one large-scale survey. Although the metropolitan lists come from two reputable sources (the Minority Business Enterprise Legal Defense and Education Fund and the Joint Center for Political and Economic Studies), the data are conflicting and incomplete.[85] The survey is an improvement on the metropolitan lists, but still problematic. George La Noue reports there were 234 MBE programs confirmed by surveys at the time of *Croson*, and perhaps upward of 2,400 once sampling vagaries and nonresponses are accounted for.[86] But the actual number and location of these other programs are not much more than conjecture. Further, the hope of ever completing a comprehensive list is doubtful, given (1) the wide range of levels of government that employ MBE programs and (2) the incomplete maintenance of local government records, in either electronic or hard-copy form.

Instead, we must rely on using the litigation record and other secondary reports regarding MBE programs in state and local government to adjudge the legislative response to *Croson*. Two lawyers report that fifteen jurisdictions voluntarily dismantled their programs within the first year of the *Croson* decision, and another fifteen programs were dismantled by 1993.[87] E. Mabry Rogers and Rodney Ross also claimed in their ABA address that four nonfederal jurisdictions successfully defended their programs on the merits. Without specifying those cases, we can only assume that each has now been overturned by an appellate court.

A much more reliable source for evaluating some of the legislative response is provided by the Project on Civil Rights and Public Contracting (PCRPC), run by George La Noue at the University of

Maryland–Baltimore County. As a result of *Croson,* state and local governments have hired groups of consultants to conduct the statistical analyses underlying the compelling state interest component of the strict scrutiny review. These reports have come to be known as "disparity studies" and cost on average $500,000. La Noue has catalogued all of the disparity studies in the public domain. According to his list, as of August 2006, there were 197 such disparity studies conducted in an attempt to comply with the *Croson* requirements, and at least 130 of those studies were conducted before 1996 (three studies do not list a date). A chart of the cumulative number of disparity studies from this list is shown in figure 1.1.

While the PCRPC list is the most exhaustive list with evidence of the legislative response to *Croson,* inclusion on the list does not translate neatly into a full-fledged legislative response. For example, the City of Miami commissioned a disparity study in 1991, yet the city's legislation has not changed one word since the *Croson* decision was announced.[88] Rather, as explained in chapter 4, the City of Miami responded bureaucratically, maintaining the MBE program on paper and limiting the actual program implementation. Further, while both Philadelphia and Portland, Oregon, appear on the PCRPC list as using disparity studies, Philadelphia opted to

FIGURE 1.1 Total number of disparity studies, 1989–2006

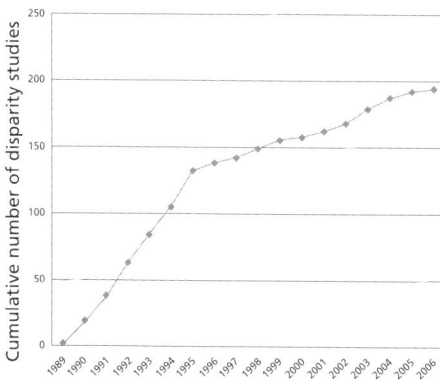

Source: University of Maryland, Department of Political Science, Project on Civil Rights and Public Contracting, directed by George R. La Noue. Chart created by author from aggregated data. See http://userpages.umbc.edu/~glanoue/.

litigate the constitutionality of its program, while Portland voluntarily dismantled its program and co-opted the leading contractors' interest group as the city created a new program in the late 1990s. Because disparity studies were essentially nonexistent before *Croson* and commonplace thereafter, however, a tremendous legislative response to *Croson* cannot be gainsaid.

THE SUPREME COURT AND PUBLIC OPINION

Scholars have not traced the immediate effects of single Supreme Court decisions regarding affirmative action on public opinion. Yet we can begin to evaluate the effect of *Croson* on public opinion by examining the overall contours of public opinion surrounding affirmative action. Most notably, what we know is that American views of affirmative action have been mostly stable, with an overall slight decrease in support over time. Most of the decrease can be accounted for by the decreasing support for this policy among African Americans.[89] Yet while the overall numbers are decreasing, in predicting public support for affirmative action, one would still look chiefly to race and ideology. African Americans largely support its practice, while conservatives largely oppose its employ. The racial differences can be quite sharp, ranging from a 30 to 50 percentage point difference between black support and white support for affirmative action. A significant difference persists, although decreasing slightly from 20 to 30 percentage point differences, when black Democrats and white Democrats are compared.[90] There is some evidence that support for the policy is no longer associated with Hispanic ethnicity, and appears unrelated to region (in the United States), education, or union membership. Support is also unrelated to income when reflective of support for affirmative action in hiring but was found to be inversely related to income when support for the use of affirmative action in college and university admissions was examined in 1992.[91]

One area that has seen significant variation over time is the extent to which the media pay attention to affirmative action. From the mid-1970s up to 1991, there was a slight, steady increase in the number of stories mentioning affirmative action in both the *New York Times* and *Newsweek*. Following a three-year decline in the number of stories published in these periodicals from 1991 to 1994, which lowered the proportion of stories mentioning affirmative action back to the 1970s levels, there was a large spike in articles in 1995, the year in which the Supreme Court decided *Adarand*. Yet within two years, the number of articles again fell to the earlier low levels. A similar but less extreme uptick and fall also occurred in 2003, the year in which the Court decided *Grutter* and *Gratz*.[92] By 2006 the proportion of articles mentioning affirmative action in these periodicals almost exactly mirrored the level thirty years earlier. Media attention to affirmative action may episodically increase, but it appears to reset to earlier levels just as quickly as it rose.

The balkanized views of affirmative action appear to be unrelated to Supreme Court decisions. While the level of attention on the part of the media changes in relation to Court cases, no discernible differences are apparent in support for or opposition to affirmative action by race or ideology in relation to these same Court cases. The overall stability of views and generalized decrease in support for affirmative action appear to reflect more societal characteristics or views than views of judicial decision making.

THE SUPREME COURT AND BEHAVIOR

Researchers examining how Supreme Court decisions, including *Croson,* ultimately affect individuals' behavior also face major limitations. Just as in the realm of public opinion, there is very little variation in the behavior from before a Court case is heard to after a Court decision. The Court's decision in *Croson* ending affirmative action plans should have meant that minority contractors would have received fewer contracts from the government, especially in construction. Since much of government construction work is essentially transitory, a low level of skill is necessary to compete for the jobs, and the industry enjoys relatively high wages with few barriers to entry to firm formation, especially in terms of capital, construction is the dominant landscape for affirmative action programs.[93] This diminishment in contracts would also mean several ancillary behavioral effects, including fewer MBEs, lower capacity of MBEs, and less minority employment. Yet the evidence for these effects is lacking, mostly because there is very little evidence that affirmative action programs produce any substantive gains (e.g., more MBEs, greater capacity, or more minority employment).

There is no statistically significant association between the growth of black-owned businesses and the existence of affirmative action programs. The growth rate of black-owned businesses in cities with MBE programs was not different from the growth rate of black-owned businesses in cities without MBE programs for the years 1982, 1987, and 1992. However, researchers have found that sales for black-owned businesses may grow in cities with black mayors, even without corresponding MBE programs in place.[94]

One study examined the number and size of contracts for MBEs before, during, and after the period in which the State of New Jersey created and ran an affirmative action contracting program. Researchers found that existing disparities between black- and white-owned businesses actually became worse during the affirmative action time period. Although the number and size of contracts let to MBEs increased while the program was in effect, the more substantial increases for white-owned firms during the same period suggest that the affirmative action program itself was not responsible for the gains. These findings are bolstered when one considers that even as MBEs conducted more work for the government, the survival rates of these same businesses did not increase. In fact, businesses that derived more than one quarter of their revenues from the government were less likely to survive than firms with a more diversified clientele.[95]

Finally, there is little evidence that MBE programs increase black or Hispanic employment. Instead, minority construction employment in Philadelphia, Portland, and Miami appears related to larger overall trends in the construction industry and increased during periods of government growth, rather than during periods in which these cities operated government contracting affirmative action programs.[96] Similarly, these affirmative action programs also were unrelated to addressing existing disparities in employment rates within the construction industry.

Because there is very little evidence that affirmative action programs in government contracting result in tangible gains for affirmative action beneficiaries, a Supreme Court decision ending affirmative action is not particularly poised to limit affirmative action beneficiaries. This is not to say that a contractor who may have received a contract under an affirmative action program would have received a government contract without the program. Rather, it is to recognize that the effects of Supreme Court decisions in this area are limited in their scope. Just as some schools may have desegregated in the immediate aftermath of *Brown v. Board of Education* and some women may have been encouraged to seek an abortion in the aftermath of *Roe v. Wade,* but in neither case were the behavioral responses on the ground widespread, the same appears to be the case with *City of Richmond v. J.A. Croson Co.* and the lives of minority contractors. In subsequent chapters I analyze how different cities have coped with the Supreme Court's affirmative action policies and untangle how the same Court case could have different effects in different parts of the country at the same time.

Croson, Dialogue, and the Contours of Checkmate

Since the Supreme Court's *Croson* decision, two apparently contradictory effects have materialized. First, the Supreme Court and the lower courts have maintained a consistently hostile stance toward affirmative action in government contracting programs. The Supreme Court extended the *Croson* analysis to cover federal affirmative action programs in *Adarand,* and the lower courts have knocked down almost all challenged programs, only restricting challenges using aconstitutional reasoning. Second, this same time period witnessed a massive surge in new constitutionally suspect affirmative action programming and the maintenance of existing constitutionally problematic affirmative action programs. Only a handful of jurisdictions voluntarily dismantled unconstitutional contracting programs. That is to say, there have been two very different institutional responses to the exact same Supreme Court decision.

The different institutional outcomes are not particularly problematic as long as a mechanism exists for a constitutional dialogue to take place. If judicial decisions leave room for legislative and executive responses and if elected branch decisions can be reviewed by the courts, the notion of separate institutions sharing powers rings true. Yet what we see here is different. While there have been approximately sixty different judicial decisions regarding MBE programs since *Croson,* there are several hundred, if not more than a thousand, different legislative or executive MBE programs. This massive discrepancy between the institutional outcomes suggests that there has been a breakdown in the ongoing constitutional conversation about affirmative action.

While in the next three chapters I detail many of these different institutional responses in three large metropolitan cities, one can begin to see the social, legal, and political factors that have contributed to the institutional discrepancies. There are quite stable public views of affirmative action, with notable differences based on race—but not based on judicial decision making. There are some aconstitutional grounds for resisting challenges levied against affirmative action, most notably, but not limited to, standing. And in the policy realm, we have seen at best only very limited evidence of isolated behavioral changes resulting from affirmative action policies.

As this story now turns from the Supreme Court and the national responses to the decision, the individual pieces of those cumulative responses come to the fore. Philadelphia, Portland, and Miami provide a high-quality collection of cases with which to analyze affirmative action in action. The study of these cities offers geographic, racial, and governance diversity that can then be extrapolated to a wide array of other U.S. cities and contexts. To generalize, Philadelphia represents a black-and-white, eastern, unionized, strong-mayor industrialized city of the past. The Philadelphia experience can speak to Baltimore, Boston, Cleveland, and Pittsburgh. Portland is western, largely white—with coalitional minority groups—has a commission form of government, and is a new modern city. Portland speaks to Minneapolis, Denver, San Francisco, and Seattle. And Miami is very different. While Miami operates with a council-manager form of government and, like Los Angeles and San Antonio, has a large Hispanic population, the Cuban exiles among Miami's population place the city in its own category. How these cities' reactions vary, including the various forms of checkmate they employed, demonstrates the contingent and varied responses to Court cases. A look at these individualized responses begins with Philadelphia, for much of the early affirmative action history was effectively written in Philadelphia and the city's response serves as a model of successful Supreme Court–elected branch continued interactions.

2

PHILADELPHIA AND THE
ONGOING DIALOGUE

Philadelphia, it is said, is a city of firsts.[1] Philadelphia had the first American stock exchange, theater, merry-go-round, and daily newspaper. It also had the first stone bridge, paper mill, insurance company, telephone book, and public schools in the colonies. As the city that gave birth to the U.S. Constitution, it is thus only fitting that Philadelphia has figured so prominently at the beginning of the country's history with affirmative action. Not only did Presidents Johnson and Nixon develop the first federal race-based affirmative action contracting program, the aptly named Philadelphia Plan, for Philadelphia, but Philadelphia was the site of the first post-*Croson* lawsuit, by Associated General Contractors (AGC), and the first trial over a post-*Croson* minority business enterprise (MBE) program.

While Philadelphia is first in many respects, it is also a typical northern postindustrialized city. Like Cleveland, Detroit, and Milwaukee, Philadelphia in the last half of the twentieth century saw a large growth in its African American population and a large decline in its manufacturing base. The eroding tax revenues and increased pressure on local spending resulted in, in the words of a local reporter, a city "on the brink."[2] From 1970 to 1980 the city's manufacturing base was slashed in half, and the number receiving public assistance increased from 200,000 to almost 350,000.[3] For a city that once was the preeminent American city, an icon of freedom and liberty to developing nations across the globe, modern

Philadelphia had become a stereotypical declining American urban morass.[4]

The economic downturn and the white flight to the suburbs that plagued Philadelphia posed substantial obstacles for local politicians seeking to fix the harsh conditions afflicting the black community. Beginning in the early 1980s, Philadelphia began to pass a series of local ordinances designed to assist African Americans. This legislative agenda included a program to involve black contractors in city contracts. Philadelphia's MBE program sought to spend 25 percent of city contracting dollars with minority-owned firms. The MBE program drew the ire of AGC in the weeks following the U.S. Supreme Court's ruling in *City of Richmond v. Croson,* and AGC filed a lawsuit designed to force Philadelphia to comply with *Croson.* And just as happened in Richmond, the judiciary struck down the MBE program in Philadelphia.

This chapter explores the largely successful court–elected branch interactions related to the Supreme Court's affirmative action policies. Philadelphia is unique in that the city has long been associated with affirmative action yet typifies the legislative-judicial cycling as suggested by the coordinate construction scholarship. Following *Croson,* the city council and the mayor defended existing policies from an interest group challenge and attempted to follow the doctrine announced by the Court in *Croson,* yet still found themselves losing the core of the city's affirmative action program to litigation in 1996. Since that time, the city has directed efforts toward increasing the contract dollars awarded to black-owned firms through qualifying some local black-owned firms for a federal "disadvantaged" set-aside program at the Philadelphia airport and through vigilant enforcement of equal opportunity legislation, but without a direct MBE program of its own. What is crucial in the Philadelphia story is the back-and-forth iterations of constitutional dialogue between the elected branches and the courts, with each branch of government offering up its own view of the Constitution. Ultimately the view from the judiciary would, appropriately, come to rule the day.

Affirmative Action in Philadelphia

Affirmative action, in a sense, was born in Philadelphia. President Johnson's Philadelphia Plan, initiated in 1969, instituted race-conscious hiring practices for both contractors and subcontractors seeking federal contracts. The trade unions and others, however, were slow to endorse these mandated inclusion efforts. As a result of the obstinacy displayed by the unions, several private lawsuits were filed in the 1970s against unions and the government alleging violation of the equal protection guarantees of the law.[5] Facing both legislative and judicial orders to end their discrimination, some trade unions began to integrate racially. In the words of Robert Beauregard, however, "Progress was being made, but at a glacial pace."[6]

Efforts to assist minority businesses, and minorities in general, had traditionally been the province of the federal or state governments. But in the 1970s, local governments, now beginning to be run by dominant minority coalitions that had taken over from the splintering Democratic machines, started to address racial and economic issues on their own.[7] With the dwindling manufacturing base, the political strength of Philadelphia's industrial unions had weakened, and the Democratic coalition of unions, minorities, and liberal whites largely disintegrated.[8] The changing power dynamics in local politics helped facilitate and then to shape the new political agenda. Political power in the city began to concentrate in neighborhoods, an example of what one scholar calls "street-fighting pluralism."[9] The newly distributed power brokers in the political world of Philadelphia caused the city to devolve into a "city of fiefdoms and feudal lands, and warring bands of self-interest."[10]

In 1980, two of the most powerful members of the city council were (future mayor) John Street and city council president (and future congressman) Lucien Blackwell, both African American men.[11] Blackwell had been approached by black contractors complaining of the lack of minority participation in city contracts.[12] Blackwell sought assistance from the city solicitor's office by asking its lawyers to draw up a bill addressing the contractors' concerns. Then mayor William Green initially resisted these efforts, arguing that affirmative action was illegal. Faced with high-profile cases of police mistreatment of blacks and crumbling housing in black neighborhoods, however, Green felt he had no choice. He agreed to let the legislation go forward if the city solicitor's office could demonstrate the constitutionality of the program.[13] For two years the ongoing negotiations between the mayor's office and the city council, mediated by the city solicitor's office, slowed the momentum of the potential contracting program.

THE HEARINGS

On February 17, 1982, the city held the first of several public hearings regarding the issue of minority contracting in Philadelphia. According to the transcripts of the city council hearings, witnesses in the first hearing included a U.S. congressman, interest group representatives, some city officials, and a few contractors. Witnesses made oral statements, and then subsequently entered their prepared written remarks into the record. No witnesses came forward from the city's Purchasing Department—the office responsible for cutting checks to contractors—and the only opposition to the proposed program came in a written statement from John Smith, general manager of the Contractors' Association of Eastern Pennsylvania, the local chapter of AGC.

Congressman William H. Gray III began his testimony arguing why the legislation was needed in the Philadelphia area. Gray suggested that Philadelphia's MBE program would "[redress] the fact of years of racism and isolationism experienced by the Philadelphia minority business community, in their efforts to fully participate in the city's procurement and contract in activity." Gray reported that of the more than $975 million spent on city-funded contracts between 1979 and 1981, minority-owned firms in Philadelphia received a total of $774,000, or less than one-tenth of 1 percent of the city's contract dollars. Gray argued that since blacks made up 37.5 percent of the population and Hispanics 3.8 percent, serious government efforts were needed to address the underutilization of minority contractors. In closing, Congressman Gray struck an ominous tone "Today's hearing serves notice to every local politician, black or white, Democrat or Republican, that Philadelphia's minority electorate will no longer tolerate crumbs off the floor when it comes to City funded contracts, but that we want our full share of the whole loaf of bread, and if need be, we will move to take over the bakery."

This combination of economic need and political solution dominated the testimony of most other witnesses as well. Benjamin Brown, vice president of Systems Research Company, a professional

services company in Philadelphia, contended that the combination
of minority politics and healthy minority economics could cement
gains for the entire city. After speaking of the MBE programs in
Portland, Oregon, Baltimore, Boston, Syracuse, and New Orleans,
Brown suggested that there was "a direct correlation between the levels of unemployment and the levels of crime as compared with that
of the business vitality of the black communities." Curtis Owens,
a contractor with Impact Associating, also thought that the MBE
program "can be an effective tool to increase the economic status
of minorities . . . provide an incentive for minority growth and ex-
pansion, and help increase employment and the tax base." And a
representative of the National Association of Minority Contractors
offered, "We realize preference programs are not a panacea for the
problems of minority contractors; however, they do provide a firm
base from which these companies can branch out and develop."
Therefore, whether one subscribed to maximus or minimus goals
for the program—to benefit the entire community or to lift up
those facing severe challenges—at the core of each type of goal was
an economic motivation. If the city let contracts to minority-owned
firms, these firms—and possibly others—should flourish.

Additional witnesses at the hearings also testified regarding the
program's initial scope—to cover "minorities" with a 25 percent
spending goal. The bill did not have separate goals for different minority groups or any spending goals for women-owned businesses
(WBEs). On further questioning from Councilwoman Joan Specter
(wife of now U.S. senator Arlen Specter) and Councilwoman Au-
gusta Clark about why women were excluded from the legislation,
city attorney Carl Singley suggested there ought to be separate hearings regarding coverage for women.

In a second hearing, which occurred the following month, the
efforts of Councilwoman Specter bore fruit. The MBE bill was
amended to include a 10 percent spending goal for WBEs. During this hearing Beverly Harper, a representative of a coalition of
minority contractors called the Brain Trust, provided information
about the origins of the spending goal figure of 25 percent. According to Harper, "The goals were a compromise. There were a number of people in the Brain Trust who wanted the goals to be much

higher. We went through several meetings where we discussed the goals, and I felt we should go in, a number of people felt we should go [in,] for higher goals and negotiate down."[14]

This second hearing also provided some additional information regarding what at least some program proponents meant by goals. The discussion between Councilwoman Clark and Ms. Harper is illustrative of the minimum nature of these goals.

> Councilwoman Clark: And we're talking about goals being the minimum achievement, not the maximum?
> Ms. Harper: Yes.
> Councilwoman Clark: So that nothing prevents the city from doing 80 percent business with women; is that not true?
> Ms. Harper: That's true.
> Councilwoman Clark: And what we're saying is that the city will not have met the minimum expectations of this piece of legislation if it gives less than ten percent of its contracts to women?
> Ms. Harper: That's true.
> Councilwoman Clark: And in all cases the goals we've established in this piece of legislation are minimum goals.
> Ms. Harper: Yes.

Thus, at least for Councilwoman Clark and Ms. Harper, the 10 percent goal for WBEs established between the first two public hearings and the 25 percent goal established for minorities were not actually goals, in the sense of rough aspirations. Rather, the figures represented a hard floor that, if not achieved, would mean the city had fallen short of the "minimum expectations." If the city did not spend at least the "goal" amount, the program had failed. No witness, however, called these goals "quotas."

Despite ballpark spending goals and stern minimum expectations, several witnesses testified at the city council hearings that Philadelphia's MBE program would withstand constitutional challenge. Rotan Lee from the Washington, D.C.–based Minority Business Enterprise Legal Defense and Education Fund informed the city council that "the Supreme Court has been very clear that there is nothing inherently unconstitutional about the evolution of programming that is identified for certain groups of people, as long as it is not exclusive and preclusive. . . . And that can be done in a way that can overcome even some of the stiffest legal challenges." Greg Wheeler, an attorney for the Brain Trust, maintained that "[the bill] has been specifically formulated to meet the Fourteenth Amendment Equal Protection standards established in a landmark decision *Fullilove v. Klutznick.*" (The *Fullilove* decision upheld a federal MBE program in 1980.) The city's attorney also suggested that by tailoring the city's legislation and actions to what the Supreme Court thought was important in *Fullilove,* the Philadelphia program would similarly withstand legal challenge. When I interviewed many of these same individuals almost twenty years later, they still believed that what was being done in 1982 by Philadelphia should have been upheld by the courts.[15]

THE PROGRAM

While the courts would one day evaluate Philadelphia's MBE program, a different and unforeseen obstacle stood in the way: Mayor Green. Even though Green had negotiated with the city council, primarily with the MBE legislation sponsor Lucien Blackwell, Green still vetoed Philadelphia's MBE program. Mayor Green accused the city solicitor's office of "working for Lucien Blackwell" and suggested that the program had been rammed down the throats of Philadelphians without careful deliberation. Even some program supporters—who admitted to not being fans of Mayor Green— concurred. According to one bureaucrat, "The City Council, especially Lucien Blackwell, had an attitude, like 'don't tell me how to do my job.' They stopped the hearings as soon as they had 9 votes [of the sixteen-member City Council]."[16] An exchange that occurred about midday during the first hearing, between city council chairman Lucien Blackwell and Councilman John Street, highlights the eagerness to bring the bill up for a vote:

The Chairman: Any questions by the committee?
Councilman Street: Mr. Chairman, I have one question.
The Chairman: Councilman Street.
Councilman Street: I would like to know whether it's time to
    vote yet.
The Chairman: I'm ready.
Councilman Street: I'm ready to vote.

>   The Chairman: If you notice, Councilman Street has been rather
>   quiet today and that's unique for him. But he is already con-
>   vinced [to vote yes]; he had his mind made up when we walked
>   in. Thank you, sir.

The attitude evinced by Street and many others was that the
public hearings were not really about garnering evidence to be used
to decide a course of action. Rather, the hearings were effectively
pro forma. Though even a casual observer of C-SPAN could ob-
serve that legislative hearings are not always about serious inquiry,
this exchange highlights how governments may simply go through
motions devoid of substantive content.

Pursuant to the local rules established for the Philadelphia City
Council, on May 13, 1982, the city held an override hearing regarding Mayor Green's veto of the MBE program. In a short hearing,
the city council managed to override Green's veto with a vote of
16–0. And beginning on July 1, 1982, Philadelphia joined Atlanta,
Portland, Oregon, Washington, D.C., Baltimore, Birmingham, Alabama, Boston, New York City, Los Angeles, Camden, New Jersey,
Oakland, San Diego, and Chicago in having its very own MBE
program.

In creating Philadelphia's MBE program, the city also created
a new bureaucracy to administer the program, the Minority Business Enterprise Council (MBEC). Launched with a staff of twenty,
MBEC certified contractors and reviewed all contracts greater than
$10,000 (later raised to $30,000) and reported back to each city
department specifying the percentages to be used for set-asides on
each contract. Based on the availability of minority and women
contractors, these recommendations could range from zero to 100
percent. In addition, in 1987 the city amended its MBE ordinance
to include a 2 percent spending goal for certified disabled-owned
businesses. But rather than disaggregate contracts into four parts,
majority, minority, women, and disabled, MBEC sought to achieve
its overall spending goals by identifying individual contracts that
should be targeted to each group. As one bureaucrat remarked,
"Trying to spend two percent of a construction contract with a
blind guy ain't gonna cut it."[17]

The results of Philadelphia's MBE program looked nothing short of astonishing. Before the program started, MBEs earned less than $1 million of the average annual $300 million contracted by the city. In 1984 MBEs grossed $43 million, and in 1988 MBEs contracted with the city for $62 million.[18] An investigation by local reporters, however, alleged that roughly half of all the contracts made with MBEs were awarded to "fronts" or "pass-through" businesses[19] and that just two companies, both based outside Philadelphia, received the bulk of those dollars.[20] Despite this likely fraudulent activity and the direction of dollars to non-Philadelphia firms, there still appeared to be sizable gains for minority employees. Although minorities accounted for little more than 10 percent of the construction workforce, minority participation on government contracts during these same years ranged from 15 to 20 percent. Compared with the paltry pre-MBE program numbers, the Philadelphia program provided significant gains for minority contractors.

Interest Group Activation and Judicial Agency

As minority contractors enjoyed success under Philadelphia's MBE program during the mid- to late 1980s, there were undoubtedly individuals who thought those successes should have been directed elsewhere. Around the country, local members of AGC, the construction industry trade association, thought that as a result of all of the new MBE programs they were now being excluded from government construction contracting and even local political participation.[21] As a result, AGC waged legal battles in different parts of the country over the constitutionality of programs similar to Philadelphia's program. While AGC went without success in most of these lawsuits, when the U.S. Supreme Court granted certiorari in *City of Richmond v. Croson,* AGC's "strategic opposition" strategy was just about to come to fruition. By systematically choosing to fight over the most egregious examples of MBE programs around the country, AGC designed its litigation efforts to culminate in a strong opinion from the U.S. Supreme Court eradicating these programs nationwide.[22] This strategy is in accordance with the literature on interest group litigation strategy, generally in support of "repeat players."[23]

Emboldened by the Court's ruling in *Croson* striking down Richmond's MBE program under strict scrutiny, and true to the history outlined in the legal mobilization literature,[24] AGC began a second litigation campaign. Now that AGC had achieved a positive ruling from the Supreme Court, the association sought to use the *Croson* standards to dismantle programs across the country. In the words of a closely allied interest group, "State and local minority business programs will fall like dominoes because of the ruling."[25] Within four years of *Croson,* AGC would initiate lawsuits in fifty-five cities around the United States. A lawsuit against the City of Philadelphia over its MBE program, commenced within just three months of *Croson.*

The City of Philadelphia attorney assigned to defend the program knew that Philadelphia's program could not withstand judicial scrutiny in light of *Croson.* The city clearly lacked the detailed quantitative evidence sought by the Supreme Court, and its goals were simply the result of political compromise—one of the factors that led to the demise of the Richmond program. Nevertheless, Philadelphia decided on a multipronged defense. First, Philadelphia would defend its program in court, hoping for a favorable judge to be assigned the case. Second, Philadelphia would attempt to go through the disparity study process outlined in *Croson* and argue that postenactment evidence would be sufficient to sustain Philadelphia's MBE program. And third, the city developed a backup plan in the form of an executive order that delineated spending goals similar to the legislation.[26] If the city's legislative program were shut down, Mayor Rendell, with the stroke of a pen, would enact a new program to take its place.[27] This posture of defense, in the face of doctrinal loss, would at the very least serve to maintain some semblance of a program in the interim and position the city as still attending to minority interests.

During the up-and-down course of litigation, which resulted in three federal district court opinions and three federal circuit court opinions, the government's strategy of delay began to gain momentum. A graphical representation of the snakelike litigation route is presented in figure 2.1. By fighting the AGC and using its backup plan as needed, the city was able to operate its program—despite its unconstitutionality—for a lengthy period of time. Based on these court opinions involving the Philadelphia program, one can trace the judicial responses to *Croson* at the local level.

AGC's lawsuit, filed in federal court in Philadelphia on April 14, 1989, traversed the discovery phase and resulted in the typical cross-filing of summary judgment motions. Summary judgment motions ask the judge to rule as a matter of law that the movant is entitled to relief because the relevant facts are not in dispute; parties, depending on the local rules, may file for summary judgment in part or in whole. On April 5, 1990, Judge Louis Bechtle, a Nixon appointee in the Eastern District of Pennsylvania, granted the plaintiff's summary judgment motion and ruled that Philadelphia's

FIGURE 2.1 Philadelphia's affirmative action litigation route in *Contractors Ass'n of Eastern Pennsylvania Inc. v. City of Philadelphia*

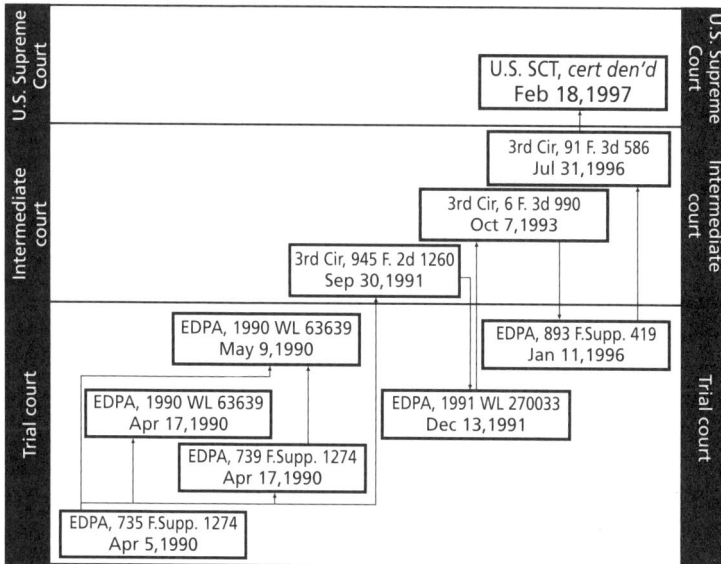

Source: Based on Case History Graphical Representation, 2006. Reprinted in part from a KeyCite display on Westlaw, at www.westlaw.com, and used with permission. Copyright © 2009 Thomson Reuters.

MBE program was unconstitutional. Bechtle found that *Croson* "is centered on a discussion of the difficult level of proof with which a government must comply to pass muster under the strict scrutiny test. The focus seems to be on the methodology and process a government must employ in enacting a set-aside provision." The court found that the city's multiple program goals of encouraging minority participation on city contracts, increasing employment, remedying the pattern of past and present societal discrimination, and growing minority businesses were all insufficient under the guidance of *Croson*. Further, the court chastised the city for the political compromises made to include women and the disabled in the set-aside provisions.

The city appealed Bechtle's decision granting summary judgment for the plaintiffs to the Third Circuit Court of Appeals and won a partial victory, being granted an extension of the discovery period to come up with more evidence, on September 30, 1991. The city's victory, however, was short-lived. In reviewing what transpired during the additional sixty days granted for discovery, Judge Bechtle found on December 13, 1991, that the city still "has not produced any evidence which could cause the court to reconsider its prior ruling."

The city again appealed Bechtle's ruling to the Third Circuit Court of Appeals. This time, however, the city's case was assigned to a different panel of three judges and scored what appeared to be two large victories. First, in the Third Circuit's October 7, 1993, ruling, the court found that AGC had standing only in relation to construction, and limited the scope of the hearings to construction. The city's program, as far as it applied to vending and nonconstruction services, would not be subject to this litigation.

This victory for the city, however, was not of much solace to the proponents of the program, for two main reasons. First, denial of standing does not address the merits of the issue but rather states only that there are better parties to bring the case. If a more appropriate party came forward, the city's program would still be subject to attack. And second, construction is the primary focus of just about all local affirmative action programs.[28] The second victory for the city, however, seemingly had more import for the crux of the program. The Third Circuit held that Judge Bechtle had improperly allocated the burden of proof in the case to the city, and remanded the issue of construction set-asides for minorities back to Judge Bechtle for a full hearing.

What followed in Philadelphia was the very first trial over a post-*Croson* MBE program. Although litigation in similar cases had become part of the AGC strategy nationwide, the cases had been decided either on the pleadings or on summary judgment motions. During the nine-day bench trial in Philadelphia, AGC presented just two witnesses and entered about 100 exhibits into evidence. The main expert witness offered by the plaintiffs was political science professor George La Noue. La Noue testified that the social science evidence relied on by the city in its case was methodologically flawed, just as he had said in his many depositions and expert witness reports in other cases. The city's main expert was an economist, Andrew Brimmer, who conducted a disparity study for the city, just as he had done for several other cities. The legal resolution over the reinvigoration of the urban black core had come largely to rest on the testimony of a political scientist and an economist.

As he had done twice before, Judge Bechtle in 1996 found Philadelphia's MBE program unconstitutional. This time, however, Bechtle tried to make sure he would not have to deal with this case yet another time. Just in case some part of his ruling would be deemed insufficient by a higher court, Bechtle held that the legislation was unconstitutional for five separate reasons, any one of which would have been constitutionally sufficient. Bechtle ruled that the disparity study used by the city was not statistically refined enough to account for nondiscriminatory disparities, the city was not shown to be a passive participant in a discriminatory marketplace, the goals used in the legislation were not tied to availability, race-neutral measures were not considered by the city, and the scope of the program was not limited to the Philadelphia marketplace. Despite the city's efforts, the MBE program did not comport with U.S. Supreme Court precedent.

Thus it was not terribly surprising when the Third Circuit yet again reviewed Judge Bechtle's decision and found that the city's program violated the equal protection guarantees of the Fourteenth Amendment. After the Third Circuit denied the city's motion for rehearing in July 1996 and the U.S. Supreme Court denied certiorari in the case in February 1997, it all finally came to an end: Philadelphia's MBE program for minority construction workers had been ruled unconstitutional.

Constitutional Dialogue

The Philadelphia saga offers a window onto legislative and judicial constitutional dialogue. Philadelphia's city council crafted its MBE program with an eye toward compliance with Supreme Court doctrine. After the city initiated the policy, a city agency, MBEC, implemented the decision. In the interim, the U.S. Supreme Court again ruled on affirmative action, and subsequent to that ruling an interest group filed a federal lawsuit in Philadelphia. Following a series of judicial decisions from the district court and rulings on appeals by the Third Circuit Court of Appeals, the City of Philadelphia resigned from its efforts to stray from the Supreme Court's jurisprudence. After fourteen years of attempting to push its view of the Constitution, the city came to understand that the Court's view of the issue would rule the day. The back-and-forth nature of the dialogue between the courts, the elected branches, and even nongovernmental actors is the mark of a successful constitutional dialogue. Tracing this conversation demonstrates that while the City of Philadelphia maintained a view of the Constitution different from the judiciary's, ultimately a concept of judicial primacy prevailed.

To create Philadelphia's program, a member of the city council directed one of the attorneys from the city solicitor's office to draft the bill. This attorney canvassed court opinions, notably *Fullilove v. Klutznick* and other municipal legislative efforts of a similar ilk. After reviewing other programs and drafting Philadelphia's program to be in line with the rules set out in *Fullilove,* Philadelphia held a series of public hearings over the proposed bill beginning in 1982. Throughout these hearings, witnesses identified not only the perceived need for such a program but also potential problems with the proposed program. As a result, the Philadelphia City Council amended its original draft of the program to accommodate set-aside efforts for WBEs. Philadelphia again amended its program five years later to include disabled-owned businesses.

Philadelphia at this time made some rather reasoned responses to the economic situation facing African Americans in the city, and with reasonable interpretations of Supreme Court jurisprudence. Just as Congress had selected a 10 percent spending provision for minority contractors in the program upheld by the Supreme Court in *Fullilove* using a compromise, so too did Philadelphia use a compromise in selecting a 25 percent spending goal for minority contractors. Justice Powell's concurrence in *Fullilove* suggests that Congress adopted the 10 percent set-aside as a compromise between the 4 percent of minority contractors and the 17 percent of minorities in the general population.[29] In Philadelphia, less than 1 percent of contract dollars had been won by minority-owned firms, yet Philadelphia's minority population made up about one-half of the general population. Philadelphia, also like Congress, used a broad notion of minority in establishing its program, not differentiating among Hispanic-, Asian-, and African American–owned firms. Although these factors, or more precisely the lack of relationship between the spending goal and the actual availability of each minority classification within a given field, ultimately proved decisive in the downfall of Philadelphia's program, at the time of their adoption in 1982 these choices were certainly a reasonable view of the Constitution in light of the Supreme Court's jurisprudence at the time.

The Supreme Court's decision in *Croson* answered Philadelphia's view of the Constitution with a fairly strong rebuke. Not only did the *Croson* Court strike down Richmond's MBE program but the Court delineated the standards by which future similar cases should be adjudicated by the lower courts. Almost immediately after the Supreme Court's decision, an interest group, AGC, instigated a lawsuit in federal court against the City of Philadelphia charging— correctly, as it turned out—that Philadelphia's MBE program did not adhere to the then just announced standards.

While Philadelphia's view of the Constitution was quite reasonable in terms of *Fullilove,* the Supreme Court distinguished that case before pressing ahead with its ruling in *Croson.* At issue in *Fullilove* was a congressional program, and in *Croson* the Court adjudicated a local (state) program. Congress, according to the Court, possesses different powers than do the states, notably powers granted specifically to Congress under Section 5 of the Fourteenth Amendment. Philadelphia's powers, in terms of adherence to the U.S. Constitution, are the same as Richmond's—not as Congress's. The Court in

Croson also specified that the goal percentages must be related to the availability of minority contractors, differentiated by race or ethnic group. According to Justice O'Connor's opinion in *Croson,* that Richmond included Aleuts and Eskimos among the program beneficiaries without demonstrating a history of discrimination against those same groups proved constitutionally problematic. This too would pose an issue for Philadelphia, even though it did not for the federal program in *Fullilove.*

Just as Philadelphia responded to the Supreme Court's *Fullilove* decision, so too it would respond to the *Croson* decision. Philadelphia directed economist Andrew Brimmer to conduct a disparity study of Philadelphia's contracting system, attempting to match its efforts to the doctrine announced in *Croson.* Whether Philadelphia could utilize post-policy-enactment evidence to justify an existing program had not been definitively ruled on by the Court in *Croson,* as the issue was not raised by the Richmond case. Again, Philadelphia came up with a reasonable interpretation of the Constitution given the Supreme Court's jurisprudence. In the resolution of the lawsuit facing Philadelphia, the judiciary did not precisely rule on the question of whether postenactment evidence would suffice for constitutional analysis. Instead, the courts held that *even if* postenactment evidence sufficed, the actual evidence used by Philadelphia still fell short of the constitutional standard announced in *Croson.* Among other things, the disparity study at issue in Philadelphia did not statistically account for nondiscriminatory disparities between black and white contractors. The judiciary ruled that Philadelphia's program violated the Constitution, and the dominant track of affirmative action in the city came to an end.

Ultimately Philadelphia's view of the Constitution failed, and the judiciary's won out. Yet what is particularly noteworthy is the back-and-forth dialogue between the branches of government. Philadelphia's program reflected reasonable attempts to navigate through the Court's doctrine. On two separate occasions Philadelphia shaped its legislative efforts to comport with Supreme Court decisions. Both the judiciary and the elected branches offered their views of the Constitution, and instead of endless cycling, this process ended by giving deference to the judiciary. Philadelphia did not, however, suddenly become an anti–affirmative action city; notably, in the face of ending its program, Philadelphia still maintained its MBEC offices, and its citizens eventually even elected Councilman John Street. The Supreme Court in its decisions left room for policy innovation among the various components of the elected branches but was still the definitive voice in terms of deciding the larger meaning of the equal protection clause of the Fourteenth Amendment. The Supreme Court did not rule as a club and command compliance but instead decided and requested, in its doctrinal direction to the lower courts, to give primacy to the national court structure. The right to equality means the same thing in Richmond, Virginia, as it does in Philadelphia, Pennsylvania.

In the next two chapters, I show that both Portland, Oregon, and Miami, Florida, have affirmative action programs likely to be adjudged unconstitutional, yet both jurisdictions have adopted strategies that have staved off litigation. These strategies have blocked the judiciary from ruling against each city's MBE program and have made it likely that these cities will be able to continue to maintain these programs without allowing the judiciary to continue the constitutional dialogue. The right to equality has a different meaning in Portland and Miami than it does in Richmond and Philadelphia, and this difference directly challenges the notion of judicial primacy that I advance in this book.

3

PORTLAND AND UNSUCCESSFUL COURT–ELECTED BRANCH INTERACTIONS

In the 1983 movie *War Games,* a computer programmed to think and speak runs through several simulations of both tic-tac-toe and the "real-life" game Global Thermonuclear War. Failing to find a winnable pattern to ensure victory, the computer declares, "Strange game. The only way to win is not to play at all." The City of Portland, Oregon, has similarly learned how not to play the litigation game. Rather than constantly amending its affirmative action program for government contracting in reaction to the courts, the city has been able to maintain its unconstitutional affirmative action program by blocking the threat of litigation against the city.

When the U.S. Supreme Court decided *Croson* in January 1989, Portland's city attorney, Madelyn Wessel, believed the city had few options. Wessel read the decision, and especially the Court's doctrinal discussion of how to craft a constitutional affirmative action program; she recommended to then mayor J. E. "Bud" Clark that Portland's minority business enterprise (MBE) program would not withstand legal challenge and must be repealed. Mayor Clark made it known to the city commissioners that the city's affirmative action program, which dated to the 1970s, would have to be eliminated.

In the mid-1990s, however, new Portland mayor Vera Katz led a consortium of governments in the process of establishing new affirmative action programs. In attempted partial compliance with the Court's opinion in *Croson* and related decisions from the U.S. Court of Appeals for the Ninth Circuit, local governments banded together in their efforts to undertake the costly disparity study process. This process resulted in a hefty fourteen-volume report detailing even arcane historical artifacts, past government and private sector practices, and contracting results, which was used by the city and other local governments to establish new MBE programs designed from the contours of *Croson*. But even as Portland put forward its new affirmative action program, built in line with the *Croson* doctrine, the city also knew that litigation was a dead end. The judicial standards had proven to be illusory, and the only way to maintain the program would be to insulate it from legal challenge. Portland, rather than assuming an adversarial posture against Associated General Contractors, brought AGC into the fold and made concessions to the interest group that ensured the survival of the affirmative action program despite its unconstitutionality.

The Road to, From, and Back to Affirmative Action

In the 1970s, the City of Portland began to pass a series of civil rights ordinances designed to address the needs of its minority communities. Though there had been a number of protests and lawsuits against the city or the local unions in the 1960s, it was not until black, Hispanic, and Asian populations began to move into the city from the outlying areas in the 1970s that the city's legislative agenda appreciably changed. In 1974, Portland passed a contract compliance ordinance that required all firms contracting with the city to be certified as equal opportunity employers. By 1979 the city had passed what it thought was a comprehensive approach to encourage MBEs to contract with the city, including a 10 percent utilization requirement on contracts in excess of $100,000.[1]

To be sure, the city's mostly white population was not uniformly enthusiastic about the plan. The disdain of one contractor, then a supplier of heavy duty trucks to the city, was reported in the local papers after Portland passed yet another affirmative action ordinance in 1976: "We're not able to go out to some pig trough somewhere and pick up some kind of revenue sharing money to meet affirmative action plans."[2] Despite some vocal and active opposition from the white community, in the late 1980s the City of Portland maintained its 10 percent MBE participation rate on municipal construction contracts.[3]

In the late 1980s, however, two judicial decisions changed the landscape of minority contracting in the Portland area. First, in late 1988 a federal judge in Oregon struck down Multnomah County's (the county fully encompassing the City of Portland) MBE program in response to a lawsuit brought by a white contractor and an interest group, AGC. Then in January 1989, the U.S. Supreme Court issued its opinion in *Croson*. Madelyn Wessel, Portland's city attorney, studied both opinions and knew Portland had not collected data in a fashion that would withstand legal challenge. Wessel informed populist Mayor Clark that defending the city's MBE program would be fruitless. The city's program was subsequently eliminated in direct response to the *Croson* decision.[4]

The judicial dismantling of the county's program, combined with the legislative dismantling of the city's program, nearly crippled the minority business communities and sent local governments scurrying for cover. In the first year following *Croson*, the city's MBE participation rate, or percentage of minority employment on government contracts, fell from 10 percent to less than 3 percent, and the county's MBE participation rate fell from almost 20 percent to under 1 percent.[5] According to a former city and county commissioner, the city and county were terribly concerned with "getting around *Croson*."[6] Meanwhile, the city developed some alternative programs and spent nearly $800,000 on programs that wound up contracting with only one or two minority suppliers over several years. Yet city projects completed in North-Northeast Portland, where the black community is concentrated, continued to use white workers—much to the chagrin of local residents. The perception among minority communities was that the city was not an effective agent for social change.

By 1992, "there were significant protests, organized by an ad hoc group of contractors, about the fact that non-white contractors were not getting their fair share of City work."[7] As a result of both the visible nature of the minority contracting protests and the long-held personal views of then mayoral candidate Vera Katz, affirmative action became a major theme of the mayoral race in 1992. A victorious Mayor Katz set to work on the affirmative action issue right away in the early days of her administration in 1993, assigning responsibility for the issue to her chief of staff, Sam Adams.

Given the decidedly anti–affirmative action outcome in both the Multnomah County case and *Croson,* one might think that the city's options would be limited. Legal analysis from the early 1990s, however, by the State of Oregon's Department of Justice and the City of Portland's city attorney's office cast a more optimistic light.[8] While the outcome of both court cases wound up dismantling existing affirmative action programs, the text of the opinions spelled out for state and local governments how to enact an ostensibly constitutional affirmative action program. The city and the state recognized that rigid quotas were now dead-letter law, absent activities on behalf of the government that would subject the government to a race discrimination lawsuit. But according to their analysis, a host of other affirmative action options was available to governments, without resorting to rigid quotas.

Legal analysis was not enough for the City of Portland. The city also sought input on the process from the local policy stakeholder communities that ultimately would be affected by a potential program, including majority and minority contractors' groups. According to one organizer, "One of the first things we did was establish an advisory group—the Fair Contracting and Employment Forum [FCEF], to both get educated in qualitative issues from the perspective of contractors, or potential contractors—and to also educate them. . . . My perception was that, after reviewing what other cities had done, what we had done, and what we had reviewed in the court cases, which were frankly leading, requiring, toward a fact based approach. It seemed like the obvious thing to do."[9]

In 1993, Mayor Katz moved forward with her plan to establish an MBE program that would not be struck down by the courts, and sought the Portland City Council's approval to conduct a fact-based disparity study, in accordance with the guidelines elucidated in *Croson* and, by that time, several lower court opinions implementing *Croson.* In a statement regarding the disparity study, Mayor Katz left little doubt about the reason for conducting it: "The decision to fund the study was first and foremost a response to the United States Supreme Court decision in *Richmond v. Croson,* 1989, so that the City would be in a position to support appropriate growth and advancement opportunities for minorities and women, without the constant threat of legal liability."[10] Rather than seeing it as a laborious task heaped on unwitting governments by the Supreme Court, City of Portland personnel willingly subscribed to the rationale behind the disparity study:

> In a City as complex as the City of Portland, which has a Commission form of Government, with 30 odd bureaus divided among five Commissioners and [which] operates in silos, unfortunately, more than it should, that [our earlier] work done based on perceptions wasn't accomplishing much. We needed to get below the surface and establish a baseline and track our results. So we did a disparity study, which is not only required by law, but I embraced the disparity study and encouraged the depth and breadth of it that we have, on the advice of [city attorney] Madelyn Wessel, because it was a way to define the problem. I thought it was great that the Court was requiring that, because in a lot of public policy issues . . . you don't have the luxury of going in and defining the problem. All the solutions that stem from an ill-defined or inadequately defined problem usually have an ill-defined or inadequate solution.[11]

The city spared few resources in seeking the best possible disparity study that money could buy. It hired George La Noue, the University of Maryland–Baltimore professor who usually served as an expert witness to testify *against* the soundness of disparity studies (including in Philadelphia) as a consultant to help *design* the disparity study.[12] This strategy of bringing one's opponents to the table foreshadowed how the city would engage with AGC. The city joined forces with nine other governments and still managed to spend more than $700,000 over three years to obtain their fourteen-volume report in 1996. While the outside consultants conducted their disparity study work, the city began to hire staff specifically to track data on city construction contracts internally.[13]

Those individuals intimately involved in the decision to create the disparity study maintain that the process was fair. According to one bureaucrat, "I didn't care what the disparity came out saying, as long as it was as accurate a reflection of the facts as we could assemble them. And it has its weaknesses because the facts hadn't always been well tracked along the way. I was interested in the facts, and then I was interested in having our constituents and our bureaucracy wrestle with those facts—as opposed to wrestle with the generalized issue."[14] But outsiders, both affirmative action supporters and opponents, took a less sanguine view of the city's motivation, including one former legislator who remarked, "They knew what they were doing when they paid $700–$800 thousand for consultants."[15] In this view, the disparity study was not really about studying an issue but about buying a package of information to satisfy the courts.[16]

The city did not stop in its efforts with the publication of the disparity study. The disparity study was merely one more step along the way in policymaking. Those close to the mayor argued that the disparity study was an incomplete piece of the policy creation puzzle: "My experience in these 17 years has been when I look at what other cities have done, the court cases served as their strategy. The disparity study has nothing close to a strategy. Sure, there is a list of recommendations. But that is still far from a strategy. So there was no way we were going to put together a strategy without getting advice."

So the city created yet another committee, the Contract Coordinating Committee (C3), lead by Adams, Wessel, and the city's director of purchasing, Sue Klobertanz, to come up with such a strategy, starting with what was contained in the disparity study. As one legislator later remarked,

Fundamental to this effort has been the effort of Sue [Klobertanz], Madelyn [Wessel], and Sam [Adams]. Sue with the operational side of it. Sam on the politics side, and Madelyn on the legal side. . . . Without any one of them, I don't think it could have succeeded. Sue is very hard charging, and she's been able to accomplish in terms of implementation is frankly amazing. Along the way as a result of that sort of hard charging attitude, she ruffled a lot of feathers. The system doesn't change without someone there dragging folks along. There are some Bureau Managers who don't really like her much. Madelyn is key, because she has some national expertise on this issue. She's able to bring to the table not just her own great legal mind, but also to offer a comparative insight to what other places are doing or not doing. The fact that it has been run out of the Mayor's office, and by the Mayor's Chief of Staff, has also contributed. It wasn't done just by staff. This has been done under the close thumbprint of the Mayor. She gave Sam her full support and he used it to full advantage.[17]

This "iron triangle" of politics, law, and operations led the city's exhaustive efforts to create a comprehensive program tailored to the factual predicate laid out in the fourteen-volume disparity study.

C3, however, also brought in the folks from FCEF who had previously helped steer the city's course of action in obtaining the disparity study. Of note, FCEF membership included not only affirmative action supporters but also several representatives from AGC, as well as black contractors who were convinced the city's efforts were only smoke and mirrors, intended to keep the status quo in place.

C3 and FCEF were charged with using the disparity study findings to develop a workable program. According to a bureaucrat who led much of this effort,

> We spent months going through every single page of those 14 volumes. I worked them. I was the "bad-ass" who forced them to go through every single page relating to the City of Portland because I wasn't going to ask for all that effort and then have it not go anywhere. I needed all [of them] at least wrestling with the same facts that we had to wrestle with. So we did that, and as we did that I think that their views changed. Mine changed. I don't know if they necessarily recognize[d] it, but it allowed them to get more sophisticated [about] where to apply the pressure. As opposed to railing against the City, they were able to apply pressure to not only the right bureau managers, but also the right sectional leaders within bureaus—the people who manage the project managers, the project managers that had the big, big projects. So it allowed them to get a lot more sophisticated and to get better results.[18]

This laborious presentation of information not only provided city officials and committee members with important information but served to cement relationships with fractious parties.

The results of the C3 and FCEF efforts included a ninety-two-

page document, known as the "Strategy," structured as if designed
by an academic policy analyst. The Strategy provided background
on the issue, defined the problem, set out the goals to be achieved
in the program, specified long-range outcomes that should result
from the program intervention, assigned responsibility and a budget
for each program element, and provided a timeline for implementing each phase of the program. Mayor Katz introduced the Strategy
to the Portland City Council on August 27, 1997, and it was unanimously adopted.

Portland's MBE Program

The guiding principle behind Portland's new MBE program is
an aspiration toward "race and gender parity in the amount the City
spends to procure goods and services by awarding contracts to a
diverse and competitive group of local contractors while providing
significant employment opportunities to minorities and women."[19]
Among the specific goals identified in the Strategy is that "the City
achieve, and sustain for three consecutive years, parity in the number of contracts [and contract dollars] received by a diverse group of
[contractors] so that race and gender specific program criteria may
be removed." The Strategy also identifies several specific objectives
of the program, including "graduating at least ten firms per year
from [a specific program component] after it has been in operation
for three years."

The program has many race- and gender-neutral components,
including better training of managers, program outreach, and the
provision of general business assistance to any contractor who asks
for help. In the words of one bureaucrat, "Don't underestimate
that a lot of what we have done here is simply improve the City's
purchasing system in general. The large contractors, unlike the
small minority contractors, can pay to have someone on staff wade
through all of the red tape and bureaucratic regulations."[20] Other
components of the MBE program address apprenticeships, subcontracting, equal employment opportunity certification, public-
private partnerships, and a sheltered market program. While all of
these components are directed in some fashion toward establishing
overall spending parity, the program is far from simple-minded. A
high-level city official explained, "This is a very complex problem,

and this is a complex solution. And we take shit for that sometimes. And the fact of the matter is that I think your efforts need to be as complex, at least you have to consider them to be as complex, as the problem."[21]

Some aspects of this program are indeed richly complex and multifaceted. There are fifteen basic components to the plan: a Sheltered Market Program, Direct Services Contracting, Expanded Informal Contracting, A&E Procurement Plan, Reformed Good Faith Program, Technology Pool, Regional Mentoring Program, Regional Bonding and Financial Solutions, Coordinated Referral System, Monitoring of Actual Use, Restrictions on Substitutions, Uniform Data Collection, Enforcement of Non-discrimination Policies, Project Manager/Inspector Training, Centralized Monitoring, Performance/Evaluation Standards, Frequent Public Reporting, Regional Workforce Development, Continuation of Pressure to Enforce State Training Standards, and an Expanded EEO Program. But there is one component that is quite straightforward and decidedly controversial: the sheltered market program, which was begun in January 1998. The apprenticeship program, good-faith efforts at subcontracting with MBEs, and other pieces of the program, while not completely ignoring race, at least have enough race-neutral components not only to pass constitutional muster but to do so in a way that does not ruffle the feathers of affirmative action opponents. In fact, the leading interest group nationwide opposed to affirmative action, AGC, actually pushed for the apprenticeship program as part of Portland's efforts.[22] The sheltered market program, however, has not remained free of criticism.

Portland's sheltered market program allows certified MBEs, women-owned business enterprises (WBEs), and emerging small businesses (ESBs) an opportunity to bid only against each other on designated construction contracts under $200,000. In the blunt words of one contractor who was involved in FCEF, "It's unconstitutional as hell!"[23] City officials responsible for the program direction, while not using the same language, also suggested in interviews that "there are some areas of the program which we feel more comfortable about than others."[24] While whites can—and do—qualify for the program as part of the State of Oregon's certification as an ESB (as can minorities and women), white males cannot qualify for the program as an MBE or a WBE. Black contractors and white contractors are not competing for government contracts on equal terms.

The different treatment by race is not per se unconstitutional, as *Croson* and its progeny make clear. In fact, even if a jurisdiction successfully navigates the labyrinth of requirements elucidated by the Court, governments purportedly remain free to institute race-based programming—though short of a rigid quota system. According to Portland's disparity study, "Justice O'Connor speaking for the majority postulated various methods of demonstrating discrimination and set forth guidelines for crafting MBE programs so that they are narrowly tailored to address suspected racial discrimination."[25] Therefore, the two critical issues for Portland are (1) whether the program is a rigid quota system called something else and (2) whether the city followed the steps delineated by the judiciary in *Croson* and its progeny.

Portland's sheltered market program places responsibility for certification of MBEs, WBEs, and ESBs on the state. Oregon requires that average firm receipts not exceed $1 million annually, firms must have been in business for two years prior to admission to the program, and firms must agree to several evaluation assistance requirements. Once a firm has qualified for the program, these companies compete only against other certified MBEs, WBEs, and ESBs in bidding on city contracts less than $200,000.

The city disavows the notion that this program is a quota in disguise. According to the Strategy, "Based on the requirements of the *Croson* decision, the data from our study did not support minority contracting quotas or set-asides, nor were these tools desired by the Contract Coordinating Committee (3C) and these practices as they tend to distribute contract unique opportunities to a few high profile minority and women-owned firms."[26] Elected leaders voiced a similar opinion: "We probably could have come up with a quota system that was reasonable. It would have been in the Oregon tradition 'competently administered' and it probably would have done some good. But because people elsewhere might have less reasonable and more polarized [views] about these things, it, you know, got to the point where there was a *Croson* decision, and we have to live with those strictures that come down from nastier battles elsewhere."[27] Members of FCES also interpreted the Portland situation not as using rigid quotas but as setting "aspirational" or "soft" goals in its Strategy.[28]

Some white contractors, however, see the situation in another light. "You can call them good faith efforts or goals, but they're quotas. And no one stands up to say otherwise. This government has quotas."[29] And according to a Department of Purchasing employee, "The program has been a boon for work for minority contractors. Here is something where we can say to minority contractors, 'you are almost assured of getting work. All you have to do is get out there and bid.' We can't help you if you don't bid. But if you bid, you are going to get some work."[30]

Some analysis of the sheltered market program, however, indicates that if there is a quota, it is not being enforced particularly strictly. The city's *Fair Contracting and Employment Strategy: Three Year Review*[31] does list a "benchmark" for black-owned firms to receive 3.75 percent of city contract dollars. Portland segments its contracts in the *Three Year Review* to include contracts involving more than $500,000, contracts between $200,000 and $500,000, contracts between $50,000 and $200,000, and contracts of less than $50,000.

Portland's data make clear that despite the sheltered market program, white-owned firms not only still receive new contracts under $200,000 but have managed to receive the majority of these contracts (presumably because these businesses qualify as ESBs under Oregon's definition). And whereas minority firms continue to make strong inroads on informal contracts under $50,000 and on larger contracts up to $500,000, they have not done so on very large contracts. From the time of the imposition of the program up to the year 2000, black-owned firms had not received a single contract worth more than $500,000 from the City of Portland. Thus there appears to be competitive bidding on all midsize and small contracts and continued market domination by white-owned firms for the very large contracts.

Perceptions about what is occurring as a result of the program are also important in evaluating the impact of the MBE program. One bureaucrat argued that while the city has made progress, contractor perceptions and unrealistic demands have limited the minority community's view of the program: "The program has increased participation—it may not be what these contractors would call 'nirvana,' but it did increase minority participation. The numbers before were really quite minimal. What it did was encourage new businesses to start and start to educate the prime contractors."[32] One city commissioner also offered some explanation of the limited impact: "We're starting with a very small, weak, base of minority enterprises. So it's really been fostering fledgling firms . . . and trying to carve out a niche for them with the sheltered market."[33] While these perceptions and hard results do not completely rule out the possibility of the imposition of a quota system, they are at least suggestive that in enforcement, Portland has neither created a market sheltered completely by race nor given away contracts to undeserving firms simply because of a racial quota.

The fourteen-volume disparity study is an attempt by a wide-ranging number of actors to follow the Supreme Court's MBE affirmative action policies. Both from discussions with city personnel and on review of Portland's documentation, it seems clear a legitimate attempt was made to follow the judicial conception of a constitutional affirmative action program. The consultants reviewed not only the legal standards from *Croson* but also those from the appropriate U.S. Courts of Appeals decisions interpreting *Croson.* The City's disparity study reads, in part, "In *Coral Construction Company* . . . and *AGC of California v. City and County of San Francisco,* the Ninth Circuit elaborated on the requirements set out in *Croson,* and thus further delineates the careful specificity with which MBE and WBE programs are to be crafted."[34]

Croson clearly was also on the mind of many legislators. According to one city commissioner, "In terms of what we can do—based upon *Croson*—we feel like in Portland, we are at about the state of the art. . . . As far as I can tell we're doing everything that we can do legally."[35] And Portland's Strategy also makes clear that an attempt was made to craft Portland's response to the court's jurisprudence. According to the *Three Year Review* of the program, "Although many affirmative action programs are being dismantled around the country, the strategy is tailored to the legal framework established by the Supreme Court and moves the city closer to economic equity."[36]

Whether Portland's program would withstand constitutional challenge is subject to some speculation. Certainly Portland tried to follow the Court's prescriptions. But given the near unanimity among the courts, both federal and state, in finding post-*Croson* MBE programs unconstitutional, it is very likely that should Portland be subject to litigation, its program would find its way into the dustbin of history. Faced with that knowledge, it stood to reason that Portland's new legislative efforts in creating an affirmative action program had to be accompanied by actions designed to avoid litigation altogether.

Interest Group Co-option

Throughout the 1980s, and again in the immediate aftermath of *Croson,* AGC, the nation's leading contractors' interest group, instigated dozens of lawsuits nationwide against governments operating MBE programs.[37] AGC's lawsuits and threats of lawsuits resulted in the dismantling of MBE programs across the country, from Connecticut to Cincinnati to California. Wherever MBE programs existed, a local AGC chapter was a direct threat to their existence. Portland's AGC chapter was no exception, having successfully sued in the late 1980s to dismantle Multnomah County's MBE program in *Matson v. Multnomah County.*[38]

Despite AGC's history of antagonism toward MBE programs and the seeming interest of AGC's contractor membership, AGC leadership reports today that AGC will not support litigation against the City of Portland for its MBE program. The decision not to support such litigation could be explained as the result of a belief that AGC would be unsuccessful in its efforts. A review of the AGC's litigation history, coupled with the fact that one of the contractors quoted above as claiming Portland's MBE program was "unconstitutional as hell" is an AGC leader, suggests otherwise. In fact, what has occurred is that the City of Portland successfully co-opted the local AGC branch into supporting the city's agenda.

AGC's conversion, or in the words of a different AGC leader, "our Road to Damascus," occurred for several reasons.[39] First, generational differences between the older AGC membership and its new leaders have allowed today's AGC to be more amenable to working with the city. Second, AGC leadership's inclusion in the

Fair Contracting Employment Forum provided AGC and the city with a level of mutual trust and an openness to receiving ideas from one another. And third, specific capitulations made by the city to AGC have sufficiently mollified the needs of AGC leadership and resulted in AGC's agreement not to support litigation against the city.

Just as in Philadelphia, the former Portland AGC leadership—the leadership that spearheaded the litigation against Multnomah County—was drawn chiefly from the World War II generation. Largely coterminous with the Court's ruling in *Croson,* AGC leaders either retired or passed away. And just as death and retirement were the leading cause in the party transformation of southern senators during the 1940s and 1950s,[40] factors related to age have been responsible for a changing of the guard in Portland's AGC.[41] The new AGC leadership is comprised of men who are figuratively if not literally the sons of the earlier leaders. The World War II generation passed the baton to the Vietnam generation.

The generational difference between the leadership of AGC has had substantive ramifications. In the words of one bureaucrat, "They went, or didn't go, to Vietnam. They are our age—late 40s. They understand keeping people employed, and not having an underclass—especially based on race—is healthy for everybody."[42] These differences in understanding "life's realities," however, also involve differences in political choices. The new AGC had become "sick of the portrayal as obnoxious, combative, white guys" associated with the old AGC—and "we decided to do something about it."[43] AGC's choice was to work hand-in-hand with the City of Portland in creating a new MBE program.

The inclusion of AGC in the city's FCEF alarmed several other members of the FCEF. According to one FCEF member, "AGC was slowly but surely starting to become our partner, though I, and others, were waiting for that little stab."[44] Another FCEF member reported, "While I give 'em credit for trying to change, for me, the jury's still out [on AGC]."[45] But the city's and AGC's continued exposure to one another and the long-continued meetings fostered a collective sense of ownership in the new MBE program. In fact, during my interviews with them, AGC leaders routinely referred to Portland's MBE program as "our" program.

The amenable new leaders of AGC, coupled with good will fostered by inclusion in the policy creation process, may have been sufficient to safeguard Portland's MBE from AGC-supported litigation. The city, however, did not stop there. Portland gave in to AGC demands on both the apprenticeship and mentoring components of the MBE program and, more important, limited the sheltered market program to only those small contracts worth less than $200,000.

AGC's insistence on the apprenticeship and mentoring program provides AGC with two key pieces. First, the programs help AGC with its own ongoing labor supply issues. Second, the programs allow large companies to take MBEs "under their wing," which ensures that the larger companies have a hand in how new MBEs function. At least one bureaucrat was quite cynical in explaining AGC's support for the apprenticeship and mentoring programs: "Of course, later on they can say, 'well we ran all these training programs and no one showed up.'"[46]

The relatively small cap on contracts at $200,000 for inclusion in the sheltered market program has enraged a few minority contractors and been a substantial coup for AGC. Typically, profits on construction contracts are somewhere around 5–7 percent of a contract. Even if a minority contractor was lucky enough to get one the largest contracts available under this program, the most the contractor could make would be $10,000–$14,000. A bigger problem than the lack of profit, though, is that the City of Portland, like most governments, has a "hold back" provision in its contracts that typically withholds 5 percent of a contract until one year after a job has been completed in order to check for long-term stability. Thus, these businesses have to float themselves on no or very little profit before reaping the rewards of their work—hardly a recipe for a relatively new business to thrive. The sheltered market program, therefore, has left the large contracts—those that are typically bid on by AGC's constituent contractors, and certainly AGC's leadership—largely untouched.

Although AGC nationally has been a staunch affirmative action adversary, Portland's AGC chapter has agreed not to support litigation efforts against the City of Portland's MBE program. AGC has done so for many reasons, including the new leadership's views on race and economics and the benefits AGC enjoys because of the MBE program. While the agreement by AGC not to back litigation against Portland does not completely forestall the possibility of litigation against the city, knowing that any prospective plaintiffs will lack the financial resources that AGC could bring to such a lawsuit is an important victory for the city. Thus, any plaintiffs seeking to dismantle Portland's program would likely need to be economically self-sufficient or savvy enough to avail themselves of interest group support outside Portland. But since Portland has specifically limited the scope of its sheltered market program to just small contracts, those bid on by small, emerging, not very well-connected firms, most aggrieved parties will be businesses competing for these small contracts—exactly the type of firm that lacks the ability to sue the city. And even though there has been a proliferation of conservative interest groups around the country capable of waging an expensive litigation campaign against Portland, finding a local aggrieved party who does not mind having all the major local players disrupted is apparently more difficult than affirmative action detractors might have hoped. Portland's affirmative action program continues to treat black- and white-owned firms differently and has yet to invite litigation.

The Threat to Judicial Primacy

Following *Croson,* in early 1989 Portland eliminated its MBE program. Knowing that litigating the city's MBE program would have been fruitless, Portland quietly dismantled the affirmative action program by the end of 1989. By the mid-1990s Portland had witnessed the lower courts implement the Supreme Court's affirmative action policies with near uniformity, striking down program after program. Portland, however, sought to avoid such an outcome-determinative option. In rebuilding its MBE program after a multiyear hiatus, Portland not only followed the Supreme Court's prescriptive advice in how to craft a constitutional affirmative action program, it also sought to avoid having its program litigated. The city carefully crafted its program to avoid impinging on large contracts and targeted the brunt of its program to small contractors. By co-opting the large contractors' interest group, the city received an agreement from AGC not to support litigation against the city's MBE program and immunized itself from all but self-funded lawsuits.

The city's operation of an unconstitutional program and concomitant insulation of the program from lawsuit effectively limit the judiciary from engaging in constitutional dialogue. It is one issue to legislate in ways either not envisioned by the judiciary, or perhaps at the fringes of an unclear judicial decision. Portland's actions, however, are both contrary to existing law and designed to thwart judicial will by nullifying the constitutional vision of the judiciary. The ideological direction of elected branch malfeasance does little to defend against the normative problems with nullification. Instead, despite its "good faith" efforts, the City of Portland continues to treat white and black contractors differently, in defiance of *Croson*. Though Portland accomplished this task of defiance largely on the basis of interest group co-option, the case of Miami, discussed in the next chapter, makes clear that co-option is only one method by which to maintain a suspect affirmative action program and avoid litigation.

4

MIAMI AND EXECUTIVE CHECKMATE

Popular legend holds, probably incorrectly, that President Andrew Jackson, in response to a U.S. Supreme Court ruling that Georgia had improperly taken Cherokee lands, said, "John Marshall has made his decision; now let him enforce it." As we know today, Supreme Court decisions are not self-enforcing. The case of Miami demonstrates that the Supreme Court can simultaneously change behavior and appear powerless. Understood in this way and in the context of the constitutional dialogue literature, the case of Miami also demonstrates the uneasiness of the categories of successful and unsuccessful court–elected branch interactions while highlighting the need for judicial primacy.

When the Supreme Court decided *Croson,* the City of Miami, in contrast to Philadelphia and Portland, neither defended its program in court nor legislatively dismantled its minority business enterprise (MBE) program. Indeed, Miami's program has not undergone any legislative amendments since before the *Croson* decision in 1989. While Miami has not altered its legislation, the city has responded to the *Croson* decision in the implementation of its affirmative action program, officially leaving the program on the books but refusing to implement the more controversial elements of the program, and finally (recently) calling the program "not mandatory."

Despite maintaining an unconstitutional program, Miami has avoided litigation chiefly because of its program's "nonimplementation" and the concomitant lack of standing accruing to any aggrieved individuals, but also because of the small budget designated by the city for use in this program. Even if Miami's affirmative action program were implemented to the letter of the law, it would likely not ruffle enough feathers to invite litigation. But why does Miami not simply remove the nonimplemented, and likely unconstitutional, program from its books? I contend that Miami opts to maintain this hollowed-out version of an MBE program not out of a desire to assist minority contractors but because of the perceived political problems for lawmakers associated with taking a stance against an affirmative action program in a majority-minority city. The political benefits of maintaining an unconstitutional program outweigh the perceived costs of its removal.

What this means for the constitutional dialogue theory is that elected branch responses cannot always be neatly categorized as successful or unsuccessful. By one measure, Miami's case seems much like Portland's: a city maintains an unconstitutional program in the face of a contrary Supreme Court decision. Yet a deeper look at the operation of the program in Miami suggests that the affirmative action program is not actually denying anyone his or her right to equal treatment, because the government is not enforcing the legislation. While in the end, I suggest Miami's maintenance of the program is still problematic constitutionally, even taking into account the lack of implementation, this mixed nature of Miami's response to the Supreme Court is very much a mixed success in terms of constitutional dialogue. There is a public face of elected branch monologue, yet a more in-depth analysis suggests that there is a sort of a consensus among the branches of government that affirmative action in government contracting is unconstitutional.

Miami's Affirmative Action Program

Miami's affirmative action program traces its roots back to the mid-1980s. In 1984, the City of Miami's city manager, Howard Gary, an African American, hired a former Urban League executive as a special assistant to draft legislation that would address serious disparities between white- and black-owned firms in city contracting. Though the legislation would also cover Hispanic- and women-owned businesses (WBEs), the primary impetus behind the program was to address what one city bureaucrat sarcastically referred to as the fact that "less than zero percent" of city contracts were being awarded to African Americans.[1] The then mayor, Maurice A. Ferre, a Puerto Rican and the first Hispanic mayor of a major American city, had been mayor of Miami since 1973 and was a strong supporter of Miami's black community.[2] Xavier L. Suarez, the city's first Cuban American mayor, defeated Ferre before final passage of the bill, and on December 19, 1985, Mayor Suarez signed Ordinance 10062, "The Minority and Women Business Affairs and Procurement Ordinance of the City of Miami," into law.

The MBE program sought to spend more than half of all city contract dollars with minority-owned firms. As one local politician put it, "If more than half the city are minorities, they should have more than half of the contracts."[3] Miami's MBE program divided a 51 percent spending goal evenly among three groups: 17 percent of city contract dollars were apportioned to black-owned firms, 17 percent to Hispanic-owned firms, and 17 percent to women-owned firms. The program allowed the city manager to create set-asides or separate sheltered markets for each individual minority group, so that a request for proposals could be successfully bid on by only black-owned firms or only Hispanic-owned firms, depending on the bid specification. The law also required all bidding firms to provide evidence of a good-faith effort to solicit the participation of minority-owned subcontractors in the bidding process.

At first, the bureaucrats ran the program from a distinct MBE bureaucratic office, placed hierarchically directly under the city manager's office and kept separate from the Department of Purchasing. According to one bureaucrat, this was because having the MBE program in Purchasing (the agency that had been awarding contracts) would have been like having "the fox guard the hen house."[4] A little more than three years after the program began, but just a few days before the *Croson* decision, the City of Miami amended its MBE program to make a few semantic changes (e.g., changing "bidder" to "bidder, proposer, or vendor") and one substantive change: Ordinance 10538 changed the definition of an MBE to exclude businesses with more than twenty-five employees or a net worth of more than $2 million. Thus, large minority-owned companies were supposed to be ineligible for the city's program.

Around this same time, the city moved the MBE office from the city manager's office to the General Services Administration.

Croson, Dade County, and Miami's Duck and Cover

When the *Croson* decision came down, on January 23, 1989, applying strict scrutiny for both "benevolent" and "malevolent" race-based legislation, the city opted not to rescind its program. Instead, it "just kind of rode it out for a while."[5] Unlike in Pennsylvania and Oregon, where major cities are the driving economic powerhouses, in Florida counties provide the lion's share of local government spending. Thus, the City of Miami opted to "keep close tabs on [the actions of] Dade County" and the county's affirmative action program response. City personnel figured that all the cues necessary for the city to act could be gleaned from the county—whatever happened in the area would happen to the big fish first.[6] If a lawsuit were forthcoming, the county would be the richer target, and if program modifications had to be made, the county's staff could do the heavy lifting.[7]

Dade County (now aptly named Miami-Dade County), the county that encompasses the City of Miami, had enacted its first MBE program in 1982 in response to the Liberty City–McDuffie riots of May 1980. County Ordinance 82–67 provided sheltered markets for black prime contractors and established goals that were to be applied on a contract-by-contract basis for black participation as subcontractors on county contracts. The program attracted an early lawsuit, but the courts upheld the 1982 program for black contractors in its entirety in the early 1980s using the U.S. Supreme Court's 1980 ruling in *Fullilove v. Klutznick* as a basis for the decision.[8] After the Supreme Court changed its analysis of "ameliorative" race-based legislation in *Croson* in 1989 to mirror its analysis of "discriminatory" race-based legislation, plaintiffs soon brought another challenge to Dade County's program in light of the strict scrutiny standard announced in *Croson.* This challenge was settled out of court, with Dade County still operating its MBE program.

Four years after *Croson,* in 1993, the Dade County Commission expanded from a seven-member at-large commission to a thirteen-member district-based commission. The resultant change in racial and ethnic representation on the commission was stark. The commission changed immediately from five white members, with one black seat and one Hispanic seat, to six Hispanic members, four black members, and three white members. The new commission then substantially amended the county's MBE program in 1994, largely in response to the new racial representational scheme and, reportedly, the influence of political contributions from prominent members of the Latin Builders Association.[9] Rather than maintain sheltered markets and subcontractor goals only for black businesses, as had been the case since 1982, Dade County expanded the reach of the program to include Hispanic- and women-owned businesses.

This new program change was met with an immediate legal challenge in 1994. After a two-year legal battle, on September 17, 1996, Judge Ryskamp of the U.S. District Court for the Southern District of Florida ruled that the Dade County program failed both the "compelling state interest" and the "narrowly tailored" provisions of the strict scrutiny standard in *Croson,* and ruled the program unconstitutional. The subsequent appeal by the county was unsuccessful, and the county was supposed to rescind its construction-related race- and gender-based program in 1997.[10] Yet for six years Miami-Dade "did not amend, modify, or repeal the remaining sections of its MBE programs, and further litigation predictably ensued."[11] In a federal court decision in 2004, the courts struck down the program again and also assessed the Dade County commissioners personal liability for damages, though only at $100 per corporate plaintiff. And at long last, the county stopped operating its affirmative action program.

The Dade County example looks in many respects like the Philadelphia case. The government, committed to an affirmative action program, even in the face of *Croson,* fought a legal battle that eventually culminated in the striking down of the government's program. What is quite different, of course, is that the county ignored the initial judicial ruling. Only when the county commissioners had been assessed personal liability did Dade County actually end its maintenance of an unconstitutional program. Thus the county case also seems to be an example of a successful court–elected branch interaction. Yet as I was interested in how three different cities responded to *Croson,* the City of Miami presents a more complex story.

While Dade County expanded the reach of its program, the City of Miami stood pat. While Dade County fought a legal battle over the constitutionality of its program, the City of Miami stood pat. And when Dade County faced another round of litigation, the City of Miami stood pat. In fact, in the almost two decades since *Croson,* the City of Miami has made no formal alterations to its MBE program. By one take, then, it appears that the City of Miami is simply flouting the Court. The Court has declared that MBE programs are subject to the highest judicial scrutiny and has directed the lower courts to apply the elusive standard, but the city has effectively continued going about its business as if nothing had changed. There are, however, some alternative explanations for what the city has done.

One explanation could be that the city's program is constitutional and meets the standards announced in *Croson.* As detailed in chapter 1, constitutional affirmative action programs must pass the strict scrutiny test. Specifically, constitutional MBE programs must both serve a compelling state interest and be narrowly tailored toward achieving that interest. The compelling state interest in its most general sense can be satisfied by demonstrating a statistical disparity between the availability of minority contractors and the utilization of minority contractors. To pass the narrowly tailored component of strict scrutiny, governments must satisfy each of five separate requirements. Governments must (1) consider race-neutral methods in reducing contracting disparities, (2) base eligibility for the MBE program on membership in racial and ethnic groups that have suffered an injury, and use goal percentages reflective of the availability of contractors in the local marketplace, (3) use flexible goals and provide meaningful waivers from noncompliance, (4) minimize the burden shouldered by excluded groups, and (5) provide a stopping point for the program. If an MBE program fails any one of the above requirements, it is deemed unconstitutional.

The Miami program is constitutionally suspect for many reasons. First, as mentioned in chapter 1, Miami's disparity study, conducted by the firm Peat Marwick, did not demonstrate contracting disparities.[12] *Croson* clearly requires governments to produce evidence, not merely perceptions or "intrinsic feelings," in the words of Mayor Suarez, of underutilized minority contractors before race-based programs can ostensibly be put in place. In 1989, the City of Miami spent $36 million on contracts, with Hispanic-owned firms receiving 31 percent, black-owned firms receiving 6 percent, and women-owned firms receiving 3 percent of the contract dollars. Yet in light of the actual availability of MBEs, there was no statistically significant difference between the availability and the utilization of minority contractors.

Second, even if the city was correct in its perception of discrimination against *black*- and *women*-owned businesses, these disparities would not give the city a constitutional rationale to include spending goals for *Hispanic*-owned businesses. This program allocates 17 percent of contract dollars to *Hispanic*-owned firms in Miami, where the government was actually spending 31 percent of its contract dollars. To have a race-based spending goal disconnected from actual practice is constitutionally troubling under *Croson.*

Finally, and perhaps most damning, is the use of "17-17-17" for spending goals. The city attempts to spend 51 percent of its contract dollars with MBEs, spread equally among the three catgories of black-, Hispanic-, and women-owned firms. The division between the three groups amounted to a decision based on "equity" without any connection to availability, utilization, or disparity in the local marketplace. Any of these failures, let alone all three, would be sufficient to render the city's program unconstitutional. To this end, the city's own lawyers in 2005 urged the city to use the race materials only for "informational purposes" in its bid materials "in a non-binding, non-mandatory and non-encouraged way," absent a new disparity study.[13] Therefore, it seems, Miami's program has been free from legal challenge not because the program meets the *Croson* standards but for other reasons.

Examining why the city has successfully avoided the lawsuit nexus to the judiciary illustrates some additional aspects of checkmate moves. As I suggest in the next section, the absence of litigation against the City of Miami during the sixteen years following *Croson* for having an unconstitutional affirmative action program is best explained by (1) the city's efforts to not implement the program and (2) the paucity of contract dollars at stake in the entire program, which makes expensive litigation prohibitive. Even if a city administration had attempted to put the MBE program into operation,

Miami would still likely remain free of litigation. Thus, checkmate moves may also entail bureaucratic and budgetary manipulation.

Checkmate

Although Dade County was embroiled in litigation, and although Miami's program would not withstand litigation, Miami did not formally alter its program. Instead, the city's actions suggest another type of response to Court decisions, one largely involving only bureaucratic action—or inaction, as the case may be. Miami's actual MBE program administration changed as a result of *Croson* both immediately after the decision and in ensuing years, when the city attempted to limit the impact of the program by not fully implementing it. Thus, affirmative action continued to exist for the city on the books, officially as a government unit, and as a reference point for government officials who responded to constituents complaining about racial problems, but in reality Miami had effectively abandoned its MBE efforts. The city had turned a tool for economic reform into an empty shell of a political shibboleth.

The first indication that the city was interested in muting the program stems from the bureaucratic reorganization of the program and its move from the General Services Administration to the Department of Purchasing. As explained to me by the director of purchasing, "It just made sense to have the program in the place where we wrote the checks."[14] Yet placing the MBE program under the control of the Purchasing Department risked ceding authority to a department that had long been responsible for failing to select minority firms. In contravention of its earlier organization placement of the program, Miami now located the MBE office squarely under the fox's nose.

Second, program administrators reported in interviews that they behaved differently in light of *Croson*. As one former bureaucrat told me, "We quietly shifted our efforts away from using sheltered markets and the like, and we pushed joint ventures and subcontracting to small minority contractors."[15] The city did not alter the written word of its program but bureaucratically avoided use of the most controversial aspects of affirmative action—and arguably this particular affirmative action program's most potent tool. By focusing instead on the peripheral aspects of the program, the city's administrators could avoid giving a cause of action to a potential plaintiff and thus avoid or least forestall litigation.

A third sign that Miami stifled the MBE program came from the city manager's office. The city trimmed the MBE full-time staff from four to three. The cut in staff for the MBE office was particularly significant in light of how the department works. According to one department manager I interviewed, "[The staff is] where the difference is made, whether the program flies or not."[16] And in the words of one city commissioner, "It is the administrators that are key—not the program documents. The attitude and commitment of administrators differentiates a good program from an awful program."[17] Both department heads and the city manager had shown extreme deference toward the then director of purchasing, who was also the head of the city's MBE program. Those close to the program asserted that the higher-ups "rubber stamp everything that [Purchasing Director] Judy Carter does." If the director of the MBE program today calls for a set-aside, it occurs; if she does not call for a set-aside, it does not occur—"[The higher-ups] sign it and don't ask questions."[18]

According to at least one city commissioner, the city's director of the MBE program, Judy Carter, was not entirely committed to minority contracting. After rating the city's efforts a "three out of ten," one commissioner remarked about the purchasing director, "Judy Carter is a fine and knowledgeable administrator, but minority contracting is not her priority."[19] In the words of another city commissioner, Judy Carter was "just status quo."[20] The overall numbers behind the program seem to bear this out. The director of the program reported that in the Purchasing Department's latest review of the program, spending on minority firms approximated 35 percent of city dollars spent—substantially short of the 51 percent goal. When these numbers are broken down, however, the lack of program implementation becomes even clearer. Instead of approximately equal contracting with black-, Hispanic-, and women-owned firms in line with the program's 17-17-17 goals, the breakdown amounts to 3-29-3. The director reported that during her tenure, dating back to the early 1990s, black-owned firms have never received more than 6 percent of city contract dollars in a year, and in some years have received as little as 2 percent of city monies.[21]

Women, supposedly the biggest beneficiary of affirmative action, have never received in excess of 10 percent of the city's contract dollars. All the more telling is that the numbers that existed at the time of the *Croson* decision were 6-31-3, much closer to the persistent and current spending patterns than to the program goals.

So the evidence that Miami's program administration changed in response to *Croson* consists of a bureaucratic reorganization, a reduction in resources, former staff reporting a change in behavior, and particularly weak spending patterns with black- and women-owned firms. Although many local officials blamed the bureaucracy for these failures, the city's failure to contract with black contractors need not be the fault of the director. Even though the city's population is more than 30 percent black and the metropolitan area population is about 20 percent black, another plausible reason for the failure to contract with more black-owned firms is that there may not have been enough available black contractors in the particular fields used by the city to fulfill the city's goal of 17 percent. The analysis below of the availability of black contractors in Miami, however, suggests that the city in fact must shoulder much of the blame.

Unavailable Firms or Administrative Failure?

The lack of spending with black-owned firms suggests, among other things, that the City of Miami purposely did not implement its program. Such a conclusion would be warranted if the city sought, but did not find, black-owned firms with which to contract. This raises the question, are black firms available to contract with the City of Miami? If not, then perhaps the bureaucratic reorganization, staff cuts, reports of changed behavior, and dismal spending numbers are simply artifacts of the lack of availability of black-owned firms. But if black-owned firms are available and if the city is still spending such a paltry amount of contract dollars with those firms, this is some evidence that such a program is not being implemented.

To understand the meaning of the City of Miami's failure to contract with black-owned firms, it is important to understand the universe of black-owned firms from which the city could contract. According to the 2000 Census, the City of Miami population was

TABLE 4.1 Construction industry 1997, all firms, by race and ethnicity, Miami MSA (as percentage of total)

RACE OR ETHNICITY	MIAMI POPULATION	CONSTRUCTION BUSINESS OWNER- SHIP, ALL FIRMS	CONSTRUCTION BUSINESS OWNER- SHIP, FIRMS WITH EMPLOYEES
Black	19	4.7**	3.4**
Hispanic	57	68.9**	57.3

Source: U.S. Bureau of the Census, *Small and Minority Owned Business Enterprises (SMOBE) (1997); State of the Cities Data Systems (SOCDS) 2001* (Washington, DC: U.S. Department of Housing and Urban Development, Office of Policy and Research Development), http://socds.huduser.org.

Note: *p < .05, **p < .01 (difference from the Miami MSA population).

about one-quarter black and two-thirds Hispanic.[22] But the city often draws contractors from a wider population, including the major counties to the north, Broward County and Palm Beach County. The relevant universe to examine, however, is not just the total population but the relevant businesses. In table 4.1 I compare the metropolitan-wide black and Hispanic general populations to the construction business populations. Despite an almost 20 percent black population in Miami-Dade, Broward, and Palm Beach counties, black-owned firms account for less than 5 percent of all construction businesses, and less than 4 percent of construction businesses with employees.

Given the stark differences between the general population and the black-owned construction firms, one wonders why such a pattern persists. One reason why black-owned firms may not form at the same rates as other groups could be the differential treatment of these firms in the industry, thus creating a disincentive to engage in this line of business. According to a city bureaucrat, many black-owned firms have faced hurdles to complying with city requirements not generally faced by white- or Latino-owned firms. For example, some black-owned firms have been adjudged to lack the business fundamentals required by domestic sources of bonding, forcing them to seek "offshore bonding."[23] Minority contractors see this government treatment, including bonding, for contracting as needless, costly, and ripe for government abuse.[24] One of the city commissioners mentioned that government administrators—not from city government—sometimes are more stringent about paper requirements from black businesses, citing as an example a missing insurance paper.[25] An interest group representative also found that program administrators at the airport were "sticklers for every piece of meaningless paper."[26] Thus, it is not terribly surprising that within the construction industry at large, there are relatively few black-owned firms.

The fairly small numbers of black-owned construction businesses helps fuel a perception prevalent among city bureaucrats and legislators that black-owned firms do not do the kinds of work for which Miami regularly engages contractors. According to a city bureaucrat, "The City is mostly involved in street and sidewalk repair, drain clearance, sewage cleanup, and has only recently gotten into building community centers in parks." And since one city commissioner reported to me that "there are very few blacks, if any, that do sidewalk and street repair,"[27] there may be little comparative opportunity for black-owned firms to contract with the city.[28] Yet noted so far are aggregate numbers—applicable to the entire metropolitan area—and admitted perceptions. A more promising method of adducing the actual number of MBEs available for City of Miami contracts is to use the city's bidder list.

The City of Miami annually certifies businesses that are at least 51 percent owned by a minority as eligible to participate in the city's MBE program. The bidder list details each firm's contact information, trade, and claimed minority affiliation as black, Hispanic, or female. While a single individual could belong to two or three of those groups, under the city program a firm may register only as a single type of minority. Using the City of Miami certified bidder lists from 2000 and 2001, I sought to evaluate whether black-owned businesses were available to contract with the city—and if there were particular concentration patterns that could explain the lack of success of black-owned firms in contracting with the city.

After the businesses certified by the City of Miami in both 2000 and 2001 are culled (eliminating duplicates), the bidder list has 242 separate companies. These companies include 106 firms (44 percent) listed as Hispanic-owned, 78 as women-owned (32 percent), and 58 as black-owned (24 percent). In addition, the 242 companies can be divided among the four hegemonic categories of construction, goods, professional services, and other services.[29] In total, there are 72 businesses (26 percent) listed as construction firms, 22 vendors (8 percent) of goods, 110 firms (40 percent) that supply professional services, and 69 businesses (25 percent) that provide other services.

Are black firms available in significant numbers in these fields? The City of Miami does not certify non-Hispanic white-owned businesses, Asian-owned firms, and Native American–owned firms, and both black female– and Hispanic female–owned businesses have an incentive to be listed as female-owned businesses in these programs.[30] Thus, the most meaningful comparisons that can be made are between black- and Hispanic-owned firms. Given the relative percentage of blacks and Hispanics in Miami, how are these groups represented on the city's bidder list?

According to the 2000 Census, the Miami PMSA population was 2,253,362 people. Non-Hispanic blacks accounted for 19 percent, or a little over 427,000, of the population, and Hispanics of any race accounted for 57 percent, or just under 1,292,000, of the population. Yet on the city's bidder list, there are 58 black-owned firms and just 106 Hispanic-owned firms out of 242. These numbers are stark, particularly in light of the spending dollar comparison shown in table 4.2. Thus, there is some evidence that based on population alone, black and Hispanic firms behave differently in seeking clients: *black-owned businesses are significantly more likely to seek participation in affirmative action programming than are Latino-owned businesses.* Note that this difference is in the wrong direction for those who argue black firms are unavailable to contract with the government.

The City of Miami contracts for a wide array of goods and services. Because of the dual governance of the City of Miami as part of Miami-Dade County, the majority of city contracts are for infrastructure services, including street and sidewalk repair, drain clearance, and sewage cleanup. The city's certified bidder lists do not show detailed information on every company, though some listings maintain "sub-field" listings. Some construction firms listed "paving" or "excavation" as a construction sub-field; some construction

TABLE 4.2 City of Miami, black and Hispanic population versus certified bidder list availability and contract dollars received

RACE OR ETHNICITY	PERCENTAGE OF TOTAL POPULATION	NUMBER OF CERTIFIED BIDDERS	PERCENTAGE OF CONTRACT DOLLARS RECEIVED
Black	19	58**	3**
Hispanic	57	106**	29**

Sources: U.S. Bureau of the Census, General Population and Housing Characteristics 2000 (Washington, DC: U.S. Department of Commerce, Bureau of the Census, 2000); City of Miami Certified Bidder Lists, 2000, 2001 (Miami: Department of Purchasing) (on file with author); bureaucrat interviews by author, 2001.

Note: $*p < .05$, $**p < .01$ (difference from Miami MSA population).

TABLE 4.3 City of Miami, number of black and Hispanic certified bidders by subcategory, construction

RACE OR ETHNICITY	STREETS AND SIDEWALKS	GENERAL CONTRACTORS	CONSTRUCTION
Black	7*	13	19
Hispanic	5*	23	33

Source: City of Miami Certified Bidder Lists, 2000, 2001 (Miami: Department of Purchasing) (on file with author).

Note: $*p < .05$, $**p < .01$ (difference from Miami MSA population).

firms listed merely "construction." With respect to the particular services most sought after by the City of Miami, are black firms available to contract? In table 4.3, I categorize firms according to the relevant listed sub-fields that may accord with the city's needs. "Streets and Sidewalks" in table 4.3 corresponds to bidders who claimed expertise in asphalt, concrete, or paving. I have also included the broader categories of "General Contractors" and bidders who merely listed "construction" under the city's heading of "Trade."

As table 4.3 illustrates, there is little support for the specific claim by the city commissioner that black-owned firms are unavailable to do street and sidewalk repair. There are actually more black-owned firms with this specialty than Hispanic-owned firms, not to mention relative to the Miami population. In each of the three categories of bidders (streets and sidewalks, general contractors, and construction) the percentage of black-owned firms *exceeds* the relative black population. In fact, black-owned firms are significantly overrepresented and Hispanic-owned firms are significantly underrepresented compared to the relative group population in the Miami PMSA under "Streets and Sidewalks."

It should be noted, however, that the city bidder list does not include all firms that conduct business in Miami, only the number of firms that voluntarily sought certification under the city's MBE program. Given the comments from black contractors who avoid working for the city, this analysis may underestimate the number of black firms qualified to engage in street and sidewalk repair. To examine all firms that conduct business in the city is a methodological dilemma that has long dogged program stakeholders and the courts.[31] The problem is locating businesses comparable to those on the city's bidder list that have not bid on city contracts. The city's own list is too narrow, as it only has firms that have contacted the city, and the Census Bureau's information is too broad, as it does not demarcate between firms that are "capable and available" for city contracts.

While there is no support for the business concentration theory advanced by the city commissioner and bureaucrat in the construction trades, there may be evidence for the concentration theory in other fields. Though most city work focuses on construction—and even narrower fields within the generalized construction trade—Miami also contracts with firms in fields other than construction. Whether the city is purchasing office supplies, contracting for bonding issues, or selecting companies to prune trees in the city parks, racial disparities in these trades could partially explain the city's lack of success in contracting with black-owned firms. Table 4.4 compares the relative group populations in the fields of "Goods," "Professional Services," and "Other Services."

A comparison of the relative group populations in the fields listed in table 4.4 shows a slightly different picture than when comparisons are made only within the construction trades. Just as black-owned firms appear to be overrepresented in the construction field and sub-fields, black-owned firms are significantly overrepresented on

TABLE 4.4 City of Miami, number of black and Hispanic certified bidders by subcategory, nonconstruction

RACE OR ETHNICITY	GOODS	PROFESSIONAL SERVICES	OTHER SERVICES
Black	3	19	24**
Hispanic	12	53	21**

Source: City of Miami Certified Bidder Lists, 2000, 2001 (Miami: Department of Purchasing) (on file with author).

Note: *$p < .05$, **$p < .01$ (difference from Miami MSA population).

the city's bidder list—as compared to the population at large—in the "Other Services" sector. Concomitantly, Hispanic-owned firms in the "Other Services" sector are underrepresented in a similar comparison. However, if these same comparisons are made using the city's bidder list instead of the metropolitan area population, black-owned firms are underrepresented in the "Professional Services" sector (although the confidence interval is only 90 percent) and Hispanic-owned firms are overrepresented in the same sector.

What begins to emerge from an analysis of the city's bidder list disaggregated by race and sector is very different from the perceptions voiced at higher levels of the city administration. Instead of black-owned firms being unavailable to provide the services sought after by the government, black-owned firms are overrepresented on the city's bidder list in the specific sub-fields most utilized by the City of Miami. At the same time, however, black-owned firms by some definition are underrepresented in the professional service trades. Class, or perhaps structural constraints regarding access to education, may explain why black-owned firms are uniquely underrepresented in the area of professional services.

Black-owned firms have positioned themselves to take advantage of this government program—except perhaps in the case of professional services. Black-owned firms are overrepresented in the areas most often utilized by the City of Miami in its contracting services, are the recipients of a 17 percent spending goal, and yet still receive only approximately 3 percent of city contract dollars. How can this disparity be explained? There are two possible expla-

nations: black-owned firms have simply not been the lowest qualified bidders on city projects or the city's MBE office has not fully
implemented the city's program.

If we consider that under the MBE program, city projects can
be bid out to black firms only, and not just to minority (in general) firms, some measure of accountability must be leveled at the
city's MBE office itself. Why has the city not utilized more black-
firm-only bidding? Given that spending with black-owned firms
has never exceeded 6 percent of city spending, why has the city not
pursued a different remedy? One answer is that the city's interest
in maintaining the program is different from the goal of reducing
racial disparities in contracting. In fact, as I discuss shortly, the city
maintains multiple goals in its affirmative action contracting program, including explicitly political goals.

A second answer, however, is that the city has purposely resisted
fully implementing the MBE program. The city's efforts not to contract with black-owned firms are a response to the Court's *Croson*
decision. Instead of directly following *Croson* and dismantling its
program, Miami has opted to maintain the program, yet render it
impotent. By virtue of the administrative placement of the program
in the Purchasing Department, the cut in staff size and concomitant
increase in employee duties, and the long-term actions by the Purchasing Department to contract with business owners other than
black business owners, the city has ensured itself the continued,
though highly ineffective, operation of the MBE program—despite
Croson.

Even if a change in administrations and administrators of the
MBE program occurs, and these individuals fully implement the
MBE program, there is reason to believe that the City of Miami
could still operate its program free from litigation. Quite simply,
the program is too small to justify the allocation of scarce resources
toward its dismantling. Typical contracts run out of the city's Public Works Department for construction-related projects range from
only $200,000 to $400,000, with one or two very large projects
topping out at around $2 million. The entire ongoing operating
budget for Public Works Department contracts almost never exceeds $20 million, and is usually around $12 million.[32] For the sake
of comparison, the former Dade County, recently renamed Miami-

Dade County, has a general expenditure budget exceeding $4 billion; the City of Miami spends barely 10 percent of that amount annually.[33] Indeed, a single Miami-Dade contract may exceed what the City of Miami spends on all contracts in a fiscal year. Without such an attractive contracting program, the city has not created the financial incentive for contractors to bring lawsuits against it. While the program is not large enough to provide lots of dollars for minority companies, it also is not large enough to attract the attention of AGC and other potential litigants. In the words of one of the commissioners, "You see, our liability [in not having enough money for contractors] is our asset."[34]

The lack of implementation and the low volume of city contracts have successfully forestalled litigation against the city. In 1998, Miami was approximately $68 million in debt and the city was on the verge of bankruptcy. But within just a few years a number of projects paid for by the county, state, and federal governments have directly and positively affected Miami. With approval of a new baseball stadium in 2008 there is a renewed optimism among some that once again the city will be "flush." Yet according to one of the city commissioners, "that's when the vultures will come in."[35] It is possible that these "vultures" will subject the city to litigation over its MBE program should added city revenues actually be transferred to additional contractual spending with minority contractors. That, however, will likely require either a change of administration or a serious change in the manner in which the city conducts business.

Interests Served by Miami's MBE Program

While Miami may remain free from litigation over its MBE program, why has the city's legislative body not voluntarily dismantled the program? What interests are being served by maintaining a feckless MBE program? To understand the purpose of Miami's program, in 2001 I formally and informally interviewed approximately thirty different policy stakeholders, including the person who wrote the legislation, legislators who annually fund the program, administrators directly involved with administering the program on a daily basis, administrators from other departments who are affected by the program, contractors, and other interest groups that have a stake in the outcome of the programs, including contractors' groups, lobbyists, business organizations, and unions. When asked about the goals of the city's MBE program and the goals of MBE programs in general, respondents predominantly expressed aims that can be divided into (1) wealth redistribution, (2) increasing the longevity and profitability of MBEs, (3) increasing the number of MBEs, (4) increasing employment among minority communities, (5) city benefits, (6) electoral benefits, and (7) compliance.

Each of the city commissioners reported that the city's choice to use race and gender in its MBE program was done benevolently. One commissioner said, "The City has to help. This must be about equality and fairness. Anytime [one] mentions equality, [one] must also mention fairness."[36] Yet another commissioner thought the program's plan was "to lift up people who are at the bottom of the ladder, to give them an opportunity to raise themselves up."[37] Government administrators not involved in the day-to-day operations of the MBE program echoed more of this sentiment, which was expressed by many of the city commissioners. One thought that the government was trying to "create opportunities in, really, the same manner as integration."[38] Thus, the civil rights aspects out of which President Johnson began the Philadelphia Plan in the late 1960s still resonate with policy stakeholders today.

Beyond issues of equity, the particular contracting program employed in Miami is also designed to assist and grow minority businesses. One of the commissioners professed that in general, "programs need to provide technical assistance since minority contractors lack education, though they are willing to work and are savvy."[39] Another of the commissioners who sometimes reviews city bids as a way of staying involved in the process remarked that "black bids were often way off the scale [noncompetitive] and not structured right."[40] The city's MBE program should give technical assistance to minority businesses to "build the capacity of these firms," but only to level the playing field. The program "has to provide for starting off, until companies can compete on their own, then the City should stop."[41] In the words of a city official, this program is designed to "allow businesses to grow, in order to compete in the marketplace. They can grow to a point in time that they will not have to rely upon the public sector."[42] But critical to this growth is the provision of business assistance programs. In the words of another administrator, "You can put the whole pie out there, but . . . if they don't have a knife and fork, they can't eat."[43]

The most useful purpose for the city's MBE program is, according to one city commissioner, "building the résumé and capacity of a firm."[44] Capacity building and assisting firms have several components beyond the literal provision of technical assistance. First, firms must simply survive. There must be enough money in the projects for these firms to meet the costs associated with participation, including equipment, payroll, insurance, and bonding. Second, there must be an incentive to maintain such businesses—they must be profitable. Small business owners must be convinced that entrepreneurship provides a means toward economic mobility. Firms must see that the industry will not evaporate once they have graduated from the government's programs.

For most respondents, growing minority businesses also translated into increasing the number of "minority" and "local" employees. One of the Cuban commissioners clarified for me these terms as used in Miami: "minority" means "African Americans," and "local" really means "Cubans."[45] By contracting with black- and Hispanic-owned businesses, the city would spur these same businesses to employ, in turn, members of those same communities. Thus, when another Cuban commissioner spoke of the city using "local companies employing local people" in its contracts,[46] at least one interpretation was that this program should aid in creating Cuban-owned companies that employed Cubans. These respondents appeared to subscribe to—and one member used the phrase himself—a "trickle-down" theory about racial job creation: minority business ownership leads to minority employment.

Contractors also focused heavily on the notion of employing people of color in these businesses: "Affirmative action can create owners of black corporations, and it can also create jobs for those black communities."[47] Another contractor lamented that these programs did not have "required participation" as a component of every government contract.[48] All of these respondents, both legislators and contractors, uniformly believed that an effective MBE program would benefit minority communities.

The city itself should also benefit from the MBE program, according to one of the commissioners. One of the commissioners broke down the goals of the program into having a "long- and short-term component." In the short term, the goals are "compliance and quality." The long-term goal, however, is to "encourage people to live in the city, by creating incentives for business to move in and to do work. Selling 1,000 police cars to the city should be a big incentive."[49] Perhaps because of the perceived dominance of Cubans in Miami, one of the Cuban city commissioners would not differentiate between the city's MBE program and a "city" bid-preference program that allows a Miami resident bidder that bids within 10 percent of the lowest responsive bid from a non-Miami resident to match the non-Miami resident's bid price. The commissioner seemed to take the position that city programs that benefit Miami residents necessarily benefit Cubans, either directly or via a higher tax base that indirectly benefits Cubans in Miami. According to noted Florida International University professor and Cuban scholar Dario Moreno, "Cubans identify with conquerors, not the conquered."[50]

Benefit to the city could also encompass something more than an increased tax base. One of the contractors was adamant about the interrelated nature of this program and possible social outcomes. "The Government needs [to] . . . bring down the social costs of government: welfare, crime rate, idle time to find drugs, more intact families, less juvenile crime, domestic violence, less hospital expenses from drug deals going down."[51] The implication of this statement is that the chain of events created by the MBE program is expected to encourage minority ownership of businesses; these owners will employ people from minority communities, and such employment will improve other social indicators. Without jobs, according to one black contractor, these individuals "will probably [be] creating a whole lot of reasons to build more prisons."[52]

While most of the comments from the commissioners addressed the aforementioned program goals, one of the commissioners recognized the electoral benefits of the program:

> The real reason for maintaining the program is the law of physics—inertia. Unless the courts or a stampeding constituency come in here, the city will maintain the program—despite its ineffectiveness. These programs allow commissioners to declare "we have

a program" and that is a statement of pluralism, and that the city
is holistic in its approach. The city is providing access to capital
and contracting opportunities, and the city can say "we are doing
our part." The program validates the concerns of the constituents.
It is now an electoral need.[53]

In other words, the affirmative action program provides a low-cost,
high-return placebo to the city as a way of palliating the concerns of
minority communities, and it will continue to do so until enough
people figure out what is occurring.

There are several different, though certainly related, implications
of this commissioner's "political" explanation. First, it establishes
the political connections between constituents and legislators over
the distribution of government contracts. Dahl characterized the
situation in New Haven as one of "ethnic politics" whereby politicians bestow "divisible benefits" using ethnic criteria to try to win
votes.[54] In this scheme, legislators ensure contracts go to black contractors to garner votes from black constituents. Second, this argument asserts that coming out against an affirmative action program,
especially in a city like Miami, would have attenuated political costs.
The status quo is the program, and action to dismantle the program
would no longer address constituents' concerns. And third, this argument also reveals that, for some legislators, affirmative action may
be a placebo for constituents. By all appearances, the program, like
a placebo, is designed to help. Yet the city commissioners, like doc-
tors, know full well its ineffectiveness. This placebo notion need not
be interpreted as sinister. Rather, in the same way that some patients
do respond to placebos, the symbolism contained in the program
itself may satisfy some constituents.

Some bureaucrats and contractors interviewed viewed the goals
of the program as more focused. For example, the purchasing director claimed the "goal is singular and clear": to achieve 51 percent of city contract dollar disbursement to Hispanic-, women-,
and black-owned businesses. Pressed further, the director also spoke
of the sub-goals of the program, to spend approximately 17 percent of city contract dollars with each of the three program target
groups, and if she had her druthers, she would like to see 25 percent minority participation or one quarter of the workforce on city

contracts to be minorities.[55] This more focused view of the goals of the program was also echoed by some of the contractors. One of the contractors believed that the program should have required participation divided by race, gender, and small businesses, project managers who judge people without double standards (implying that black contractors are more often scrutinized than are white contractors), quick and full payment, outreach to minority communities, mediation for disputes, general contractor and subcontractor monitoring, and the provision of working capital.[56] Interestingly, the bureaucrats and some contractors—presumably those individuals most closely affected by the program on a daily basis—held this narrowed view of what the city's program should accomplish. Some of this limited view may be explained by positions or stakeholder typology. Bureaucrats are paid for their own employment, and their job entails carrying out the will of the legislature as announced in legislation. Government contractors are forced to operate within detailed guidelines, both in responding to requests for proposals and in conducting government work, and thus may desire that the government be strictly bound by its regulations.

In answering the question of what affirmative action is supposed to do, the MBE policy stakeholders proffered several responses. Many of the identified goals resonate with either the theoretical affirmative action scholarship or the more recent empirical evaluations of MBE programs. As Jonathan Skrentny elucidates, affirmative action serves political, economic, and racial justice goals.[57] The city benefits, electoral benefits, and compliance are "political" goals, increasing the number, longevity, and profitability of MBEs and increasing minority employment are "economic" goals, and the civil rights–type goal of wealth redistribution fits the "racial justice" category. But of course, these goals asserted by the Miami MBE policy stakeholders are much more specific than the generic "political, economic, and racial justice" goals used by Skrentny. Interestingly, not one individual of the nearly thirty people interviewed for this study spoke of the program goal of making sure that tax dollars are not implicated in a discriminatory system—the one state interest found by the U.S. Supreme Court to be constitutionally permissible.

Miami's MBE program is designed to serve many different interests, including political interests. Thus, even if Miami's program does not achieve any of its substantive economic goals, or even the more ephemeral racial justice goals, the city's legislature has a strong incentive not to dismantle it. To be sure, the lack of a litigation specter has helped the city's legislators maintain the program, but so too has the fear of a backlash against legislators who vote against a program designed to help blacks, Hispanics, and women. In Portland, where the legislature dismantled the program, white males made up at least 40 percent of the population and an even higher percentage of the voting population. In Miami, white males make up approximately 10 percent of the city's population. With an ordinance covering potentially 90 percent of the city, it is unlikely we will see the City of Miami's commission dismantle the program any time soon.

Flouting the Court, and the Future of Affirmative Action

At first glance, the situation in Miami presents a serious challenge to those who argue that Supreme Court decisions direct behavior.[58] Instead of repealing its affirmative action program after *Croson,* as did Portland and a few other governments, or engaging in litigation over the constitutionality of its program, as did approximately fifty-five other governments, or enacting a new or revised program following the *Croson* guidelines, as did more than 150 other governments, Miami appears to have done nothing. Miami today has the exact same program on paper as it had in the days preceding the *Croson* decision in 1989.

Miami's continued operation of the program has occurred not because it is operating a constitutional affirmative action program. In fact, Miami's program clearly violates at least three different components of strict scrutiny analysis. Despite Miami's continued operation of its program, however, it does appear on close analysis that Miami has not flouted the Court. Instead of formal changes to the legislation establishing Miami's MBE program, Miami has avoided litigation of its program because of informal changes in the implementation and administration of the program. The City of Miami Board of Commissioners has not voluntarily abandoned its program because of the political interests served by maintaining the program, and the anticipated problems associated with suggesting that affirmative action should be forsaken in Miami. The city has gone out of its way to reduce any potential impact of the program and has instead opted to maintain a program successful only in establishing political cover for its politicians.

The municipal policymaker in Miami thus faces severe hurdles in the MBE arena. The city does not have the resources in its spending budget to make much of a difference with its program, even assuming full compliance on the part of program administrators and a lack of resistance on the part of other bureaucrats. Contractors have a set of beliefs about the City of Miami that casts the city as either the enemy or unimportant. Statewide efforts to dismantle other affirmative action efforts are beginning to take hold. And litigation has burned the largest local program most likely to assist these same targeted contractors.

According to one city commissioner, policymakers in Miami today must focus on achieving the same results sought in the MBE program without using race as a category in their legislation. Those who use race do so at "their own peril."[59] Instead, the most likely reforms in Miami will come from a reversion to race-neutral methods, or at least *apparent* race-neutral methods. One specific proposal bandied about in Miami now seeks both (1) to avoid and/or survive any future litigation and (2) to provide additional opportunities for black contractors. The idea is to ease franchising opportunities for black Miamians, but, as opposed to race, the avenue is geography. The proposal considers allowing additional opportunities for residents of the Overtown neighborhood (an area that is nearly all black), former residents of Overtown, and "direct descendants" of Overtown residents. The substitution of geography, in the mind of this commissioner, while seemingly a modern-day take on Jim Crow–grandfather legislation, keeps in mind the segregated housing market for blacks in Miami and detours around race-based legislation that is anathema to Fourteenth Amendment legislation.[60]

Miami has long been a city segregated along racial lines.[61] Yet since 1960 the city has undergone stark changes that, while not directly questioning a geographic-based focus, may perhaps limit the prospect for success. Miami is still more segregated than most southern cities, yet the city has become steadily more integrated racially in the past forty years than has the rest of the country. The bigger problem facing the City of Miami, however, is the "startling[ly] high level of black suburbanization" in Miami-Dade County.[62] Many of the black contractors in the Miami area do not live within the city limits and thus may be excluded from geographic programs designed for their benefit.

While the Overtown Franchise program has yet to be developed fully, the city's MBE office has already taken steps to include geography as part of its program. As neighborhood-specific projects are developed, part of the calculation of whether to use the project as a "set-aside" or a "goals" contract combines race and geography. When projects are to take place in a predominantly black neighborhood, the MBE office works with a nonprofit contractors' group to locate enough black companies to provide for "black-only" set-asides; when projects are to take place in a predominantly Hispanic neighborhood, the MBE office almost always uses the "goals" program and lets market forces and population dynamics hold sway.

Whereas higher education has opted to use race-neutral "class rank" methods of achieving the same results sought after in older models of affirmative action programs,[63] government contracting may be moving toward geography for the same purpose. This move by Miami can and should be seen as a response to the Court's decision in *Croson.* While Miami did not "perform" as did Philadelphia and Portland because of *Croson,* Miami did undertake other actions because of the decision. Though some may have been tempted to classify Miami's behavior, or lack of formal response, as flouting the Court, in fact, Miami's informal operations have exposed perhaps what may be a widespread response to Court decisions: formal insolence coupled with informal obedience. Miami's maintenance of the program supports its political goals for the program by appeasing particular constituents while simultaneously avoiding outcome-determinative litigation. By hollowing out its affirmative action program, Miami ensures that no one sustains the minimum injury that would spur a lawsuit and give the courts the opportunity to deprive Miami of its favored program.

Miami's mixed response to *Croson,* the formal insolence coupled with informal obedience, is a challenge to the classification scheme of successful or unsuccessful elected branch–court interactions. The constitutional dialogue appears to have come to a stop, while Miami maintains an unconstitutional affirmative action program.

And one only has to look at Miami-Dade County and its refusal to respond to a federal district court ruling to cease operating its MBE program and the imposition of personal liability on county commissioners to see a model for nefarious activity by the government here. Yet while Miami still maintains its MBE program, it appears that the city is not actually implementing the program. Thus, by another measure the stoppage in constitutional dialogue does not stem solely from the elected branch monopolistic interpretation of the Constitution but rather from a consensus between the elected branches and the courts about the constitutionally dubious status of affirmative action contracting programs. This may indicate that the court and elected branch interactions fall on a continuum ranging from successful to unsuccessful, with room for more mixed cases like Miami's somewhere in between. While ultimately I believe situations like Miami's are still problematic, and suggest in chapter 5 that even nonimplemented unconstitutional programs should be withdrawn from the books, one can see the mixed case of Miami to rest on a quite solid equilibrium point of law and politics.

Underbelly Epilogue

During the course of my research, I was assisted by a great many individuals. One of those individuals was City Commissioner Arthur Teele. And in the time since I finished my research in Miami and wrote this book, Teele committed suicide with a gun on the floor of the Miami Herald Building. I mention this tragedy because Teele's suicide is part of the affirmative action story in Miami.

Art Teele, an African American Republican, grew up poor in Arkansas, served the United States in Vietnam, graduated from Florida State Law School, was an official in the Reagan administration's Department of Transportation, and then became president of the National Business League.[64] Upon his return to Miami he successfully ran for the Miami-Dade County Commission. In 1996 he sought the position of mayor of Miami-Dade County but lost in an election along strict racial—but not partisan—lines to Cuban Democrat Alex Penelas.[65] Teele then successfully ran for a seat on Miami's City Commission. As the only black member of the city council in a city where district lines have been drawn largely on the basis of race, Teele was at the center of black politics in Miami.

Where the real power brokers for the white and Cuban communities were outside the government, Teele was seemingly at the center of everything related to black politics in Miami. As the head of the Community Redevelopment Agency, Teele commanded his own space in the downtown Ramada Dupont Plaza Hotel, well away from the quaint oceanside City Hall near Coconut Grove.

While I still decline to match up Commissioner Teele's quotes in this chapter with his name, suffice it to say that Teele provided a wealth of information to me. He was seemingly honest and forthright, to the point that I was taken aback by how explicit he was in regard to how affirmative action worked in Miami. As people have since found out, Teele understood all too well how affirmative action worked in Miami.

THE CRA

Miami, like many cities—including Philadelphia and Portland—hosts a variety of quasi-public agencies involved in redevelopment efforts. Miami's Community Redevelopment Agency (CRA) strove to assist minority businesses in the economically distressed northern area of downtown and Overtown. While many cities have CRAs, in Miami, the agency's board of directors consists only of the city commissioners. Given the overlap between Teele's district and the charge of the Miami CRA, Teele served as the chairman of this multi-million-dollar spending bureaucracy.

For close to five years Teele operated the CRA relatively free of interference from the rest of the city commission. The Miami CRA spent close to $11 million during that time, with between $6 and $20 million left in its spending arsenal.[66] In June 2002, city commissioners Winton, Sanchez, and Gonzalez began to question financial irregularities at the CRA based on an audit from KPMG, formerly Peat Marwick—the same firm that had conducted the nondisparity study for the City of Miami a decade earlier. The audit demonstrated weak record keeping, high turnover in the position of chief financial officer, and peculiar spending. A subsequent audit, conducted by City of Miami auditor Victor Igwe, discovered more spending incidents, which gave rise to a criminal investigation.

The CRA had been purchasing property subsequently used by drug users and dealers, buying land for non-necessary parking lots

($150,000) and then selling those lots at a substantial loss ($50,000), and making questionable loans and hiring decisions.[67] The CRA staff grew such that its annual payroll exceeded $1 million, and beyond the known prostitutes in its employ, it also began to hire former contractors with lengthy experience at the airports. In Miami, the county appropriates money for the airport in conjunction with the federal government. Teele's experience in the U.S. Department of Transportation and on the Miami-Dade County Commission, in combination with these contractors, paved the way for his ultimate downfall.

THE AIRPORT

During the 1990s, Evens Thermilus headed up Urban Constructors. Thermilus's company was one of several black-owned construction firms with 200–300 employees, along with Robinson Electric, 3W Construction, Thacker Construction, and Solo Construction. By 2001, only Randy Pearson's Solo Construction was still in operation.[68] In the summer of 2004, Thermilus was arrested along with ten other individuals in a "multimillion-dollar theft ring at the Miami International Airport's fuel depot."[69] As part of his guilty plea, Thermilus agreed to cooperate in the investigation of Art Teele.

Thermilus had started a new company, TLMC Enterprises Incorporated. The Miami CRA paid TLMC more than $800,000 on a project to build parking lots, a project that originally went for a $420,000 bid. Two of Thermilus's former executives with Urban Constructors, Robert Tyler and Brian Hankerson, each wound up on the CRA payroll—including a second bout of employment for Hankerson after he pled guilty to insurance fraud on behalf of Urban Constructors. According to state charges, Teele had been helping Thermilus get contracts with the City of Miami and the CRA in exchange for cash payments that totaled $135,000.

The July 2005 federal indictment of Teele and co-defendant Jack Maxwell charged wire fraud, money laundering, and related conspiracy charges because of a scheme to defraud the Miami airport on a $20 million contract related to the federal Disadvantaged Business Enterprise (DBE) program and the county's Community Small Business Enterprise (CSBE) program. These DBE and CSBE programs included set-aside provisions for qualified businesses. The indictment charged that Teele and Maxwell used a "front" company to qualify for the contract but that the work was actually done by a large electric contractor not even based in Miami.[70] In this case, the indictment alleged that Fisk Electric Company, a massive Houston-based electric contractor, used FLP Enterprises to qualify for the federal set-aside program, paying FLP between $600,000 and $1,000,000 for doing little more than having a qualified status. FLP was headed by Hector Paultre, who hailed from Haiti. Paultre pleaded guilty to federal charges and cooperated with investigators. Art Teele was paid $59,000 for his role in this scheme, which used the very set-aside program Teele had helped start when he was in Reagan's Department of Transportation.[71]

Two weeks after the federal indictment, having been removed from office by the governor following an assault conviction against a police officer who had been tailing him as part of the fraud investigation, three months before a trial in Miami-Dade Circuit Court on the state charges, and the day before a massive exposé was to appear in the *Miami New Times* implicating Teele in these charges as well as in claims involving drugs and male prostitutes, Teele shot himself in the head on the floor of the Miami Herald Building. He was fifty-nine years old.

The salacious nature of the Teele epilogue was certainly an interesting development in Miami after I finished my research there. Yet the episode is also emblematic of the nationwide *Croson* responses. Studies suggest that on average, twenty to twenty-five percent of all set-aside projects involve fronts or "shams of one kind or another."[72] While politicians persist in rhetoric that these programs are about increasing black ownership and employment, studies demonstrate that disparities between black and white firms actually increase during the implementation of set-aside programs,[73] there is not a significant relationship between the growth rate of black-owned businesses and cities with set-aside programs,[74] there is not a significant relationship between set-aside programs and minority employment,[75] and firms that derive more than 25 percent of their revenue from the government are more likely to fail than similar companies that perform work for a wider variety of clients.[76] Although there are some very tentative claims about the positive results of MBE programs, such as increased self-employment rates for minorities in cities with programs,[77] the vast majority of the literature is less sanguine about its effects. Thus we have massive resistance to the Supreme Court doctrine all across the country, with hundreds of blatantly unconstitutional programs at all levels of the government, elected branch checkmate moves designed to stymie litigation efforts, including those that would mute any possible positive effects of program—all intertwined with the unseemly world. As the individuals involved in these programs come unhinged from the Constitution, so too do they seem to inhabit this underbelly. Whether affirmative action is alone in this regard is the subject of the next chapter.

5

BEYOND AFFIRMATIVE ACTION

The varied reactions of the elected branches to the Supreme Court's decision in *City of Richmond v. J.A. Croson Co.* in cities across America demonstrated some different techniques for elected branch monopolization of the constitutional dialogue. Faced with judicial solidarity between the Supreme Court and the lower courts, Philadelphia, Portland, and Miami struggled in different ways to maintain an affirmative action contracting program. Philadelphia and the courts engaged in a long-drawn-out litigation–legislation modification–legislation cycle that wound up with the courts finding Philadelphia's program unconstitutional. Portland engaged an interest group in crafting its new policy and made concessions to that group that lessened the likelihood of litigation; the result is the maintenance of a constitutionally dubious program. And Miami opted to maintain a shell of its program by failing to enforce the program, which substantially reduces the likelihood of litigation against the program. All of these governments engaged in a constitutional dialogue with the courts, with Philadelphia emblematic of the judicial primacy route, Portland representing the elected branch monologue, and Miami presenting the case of mixed results—formal noncompliance with informal constitutional consensus. Governments wishing to maintain unconstitutional programs may do so as long as they are able to fashion litigation avoidance techniques.

While the Court's doctrine in *Croson* is indeed unique, the pattern established by the case is not. In several other areas of constitutional doctrine, when the Supreme Court strikes down a law, the lower courts express near unanimity, while the elected branches seek out methods of avoiding litigation. This helps explain why fifteen years after the Supreme Court declared legislative vetoes unconstitutional in *INS v. Chadha*,[1] Louis Fisher still identified more than 500 unconstitutional legislative vetoes in federal legislation; less than a decade after the Supreme Court declared flag burning statutes unconstitutional in *Texas v. Johnson*[2] and *U.S. v. Eichman*,[3] Vastine Davis Platte catalogued forty-eight unconstitutional state statutes banning flag desecration or flag misuse; and after fifty-plus years of establishment clause rulings striking down compulsory prayer in schools, including *Engel v. Vitale* and *Abington Township v. Schempp*,[4] Kevin McGuire catalogued more than 150 schools in a sample of 224 schools that had failed to comply with Supreme Court precedent regarding the establishment of religion. The pattern displayed in *Croson* resonates across these areas as well. Following Supreme Court adjudication of an issue finding the government practice unconstitutional, the lower courts nearly uniformly implement the Court's policies in a series of derivative lawsuits. Faced with dead-end litigation, the elected branches scramble to ignore, evade, and trump the Supreme Court through creating social, legal, and political barriers to litigation.

About a dozen years after the Supreme Court struck down hate speech–related statutes as unconstitutional in *R.A.V. v. City of St. Paul*,[5] Jon Gould found about 350 colleges and universities still maintaining unconstitutional hate speech regulations. Colleges and universities have largely succeeded in avoiding litigation on the part of students and professors, who one might think would be among the most willing to challenge any perceived slight in a court of law. To do so is really a factor of the social, legal, and political context in which litigation against these programs sits.

The Social, Legal, and Political Context of Hate Speech

The First Amendment's admonishment that "Congress shall make no law . . . abridging the freedom of speech" is not literally true. In fact, "Congress" doesn't really mean Congress, "no law" doesn't really mean no law, and "speech" doesn't really mean speech.

Since the time of *Gitlow v. New York* (1925),[6] the First Amendment has prohibited any government at any level from abridging the freedom of speech. Congress, state legislatures, and school boards, presidents, governors, and mayors, Supreme Court justices, state appellate judges, and city magistrates, and federal bureaucrats, state bureaucrats, and town clerks—all of these government actors can be limited by the First Amendment in regulating or punishing speech. And, of course, ample regulations and punishments for speech exist that are constitutionally permissible. The government may sometimes criminalize obscenity, allow civil liability for some slander, and prevent newspapers from publishing some state secrets. Further, the First Amendment protects some types of expressive conduct without any words being used at all. As an example, flag burning can be constitutionally protected expressive activity. But despite the expansions and limitations accorded to the First Amendment by the judiciary, some principles remain sacrosanct.

When the Supreme Court in 1943 struck down a state law mandating that students salute the U.S. flag, Justice Jackson, writing for the majority, stated: "If there is any fixed star in our constitutional constellation, it is that no official, high or petty, can prescribe what shall be orthodox in politics, nationalism, religion, or other matters of opinion."[7] This general principle guides the courts in requiring the government to remain effectively neutral in the marketplace of ideas. Speakers and listeners are supposed to be able to buy and sell their wares, relatively free of government commands. Yet some types of speech have proven to frustrate the promises of an open society, and consequently the courts have allowed the governments to regulate some speech. Under some circumstances governments may restrict advocacy of illegal or violent activity,[8] "fighting words,"[9] libel, slander, defamation, and other speech-related torts,[10] and obscenity.[11] Similarly, the government may create special limits for particular types of speakers or venues, including commercial speech, speech in the public sector or on public property, speech by the media, and speech among associations, by political parties, and in political campaigns. The First Amendment also prohibits the government from creating statutes that are "overbroad," whereby a constitutionally permissible statute sweeps into its ambit constitutionally protected expression, and from passing statutes that are so vague as to become ripe for standardless administration.

Against this constitutional background, and during the rise of "political correctness," from the mid-1980s to the present day, many college administrations around the country have passed speech codes. These regulations were designed to protect students from racist, sexist, homophobic, or otherwise bigoted speech that might impair the learning environment for some students. Some universities, like Stanford, adopted their speech code in the aftermath of an incident; the impetus for Stanford's program was a student blackface caricature of Beethoven that escalated into campuswide protests.[12] Other universities followed suit, wanting to be seen in the light of protecting students from harmful speech.[13] Well intentioned as they may be, the then existing 125 college speech codes were cast into serious doubt by the U.S. Supreme Court in *R.A.V. v. City of St. Paul.*[14]

"R.A.V." are the initials of a minor in St. Paul, Minnesota, who, in the middle of the night, burned a cross in the fenced-in yard of an African American family. The city charged R.A.V. with violating the local "bias-motivated crime" ordinance, which assessed criminal liability on "whoever places on public or private property a symbol, object, appellation, characterization or graffiti, which one knows or has reasonable grounds to know arouses anger, alarm or resentment in others on the basis of race, color, creed, religion or gender."[15] According to the Minnesota Supreme Court, such a statute is construed to be limited to "fighting words," defined as "conduct that itself inflicts injury or tends to incite immediate violence" and is constitutionally proscribable.[16]

Justice Scalia, writing for a majority of the justices, with four justices writing concurrences, found the bias-motivated crime ordinance unconstitutional. Justice Scalia argued that even though fighting words are proscribable, the government may not selectively prohibit only one view. Thus, governments may not legislate against anti-black speech anymore than they may legislate against pro-black speech. Picking sides between viewpoints is a violation of the First Amendment, regardless of whether the class of speech is proscribable. Thus, not only are states forbidden from crafting statutes that are overbroad—that prohibit too much speech; *R.A.V.* stands for the proposition that states are forbidden from crafting statutes that are underbroad—that do not prohibit enough speech. The Court, however, also crafted some partial exceptions to this particular declaration. Justice Scalia found that governments may proscribe a subset of a type of speech if that subset is the rationale for that speech being proscribable. Thus, states may "prohibit only that obscenity which is the most patently offensive *in its prurience—i.e.,* that which involves the *most* lascivious displays of sexual activity. But it may not prohibit, for example, only that obscenity which includes offensive *political* messages."[17]

The Supreme Court's ruling was an overall victory for free speech, but the Court's doctrine specified how governments could regulate hate speech. The Court struck down a particular law but declared that the general type of regulation could be permissible in some specific situations. This is the identical form of the opinion in *Croson* striking down affirmative action yet detailing how governments could ostensibly craft constitutionally permissible affirmative action statutes. *R.A.V.* was not limited to bias crimes; the holding also implicated the speech codes on the nation's campuses. These codes, like *R.A.V.,* regulate expressive behavior that is considered racist, sexist, or homophobic.[18] Some of these codes punished insults, demeaning words, inconsiderate jokes, and even inappropriate laughter.[19] According to noted First Amendment expert Donald A. Downs, "After *R.A.V.,* all fighting words codes that single out race, gender, and the like for prohibition are probably unconstitutional."[20] In the years leading up to *R.A.V.,* the lower courts had already started to knock down speech codes, including at the University of Michigan,[21] the University of Wisconsin,[22] and George Mason University.[23]

How did our colleges and universities react to *R.A.V.?* Did they quickly dismantle their unconstitutional rules and regulations? In the same era as affirmative action in contracting, colleges and universities responded with the passage of 200 *new* speech codes during the 1990s. And as in the affirmative action context, these new codes, when challenged, also wither in the face of litigation.

In the first few years following *R.A.V.,* courts continued their assault on speech codes at Central Michigan University[24] and Stanford University.[25] Yet according to Jon Gould, author of *Speak No*

TABLE 5.1 Schools' actions following court cases

ACTION	ESTIMATED PERCENTAGE OF SCHOOLS	ESTIMATED NUMBER OF SCHOOLS
Kept offending policy	14	193
Adopted offending policy	9	124
Removed offending policy	2	28
Kept nonoffending policy	17	235
Adopted nonoffending policy	6	83
Removed nonoffending policy	0	0
No policy before or after court cases	51	704

Source: Jon B. Gould, *Speak No Evil: The Triumph of Hate Speech Regulation* (Chicago: University of Chicago Press, 2005), © 2005 by the University of Chicago. Reproduced by permission.

Note: Due to rounding, percentages do not sum to 100.

Evil: The Triumph of Hate Regulation,[26] within five years of *R.A.V.* the number of schools maintaining speech codes rose from about 450 to more than 650. As can be seen from table 5.1, reproduced from Gould, it is estimated that this involved the creation of 124 *new* unconstitutional policies.[27]

Even as colleges and universities have been busy creating new policies, the courts have continued to hammer away in response to the smattering of legal challenges. In the last few years, courts have found speech codes unconstitutional at Shippensburg University[28] and Texas Tech University.[29] The Shippensburg and Texas Tech lawsuits were backed by a leading campus free speech interest group, the Foundation for Individual Rights in Education, or FIRE. FIRE has initiated an anti–speech code litigation campaign and in the last few years has used court victories to secure the dismantling of speech codes at Dartmouth, SUNY–Brockport, Troy University, Citrus College, Albertson College, and Appalachian State University. Some of these victories were achieved simply by sending a letter to the college or university while others were secured after the filing of a lawsuit.

In addition to the litigation efforts of interest groups, another avenue for attacking the speech code movement has been political activism on campus. At the University of Wisconsin–Madison, a group of faculty and students organized a political movement that eventually felled a faculty speech code. By organizing a wide array of people with quite broad political leanings, staking out universal claims in the press, and appealing to the ideas underlying free speech in the university, the political machinations had the same immediate result as the FIRE litigation campaign—the end of the speech code. Yet the political efforts undertaken at the University of Wisconsin may be more lasting, as the same political group has also defeated other threats to academic freedom on campus.[30]

While interest groups have waged litigation campaigns, and academics have organized to defeat speech codes elsewhere, what must be noted is the vast number of speech codes that go untouched. To date, about a dozen unconstitutional speech codes have been removed, leaving more than 500 speech codes intact. Despite the outcome-determinative litigation, hundreds of unconstitutional speech codes fester on college campuses.

How these unconstitutional laws continue to survive is a function of the social, legal, and political barriers to litigation. For example, at the University of Wisconsin–Madison, administrators (i.e., bureaucrats) threatened students who had used inopportune language into attending sensitivity training by raising the speech code issue. Rather than challenge the policy, the students opted to attend the program, and the university dropped the matter.[31] Students who take a stand against these codes could be framed as racist, sexist, or homophobic. It is quite natural that young adults would seek a nonpublic solution when faced with threats from a university administration. Thus, one of the reasons why these codes survive has to do with the social barriers to litigation. The social stigma associated with taking a position that amounts to "pro-racist" speech can be stifling. A second reason for the survival of the speech codes is simply the legal requirement of standing. While free speech cases notoriously allow lawsuits for "chilling effects" on free speech, and sometimes allow lawsuits before one has been targeted under the law, one must be cognizant of the particular legal requirements for a lawsuit. These legal barriers also include the requirement to pay filing fees, statutes of limitation, and jurisdictional requirements.

A final reason why speech codes may persist stems from the political barriers to a lawsuit. Even if a potential plaintiff overcomes the social and legal barriers to a lawsuit, that person or entity might not sue a college or university if such a lawsuit could jeopardize the aggrieved party's relationship with the institution. For example, an untenured faculty member or a student might see maintaining a good relationship with an institution of higher learning preferable to vindicating his or her constitutional rights. A closer look at three other areas of constitutional dialogue highlights these social, legal, and political barriers to litigation.

School Prayer and the Social Costs of Litigation

Despite an essentially uninterrupted string of cases decided over forty years by the Supreme Court finding public school prayer unconstitutional, the practice is still widespread. Because the lower courts have largely been faithful adherents to Supreme Court precedent, the explanation for the persistence of this unconstitutional practice lies chiefly in the social costs of litigation.

The First Amendment contains sibling religion clauses, both designed to accommodate individual religious practice. The free exercise clause is the more obviously liberty-focused clause of the two, providing that the government may not directly dictate how one practices religion. When the state meddles in religious affairs, it risks imposing a system based on the rule of law and democracy onto a system of faith and relationship between an individual and his or her deity or deities. The establishment clause, by restricting the government's ability to sponsor religious practice, prevents the government from coercing individuals into a particular form of religious practice. When the church reaches into the state, it limits the meaning of a constitutional democracy and threatens to exclude both different-believers and nonbelievers. Thus, to some extent the two clauses are of similar ilk. Yet many today claim that the judicial enforcement of the establishment clause is an assault on the free exercise of individuals. Despite these protests, the courts have had little difficulty finding state sponsorship of religion in conflict with the Constitution.

In the early 1960s, twenty years after striking down compelled patriotism in *West Virginia v. Barnette*,[32] the Supreme Court struck down compelled religious incantations in *Engel v. Vitale*[33] and *Abington School District v. Schempp.*[34] *Engel* involved a prayer composed by the state that the state required children to recite, and *Schempp* involved not compulsion but regular recitation of a Christian prayer and "ten verses from the Holy Bible." In both cases the Supreme Court ruled that the First Amendment prohibits states from engaging in religious ceremony. Yet despite the Court's rulings, much of the country was in no mood to desist from foisting devotional activity upon public school students.

Within just a few years, scholars had demonstrated that while there was some compliance, there was also large-scale resistance to the central holdings of *Engel* and *Schempp.*[35] Robert Birkby found that only one out of 121 school districts had completely eliminated school prayer in the year following *Engel.* He found that fifty other school districts modified their pre-*Schempp* activities but did so in ways likely to fall short of Supreme Court precedent. That left seventy school districts that after *Schempp* did not deviate from the 1915 Tennessee law that mandated recitation of Bible selections in all Tennessee public schools.[36] Other scholars also found similar results, including more than 50 percent of public schools in Indiana using Bible reading or school prayer.[37]

States also attempted to navigate within the doctrinal ambiguity of these cases. In the late 1970s, Alabama passed a series of laws attempting to evade the precise words used by the Supreme Court by adding moments of silence, voluntary prayer, or prayer for willing students to the public school curriculum. The Supreme Court, however, ruled all of these statutes unconstitutional in *Wallace v. Jaffree.*[38] The Court's doctrine in *Wallace* focused on "prayer *in* public schools,"[39] and as a consequence, subsequent innovation attempted to move the prayers to graduation ceremonies or football games. The Supreme Court, however, rejected both venues as still incompatible with the establishment clause.[40]

Thus, more than forty years of Supreme Court decisions have assumed a basic anti–school prayer stance and created a series of legal tests designed to ferret out improper commingling of government and religion. From compelled Christian prayer in schools to voluntary prayer, to moments of silence, to moving the prayer outside the instructional setting, in all, the Supreme Court has been unsympathetic to devotion in the public school setting. Within a decade of the initial thrust of cases, however, the practice itself proceeded unabated. And that pattern has not slowed much since.

Kevin McGuire, in his recent work, has been estimating (1) the extent of policy compliance with Supreme Court establishment clause doctrine as it pertains to devotion in schools and (2) the factors associated with the pervasive noncompliance. McGuire surveyed 224 undergraduate college students about their experiences attending public high school in the United States. Because any single student may lack of information about the practices at an entire school, McGuire's estimates likely underestimate the extent of the issue. According to the study, McGuire found that a full two-thirds of the schools provided evidence of failing to comply with at least one facet of Supreme Court doctrine in this regard, and 40 percent of schools maintain at least two distinct violations of Supreme Court doctrine.[41]

McGuire conducted a multivariate analysis to determine the factors with which violations of Supreme Court precedent were associated. He found that schools farther south and schools in areas with a less educated populace were most likely to be associated with disregard of Supreme Court precedent. Smaller communities and communities with higher percentages of Evangelical Christians also covaried with Supreme Court resistance. About half of the schools in the South had either organized prayer, or moments of silence, or Bible reading. Just over half of the southern schools used prayer at sporting events, and almost 60 percent of southern schools had graduation prayers.

Given the Supreme Court's hostility to school prayer, how exactly do these schools continue to evade judicial review? How do these unconstitutional government actions persist? While there is a little variation in lower court rulings, again we find fairly consistent rulings coming from the lower courts. Lower courts have refined and even enlarged the Supreme Court precedent and knocked down Christian prayers at school board meetings,[42] prayers over school intercoms made by nonschool officials,[43] student-led prayers at graduation,[44] and the teaching of creationism.[45] It does not appear to be the case that governments are sponsoring religious devotion and then winning in court. Litigation in support of school prayer, like that in support of affirmative action in contracting, appears to be dead on arrival. Thus, the way for school prayer to flourish as it does in the face of a hostile judiciary is for schools to stem the tide of lawsuits.

One mechanism employed by school districts in their efforts directed toward devotional activities is simply to await a lawsuit and then fold up the official practice. Tyler Deveny, then a senior at St. Albans High School, part of the public school system in Kanawha County, West Virginia, brought a lawsuit against the school district to stop the planned commencement prayer.[46] The school district opted to settle the lawsuit, dropping the policy and paying the legal fees incurred by Deveny.

Another option is to litigate, and then simply ignore the issue. Tangipahoa Parish, in Louisiana, has been the object of three separate lawsuits over establishment clause violations, including the teaching of creationism, a preacher's proselytizing to students, and school-sponsored prayer.[47] The school board, after stipulating to a court order in August 2004 banning prayer at athletic events, continued to allow its public address system to be used at baseball games in March 2005 for prayer. A federal judge refused to cite the school board with criminal contempt as urged by the ACLU but did require the school board to demonstrate within thirty days how it had complied with the court order.[48] Outside the school context, Judge Roy Moore famously refused to obey a federal court order demanding the removal of a 5,000-pound sculpture of the Ten Commandments from the rotunda of the Alabama Supreme Court building.[49]

While the direct lawsuits and disavowals of court orders are relatively straightforward in terms of detecting and curing, many more lawsuits likely would be brought but for the social costs incurred by prospective plaintiffs. Many plaintiffs do not come forward out of fear of community reprisal. In Nebraska, two separate plaintiffs requested anonymity, as did two plaintiffs in a single case in Pennsylvania, all seeking to end school prayer.[50] All of these students feared reprisal from their classmates because they were seeking to stop the tradition of school prayer. These fears may be well founded. Tyler Deveny was beaten by a group of fellow students after he filed suit

against his school district. One of the assailants while beating Deveny taunted him for his failure to believe in a deity.[51]

Less clandestine but potentially farther-reaching efforts to stymie
litigation also exist. Congress has considerable latitude in setting
the jurisdiction of the courts and of attaching disincentives to the
bringing of a lawsuit. In July 2006, the House of Representatives
passed by 260–167 a measure that would strip jurisdiction from all
federal courts—including the U.S. Supreme Court—in any case
involving the Pledge of Allegiance.[52] The Supreme Court in the
1940s ruled in *West Virginia v. Barnette* that the state may not com-
pel public school students to salute the flag of the United States
because students possessed First Amendment rights "not to speak."
It has been black letter law for the last sixty years—both before and
after the insertion of the phrase "under God"—that students may
not be compelled to recite the Pledge of Allegiance.[53] Thus, by taking away the ability of the courts to entertain legal challenges, those
with preferences different from the courts can maintain unconstitutional laws. Similarly, companion bills HR 2679 and S 3696 would
have, if passed, barred damages and the awarding of attorney's fees
to prevailing parties when claims were made for violations of the
establishment clause.[54] Since federal law has long provided for attorneys' fees in fruitful lawsuits finding constitutional or civil rights
violations, the obvious aim of the legislation was to increase the
costs of litigating this particular constitutional right. These legal
barriers to litigation are further explored in the next section, examining flag burning regulations, showing that the judiciary itself may
be partially to blame for the persistence of unconstitutional laws.

Flag Burning and Legal Barriers to Litigation

Around the world today it has become commonplace to see individuals protesting against the United States or its policies by tram-
pling on or burning the U.S. flag. The act is both a cathartic exercise
in hatred and one that often incites anger among many Americans
who witness it. Yet flag burning has long been part of domestic
protests, with many of the same aims and results.

During the 1984 Republican Convention in Dallas, Texas, at
which the Republicans nominated President Reagan to again be

the party's nominee in the general election, Gregory Lee Johnson took part in a demonstration of about 100 motley protesters. The disheveled group marched for about a mile in the heat of a Dallas August, all the while committing several acts of petty vandalism—pounding on car and store windows, overturning newspaper stands, turning over potted plants, littering bank deposit slips, and taking food from restaurant diners' plates. Upon reaching City Hall, Johnson, in the middle of a circle of his fellow protesters, lit the U.S. flag on fire. After burning the flag, Johnson and many of his cohorts continued their behavior and cooled off in the City Hall fountain.[55]

One-half hour later, the Dallas City police arrested about 100 protesters and charged them with disorderly conduct. Authorities later dropped those charges, but charged nine of the protesters with different crimes. Police charged four of those individuals, including Johnson, with violating a 1973 law that criminalized "desecration of a venerated object." Two of the four failed to appear for their trials, one pleaded guilty and served a ten-day sentence, and Johnson went to trial. A jury found Johnson guilty and imposed a one-year jail sentence and a $2,000 fine. Johnson appealed, and the Court of Appeals for the Fifth District of Texas upheld the conviction and sentence. Johnson appealed again, and this time the Texas Court of Criminal Appeals overturned the conviction, finding that the state's law, as applied, abridged Johnson's First Amendment right to freedom of speech. Finally, the State of Texas appealed to the U.S. Supreme Court.[56]

The Court found the Texas flag desecration statute, as applied, to be unconstitutional. The Court reasoned that Johnson's conduct was expressive conduct protected by the First Amendment, and that Texas's interest was related to the suppression of free expression, in contravention of the First Amendment. As such, the Court's decision had the effect of overturning Johnson's conviction. While the outcome of *Texas v. Johnson* was decidedly against flag desecration statutes, the Court's doctrine again demonstrated some apparent wavering and presents another kind of checkmate move, the erection of legal barriers.

The Court in *Texas v. Johnson* did not elect to strike down Johnson's conviction as a facial claim but instead "as applied." The Court elected to rule more narrowly, as the Court found a person could violate the statute without expressing any idea. For example, "[a] tired person might . . . drag a flag through the mud, knowing that this conduct is likely to offend others, and yet have not thought of expressing any idea." Thus, since the statute could conceivably be used to prosecute individuals who were not expressing themselves under the First Amendment, the statutory scheme did not need to be thrown out. Johnson's conduct was offensive—but that was the point—to convey a message, and according to the Court, "If there is a bedrock principle underlying the First Amendment, it is that the Government may not prohibit the expression of an idea simply because society finds the idea itself offensive or disagreeable." The Court noted that even though First Amendment doctrine recognizes a narrow category that allows "fighting words" to be criminalized in some circumstances, here there was no "direct personal insult or an invitation to exchange fisticuffs." Thus, *Texas v. Johnson* allows flag desecration statutes to survive, so long as such prosecutions are not related to expression of an idea or where such prosecutions are directed toward flag desecration under another First Amendment exception, such as fighting words or imminent lawless action.[57]

What has happened as a result of the *Johnson* decision? Have the forty-eight states (all but Alaska and Wyoming) that banned flag burning rushed to dismantle their unconstitutional statutes?[58] Have street-level bureaucrats—police officers—refused to arrest individuals for burning flags? Have the lower courts dug deeply into the words used by the Supreme Court in a struggle to maintain prosecutions against flag burners? Perhaps not surprising to the readers of this book, our pattern generally persists. Legislatures have refused to significantly alter their statutes, and in fact, Congress passed its own brand-new law prohibiting flag burning. We have not seen a bevy of new flag burning laws, though given the exceptionally high percentage of states prohibiting flag burning, expecting entirely new laws in the face of the Court ruling is probably unrealistic. Despite the lack of new laws, however, some police officers have continued to arrest individuals for violating flag burning statutes, and overwhelmingly the courts have rejected those prosecutions, including the U.S. Supreme Court, which reversed the convictions of two individuals who violated the federal flag burning statute.[59]

In the aftermath of *Texas v. Johnson,* Congress responded with a statute of its own, passing the Flag Protection Act, a statute criminalizing the actions of one who "knowingly mutilates, defaces, physically defiles, burns, maintains on the floor or ground or tramples upon any flag of the United States." Congress exempted the disposal of a worn or soiled flag and included a standard definition of a flag.[60] The new federal statute went into effect on October 28, 1989, and protestors in both Seattle, Washington, and Washington, D.C., were arrested in the ensuing days for violating the Flag Protection Act.

Two different district courts threw out the charges against the flag burning individuals as each court found the federal law unconstitutional.[61] Congress had built into the law a special provision by which the Supreme Court would review the cases without waiting for an appeal to the federal circuit courts. The Court again found that the arrested protesters were engaged in expressive conduct and that the government's interest, despite the lack of content-based limitation, was related to suppression of that expression, in contravention of the First Amendment.

Congress also responded by attempting to amend the Constitution. In fact, in every Congress since 1990, there have been failed attempts at amending the Constitution each term.[62] The favored amendment simply allows Congress to "prohibit the physical desecration of the flag of the United States."[63] While Congress and the states have amended the Constitution a few times to overturn a Supreme Court decision (e.g., the Eleventh, Sixteenth, and Twenty-sixth Amendments), amending the Constitution has been attempted more than 11,000 times, with only twenty-seven successes.

States have not quickly abandoned their flag burning ways either. Six years after *Texas v. Johnson,* the same forty-eight states that prohibited flag burning before the ruling still prohibited flag burning.[64] Texas has passed a new statute, modeled on the federal statute declared unconstitutional in *Eichman.*[65] A few states, such as Maryland and Arizona, have limited prosecutions to misuse "intended to incite or produce an imminent breach of the peace."[66] But most states still just maintain their anti-desecration statutes unchanged, and all these statutes are likely unconstitutional. Some statutes even go so far as to make it a crime to "cast contempt upon, satirize, deride or burlesque" the flag by acts *or words!*[67] The Wisconsin Supreme Court struck down the Wisconsin anti-desecration statute as unconstitutional in 1998, after Wisconsin prosecuted a young man for violating state law by defecating on a flag in the name of anarchy.[68]

While the particular form of desecration may have been extreme in Wisconsin, the police and court behavior was not. Press accounts of flag burnings in the first decade since *Texas v. Johnson* find a little over 100 flag desecration acts, with somewhere between six and twelve incidents annually.[69] According to Robert Goldstein, there have been at least two dozen arrests of individuals around the country under laws rendered unconstitutional because of *Texas v. Johnson* and *U.S. v. Eichman.* In almost all those cases, the charges were eventually dropped or the convictions were overturned. In Ohio in 1990, a woman was arrested, prosecuted, convicted, and sentenced to jail for one year for her flag burning protest, which led to a riot. The Ohio Supreme Court overturned her conviction, as the jury instructions did not specify that flag burning is protected by the First Amendment. A Pennsylvania man who tore down several U.S. flags during a raging fight with his fiancée pleaded guilty to insulting the flag, and his sentence included writing a book report on "The Man Without a Country" to improve his attitude toward the flag. His conviction was overturned on appeal because of inadequate assistance of counsel at trial. Alabama brought charges against a man for littering, desecrating a post office, and desecrating a flag for writing in chalk on the sidewalk antiwar slogans and carrying a "wadded"-up flag in his coat pocket. Not only did this defendant have his charges thrown out, he settled a claim for false imprisonment and malicious prosecution out of court. Prosecutors twice brought charges against a man in South Dakota who burned a flag as police officers dispersed a party, and each time the charges were dismissed by the courts.[70]

The pattern in the flag burning case is that following the Supreme Court decision striking down a flag misuse statute, the elected branches effectively ignored the outcome of those rulings and held steadfast to the words of the Supreme Court—to the doctrine. Street-level bureaucrats have continued to arrest individuals, but the courts and prosecutors have effectively blocked or dropped most prosecutions. This situation matches up mostly with our discovered pattern, except for the seeming absence of a checkmate move by the elected branches. How have the elected branches kept their preferred policies from being trampled by the judiciary? Two recent cases demonstrate that the judiciary itself is responsible for erecting an unnecessary legal barrier to litigation; the Supreme Court's unnecessary reliance on the "as applied" ruling explains why these unconstitutional laws still persist.

Ken Larsen ran for governor of the state of Utah. As part of his campaign, Larsen wrote his name in ink on several U.S. and Utah miniature flags, which he then displayed and distributed to the public.[71] Larsen was not charged with a crime, but he initiated a lawsuit alleging that he feared for his safety in light of the Utah flag burning law. Kris Winsness, another Utah resident, burned a "smiley face" into a U.S. flag and hung the flag on his garage. Winsness initially claimed to an investigating sheriff that he had burned the smiley face out of boredom, though he later maintained political expression as his motivation.[72] The sheriff gave Winsness a citation for "abuse of a flag" pursuant to a Utah flag desecration law, and took the flag as evidence. Several months later the county dismissed the charges against Winsness. Winsness, like Larsen, filed a complaint against several government officials in Utah seeking to have the Utah law found facially unconstitutional. The trial court judge ruled that the plaintiffs lacked standing, and the U.S. Court of Appeals for the Tenth Circuit, in an opinion written by Judge McConnell, upheld the decision.

Similarly, while a seventeen-year-old student in Indiana, Megan Lawson participated in rallies protesting the U.S. war in Iraq. In one demonstration, the local chief of police witnessed a U.S. flag that Lawson had decorated with a peace symbol. The chief told her the flag was "contraband" and that it was "illegal to paint a peace symbol on an American flag." No one arrested or fined Lawson. Lawson brought a claim against the government. The trial court judge ruled that the plaintiffs lacked standing, and the U.S. Court of Appeals for the Seventh Circuit, in an opinion written by Judge Posner, upheld the decision.

These two cases demonstrate one danger of the persistence of the unconstitutional laws, and a different take on the checkmate move. In both the Utah and Indiana cases, street-level bureaucrats used the existence of laws on the books to harass citizens engaging in protected expressive behavior. The police ticketed, arrested, or placed the fear of prosecution in citizens, and left it up to the prosecutors' office to rescind the charges. This quashes any actual injury that would be suffered by a citizen and takes away standing—thus defeating the lawsuit and maintaining the law on the books. When these laws stay on the books, however, police officers may again use them in their harassment of constitutionally protected speakers.

Though this political motivation for maintaining the statute yet gutting its enforcement is similar to Miami's response to *Croson,* the idea goes beyond the politically messy cases. Judge McConnell in *Winsness* addressed the larger issue frankly: "There is no procedure in American law for courts or other agencies of government—other than the legislature itself—to purge from the statute books, laws that conflict with the Constitution." Unconstitutional laws persist and are ripe for street-level bureaucratic abuse, even when the laws are widely acknowledged to be unconstitutional, until a legislature takes them off the books.

This pattern of enforcement of unconstitutional laws has also been seen in matters other than flag burning, including cases involving anti-miscegenation laws[73] and Jim Crow laws.[74] In these cases, too, governments maintained such unconstitutional laws on the books only to have their attempted enforcement stopped. Three years after the Supreme Court's 1967 decision in *Loving v. Virginia*[75] that anti-miscegenation statutes ran afoul of the Fourteenth Amendment's equal protection clause, an Alabama justice of the peace refused to issue a marriage license to a couple because the applicants were of different races. It took a federal district court ruling to invalidate Alabama's law, which had remained on the books.[76]

But the case of flag burning is slightly different. Although certainly these prosecutions are largely destined be unsuccessful, and can even be grounds for false imprisonment and malicious prosecution claims, their very maintenance is constitutionally troubling. The courts fail to declare these laws unconstitutional because there is a *possible* prosecution that can occur without violating the constitution. The Supreme Court decided *Texas v. Johnson* on an "as applied" basis, as a person could have dragged the flag through the mud. Or as Judge Posner points out in *Lawson,* a prosecution could have gone forward if the student had trampled the flag "to keep her feet from getting wet. . . . In other words, the applicability of the statute to the flag desecration depends on the facts. . . . In addition, as an elected official [the defendant] is doubtless reluctant to express himself publicly in a manner that would suggest he condoned flag desecration." Because the facts could be arrayed in such a manner that a prosecution could proceed without attacking expressive activity, the Supreme Court has let the statutes stand, even though it has rejected their application in the given cases. The real problem, however, is that the persistence of these statutes may have a chilling effect on protected speech.

In 1965, Justice Brennan wrote on behalf on the Court in *Lamont v. Postmaster General*[77] that even when a statute does not directly regulate speech, it could have a "chilling effect" or deterrent effect on protected speech, and thus could be held unconstitutional. Here, the fact that the statute could be used constitutionally does little to render it constitutional when its very existence may cause individuals to forfeit their First Amendment rights. And insofar as there have been actual prosecutions, in addition to demonstrated instances of threatened arrest, it does not seem to be a large stretch to suggest that these laws are being used to chill free speech. Despite this reasoning, in both the *Winsness* and *Lawson* cases, both Judge McConnell and Judge Posner reasoned that because these statutes are of such dubious constitutional value, the risk of prosecution is too remote to allow these claims to proceed.

What is somewhat exceptional about the flag burning cases is that the party to blame for the checkmate move is not an elected branch per se (although clearly the actions of the street-level bureaucrats are part of the problem) but the courts. It is the judiciary that has made it exceptionally difficult to have a flag burning statute purged from the books, by ruling on an "as applied" basis and not on a facial basis. Although certainly the elected branches could repeal these unconstitutional laws, the judiciary could have ruled more strongly in *Texas v. Johnson.* The Court did not need to rule in the case "as applied" but could have ruled that the statute was unconstitutional on its face. Just as the Wisconsin Supreme Court found that the Wisconsin law violated the First Amendment and struck down the law facially, the U.S. Supreme Court could have done the same thing.[78] And by taking such a limited step here, the judiciary has made it more difficult for ordinary citizens to navigate through their political lives devoid of unconstitutional laws. Thus, the courts themselves can erect legal barriers to the lawsuit. Just as a player in a chess game can render himself or herself defenseless, so too can the judiciary derail the litigation process and defeat its own ability to participate in the constitutional dialogue. The political barrier to litigation, discussed in the next section, is a crucial aspect of the final constitutional dialogue presented in this chapter.

Legislative Vetoes and Political Barriers to Litigation

Jagdish Rai Chadha, a native Kenyan of Indian descent, entered the United States in 1966 with a British passport. He received a graduate degree from Bowling Green University, and his student visa expired in June 1972.[79] The INS demanded that Chadha show cause why he should not be deported for overstaying his student visa pursuant to federal law. Chadha admitted he had overstayed his visa, but he applied to the U.S. attorney general to have his deportation suspended on the basis of likely racial persecution in his country of birth or origin. The attorney general granted the deportation suspension. Chadha's name, however, along with the names of 340 other individuals who had had their deportations suspended, was submitted to the U.S. House of Representatives as required by the Immigration and Nationality Act. The House of Representatives accepted 334 of the deportation suspensions but voted to reinstate the deportation order of the INS for six individuals, including Chadha.

Chadha sought to have the Immigration and Nationality Act declared unconstitutional, arguing his case all the way up to the U.S. Supreme Court. The Supreme Court ruled that the Constitution requires federal legislation to be passed by both houses of Congress and presented to the president under Article I, Section 7, of the Constitution. Ruling that the House of Representatives' overturning of the decision of the attorney general amounted to legislation, the Court indicated that such an action would have to be replicated by the Senate and presented to the president to be constitutional. Thus, the Immigration and Nationality Act provision that provided for this "legislative veto" was unconstitutional.[80]

What has happened since *INS v. Chadha* in 1983? Have the elected branches responded to the Court? How have the lower courts responded to the Supreme Court? The pattern of responses, like those in affirmative action, shows mostly elected branch resistance and judicial acquiescence. It appears that the courts have continued to strike down legislative vetoes, whereas the elected branches have not only modified very few of the then 200 existing legislative veto statutes[81] but have created another 400 legislative vetoes in the twenty years following the case. Faced with outcome-determinative litigation, elected branch efforts have had to be directed toward limiting opportunities for litigation.

As happened in the case of affirmative action, there were some immediate legislative responses to *Chadha*. Within two years of *Chadha*, Congress eliminated the legislative veto provisions in legislation regarding executive reorganization, District of Columbia Home Rule, national emergencies, export administration, and federal pay increases.[82] Congress also has outright ignored the decision and continued to use legislative vetoes as it had before the Supreme Court's *Chadha* decision,[83] sometimes fighting it out in the courts, as Philadelphia did in response to *Croson*. Those litigation efforts had very similar results, as the lower courts almost uniformly struck down similar legislation. Congress also passed new legislation containing legislative vetoes. By 1993, Congress had passed more than 200 new legislative vetoes.[84] And by 2005 that number had reached more than 400 statutes.[85]

Courts, including the Supreme Court, have almost unanimously replicated the anti–legislative veto outcome reached in *Chadha*. In the immediate aftermath of *Chadha*, the Supreme Court made it clear that its ruling was not an aberration. The Court struck down a two-house veto of a Federal Trade Commission regulation[86] and summarily affirmed two U.S. Circuit Court of Appeals decisions striking down two-house vetoes.[87]

Faced with the anti–legislative veto sentiment of the Supreme Court, Congress has responded by fashioning new variants of the legislative veto. *Chadha* maintained that all actions taken by Congress deemed to be "legislative" in "character" would be subject to the bicameralism and presentment provisions of the Constitution. Thus, policy responses by the elected branches were, as in the case of *Croson,* faced with a nearly insurmountable standard. Legislative actions are those actions that have the "purpose and effect of altering the legal rights, duties, and relations of person . . . outside the legislative branch." This doctrinal declaration proves to be all-encompassing, rendering all of Congress's veto machinations unconstitutional.

The primary avenue for Congress, however, has been to refrain from using a full house of Congress for a veto, but instead to move these decisions to a particular committee. Thus, most contemporary legislative veto provisions charge either the committee most closely tied to a particular agency or, even more likely, the appropriations committee with being able to review agency decisions. Committee vetoes, however, do not appear to fundamentally respond to the Court's ruling that such legislation must comply with the Constitution's bicameralism and presentment provisions.[88]

Much as the City of Miami did in response to *Croson,* Congress has opted in some instances simply to not use the textual provision of a legislative veto that still exists in legislation.[89] This may not have the same direct political appeasement aspect of Miami's bureaucratic gutting of its affirmative action contracting program, but it does insulate members of Congress from having to revisit legislative decisions that can be blamed on others. Congress has also chosen to insert "notification" provisions in much of its legislation, before an agency implements a congressional directive. While notification may seem innocuous, Louis Fisher notes "'notification' is mostly a code word for a committee veto."[90] ·

These legislative machinations have not fared particularly well in the courts. Lower courts have struck down committee vetoes[91] and even congressional "recommendations"[92] that turned out to be quite coercive under *Chadha.* Further, the U.S. Supreme Court struck down a federal law that provided a veto of an airport agency to a "board of review" consisting of nine members of Congress.[93] The one case in which a court arguably upheld a legislative veto involved the General Services Administration (GSA); the GSA was required to receive congressional consent to sell items worth more than $10,000. Although the trial court struck down the provision as unconstitutional,[94] the U.S. Court of Appeals for the Federal Circuit reversed the decision after finding the notice provision merely voluntary.[95]

Thus, given the dead end for litigation, Congress has been forced to direct its efforts toward avoiding litigation, toward creating a checkmate move and boldly speaking out with its own constitutional vision. To this end, Congress has refashioned some straightout legislative vetoes as "informal understandings."[96] These informal understandings effectively push the veto out of the limelight. For example, the House Appropriations Committee places a spending cap on an agency and allows the agency to exceed those caps if it receives permission from the Appropriations Committee. This particular agreement is not published as part of the public law but instead is inserted in the conference report, where Congress usually instructs agencies how to implement a particular statute. Government agencies are not necessarily required by law to comply with these exact provisions, but (1) agencies would rather not have to seek additional funding from both houses and the president, and (2) willful disobedience of the spending authority may not bode particularly well for future agency appropriations. Thus, the agencies have no incentive to litigate themselves, and there are no parties who have been deprived of legally entitled spending, so there is no one with standing to bring a lawsuit.[97]

Similarly, Congress may opt to insert legislative vetoes in foreign affairs.[98] Typical in this regard would be the Good Friday Accords, whereby President George H. W. Bush and Congress pledged their support for the Contras in Nicaragua.[99] Under these accords, aid would flow to the Contras for one year, but after nine months President Bush would have to receive letters from four different congressional committees to continue the aid. Such a spending policy does not establish legal rights for those abroad, and members of Congress themselves do not possess standing to challenge the legislation and may create a nonjusticiable political question as well, as four members of Congress found out in their lawsuit.[100]

What Congress has done here is effectively pin the recipients of its money with unconstitutional provisions because of the continuing relationship between the parties. Another favorite tool of Congress is illustrative of this point. Congress sometimes maintains provisions in its legislation that require agencies who wish to "reprogram" parts of their appropriations from one spending area to another to come back before a committee. In 1987, a foreign aid bill forbade agencies from reallocating budget items without reappearing before the House and Senate Appropriations Committees. The Office of Management and Budget (OMB) director balked, however, and chastised Congress in a letter pointing out the dubious constitutionality of the provision. Congress responded by striking the language from the law, thus effectively freezing foreign aid spending as it had been approved by Congress in the first instance.[101] Now OMB would have to maneuver a completely new spending bill through a Congress not particularly enthusiastic about helping out the disgruntled agency.

This is the real crux of how Congress has been able to maintain the legislative veto. Congress operated the legislative veto for more than fifty years before *Chadha*.[102] Congress had been aware of the constitutional difficulties of the legislative veto,[103] but the very practical effect of the legislative veto created two groups of winners. And after *Chadha,* "the conditions that created the legislative veto over the years did not change. . . . Executive officials still wanted substantial latitude in administering delegated authority; legislators still insisted on maintaining control without having to pass another statute."[104] What did change is that agencies that complained about the persistence of the unconstitutional laws would suffer the consequences. This political barrier to litigation provides a nearly foolproof checkmate move for Congress.

Checkmate

After hate speech, school prayer, flag burning, and legislative vetoes, the case of affirmative action seems to be less of an aberration. Rather than affirmative action simply being an exception to the rule of constitutional dialogue, these cases taken together are at the very least demonstrative of the long-term advantages held by the elected branches over the courts. The Supreme Court fills its docket in any given year with cases about statutory interpretation, conflict of laws, admiralty and maritime, administrative review, and the Constitution. Despite the storied history of the Supreme Court and the Constitution, constitutional interpretation is not the Court's exclusive work.[105] Similarly, the lore of the Supreme Court's confrontation with legislatures over statutes may be overblown. In fact, many unconstitutional government decisions are the result of judicial decree, agency rulemaking, and street-level bureaucrat discretion.[106]

According to a study by Seth Kreimer of the 1990–95 Supreme Court terms, the High Court issued opinions in 595 cases, or about 100 cases per term. As can been seen from table 5.2, 292, or just under 50 percent, of these cases involved constitutional claims. Because cases can maintain more than one claim, there were 149 constitutional cases involving legislatures and 207 constitutional cases involving other government actions (e.g., judicial decree, agency rulemaking, and street-level bureaucrat discretion). Well over one-half of the constitutional claims did not involve elected officials.

What this means is that the focus on courts and the elected branches in the constitutional dialogue uncovers only part of the problem. Not only may elected branches impose a view of the Constitution at odds with the courts' view, but teachers and police officers may also pose a challenge for the courts. And once the courts have ruled, institutional responses vary both across institutions and within institutions. For example, Pickerill analyzed about forty years' worth of the Supreme Court's practice of judicial review over federal laws to see whether and how Congress responded to the

TABLE 5.2 U.S. Supreme Court, 1990–95 terms, constitutional violation claims

SOURCE	REJECTED	POSSIBLE	SUSTAINED	TOTAL
Legislative	68	21	60	149
Nonlegislative	91	60	56	207

Source: Adapted from Seth F. Kreimer, "Exploring the Dark Matter of Judicial Review: A Constitutional Census of the 1990s," *William and Mary Bill of Rights Journal* 5 (1997): 427. Reproduced by permission.

Note: 595 total cases, 292 constitutional cases.

TABLE 5.3 Congressional responses to judicial review, 1954–97 (n = 74)

CONGRESSIONAL RESPONSE	NUMBER (%)
Amend Constitution	1 (1)
Amend legislation	27 (36)
Repeal, pass new legislation	8 (11)
Repeal legislation	10 (14)
No response	28 (38)

Source: J. Mitchell Pickerill, *Constitutional Deliberation in Congress: The Impact of Judicial Review in a Separated System* (Durham, NC: Duke University Press, 2004). Reproduced by permission.

Court. Pickerill's tabulation, reproduced in table 5.3, shows that Congress has availed itself of several different options in responding to the Court.

Once the Supreme Court has declared an act of Congress unconstitutional, then, as Pickerill informs, "Congress may do nothing, amend the Constitution or pass new legislation to override the Court, pass legislation to circumvent the Court, pass legislation to comply with the Court, or repeal legislation to comply with the Court."[107] As table 5.3 shows, Congress does nothing almost 40 percent of the time and either amends the Constitution or repeals the legislation about 15 percent of the time. Only in the remaining 45 percent of cases does Congress engage in the sort of constitutional dialogue favored by coordinate construction scholars. Taking Kreimer's and Pickerill's work together, then, we see that the typical constitutional dialogue situation envisioned by scholars reflects only a limited segment of the Supreme Court's work.

What is perhaps necessary is to discuss what is wrong with the current situation, in which the Court is unable to rein in much unconstitutional action. Some may suggest that this flouting of the Court is of no consequence. If flag burning statutes, hate speech statutes, and affirmative action programs cannot be enforced, what problems exist by virtue of their continued existence? How does having unconstitutional statutes harm us? Second, it might be that the other branches of government have competing claims on the

Constitution and its interpretation. The Supreme Court is only one branch of government, and the coordinate branches of government not only have the right but a duty to consider the constitutionality of government action. While these contentions are informative to the stakes of the debate, and I provide some measured response below, it should be noted that one very big issue is the Court not getting what it wants. That is to say, it is both interesting and problematic that the Supreme Court, an institution that has been populated by some of the intellectual heavyweights of our country, is not getting what it wants in terms of issuing opinions and having those opinions followed.

What is wrong with flouting the Court? Why should it matter if our statute books contain unconstitutional flag burning statutes? If they are unenforceable, whom do they harm? First, the easy cases are those such as affirmative action or legislative vetoes, where in essence participants have agreed to not abide by the Constitution and instead operated outside its parameters. While one might believe that such a willful declaration of the rights and responsibilities of our citizens ought to be accorded respect—after all, what can be more empowering than according legitimacy to one's own choices?—this is a problematic assertion. The agreement between the elected branches and the interest group in Portland violates the rights of individuals *not* party to this agreement. The aggrieved individuals in Portland would be those treated differently by the government by virtue of their race. These aggrieved individuals need not, and likely would not (because of the limited size of the government contracts at issue), be members of Associated General Contractors. The aggrieved individuals in the case of legislative vetoes would be the recipients of executive agency spending,[108] not just the agency itself. Thus, while there appears to be a private agreement, or Coase theorem situation,[109] to not obey the dictates of the Constitution because of the externalities involved, the end result is that this agreement denies individuals who have not made such an agreement their constitutional rights.

Second are the more difficult cases, such as flag desecration statutes or hate speech laws—laws that appear to be unconstitutional and completely unenforceable. These statutes might be akin to statutes regularly featured in the "News of the Weird" type of column, such as it being "illegal to carry an ice cream cone in your pocket on Sunday" type of law. Where is the harm in maintaining such a silly law on the books? In the *Winsness* and *Lawson* flag desecration cases and in the Wisconsin hate speech sensitivity training example discussed earlier, the government harassed or coerced citizens exercising their free speech rights into curtailing their rights—and did so by reference to the laws on the books. The police in *Winsness* and *Lawson* targeted individuals engaged in protected expressive conduct involving the flag, specifically referring to these statutes. In Wisconsin, administrators referred to the hate speech law as leverage to get students to "volunteer" to go to sensitivity training. Similarly, Julie Novkov and Peter Wallenstein each have separately demonstrated that despite the Court's ruling in *Loving v. Virginia* in 1967 that the equal protection clause made anti-miscegenation laws unconstitutional, several states continued to enforce their own provisions until faced with Federal District Court orders.[110]

It is conceivable that these are simply isolated incidents that happened to make their way to litigation and to researchers. Yet it seems more likely that there are plenty of other cases where street-level bureaucrats who may even know that such statutes are unconstitutional use them as leverage against individuals who are engaged in constitutionally protected actions. To the extent that these individuals would threaten citizens with simply imaginary legislation, in the case that these unconstitutional laws no longer existed, one might conclude that these individuals would harass citizens regardless of the presence of the law. Yet one should not discount the effect of the law on behavior. We know from psychology that the presence of a justification can affect decision making. That is to say that a person will be more likely to positively evaluate a decision if such a decision is accompanied by a justification.[111] In effect, the justification itself can be important in predicting behavior. Thus it very well may be that street-level bureaucrats are affected by the presence of these unconstitutional laws. Whether having an unconstitutional law on the books rises to the level of being a causal mechanism in the denial of an individual's rights is an open question, but the potential harm from the presence of an unconstitutional law on the books vastly outweighs any remote benefit that could conceivably occur.

It seems, then, that there can be harm from having unconstitutional laws on the books. But another claim also exists, and that is simply that the Court sometimes gets it wrong, or, to put it more delicately, the coordinate branches of government may have competing claims on constitutional interpretation. Scholars such as Keith Whittington, Mark Tushnet, and Mark Graber suggest that the Supreme Court does not enjoy a monopoly on constitutional interpretation and that the Constitution is more than simply a Delphic document to be deciphered by the esteemed legal priests of the Supreme Court.[112] While undoubtedly there are instances of horrific constitutional decisions,[113] these lists often tend to be shorthand for political affiliation. *Kelo*[114] was awful because the government can now take your property (and this case pales in comparison to the takings upheld in *Midkiff*),[115] and *Dred Scot* was horrific because it treated African Americans as chattel (never mind that the Court's reading fit squarely into the Framers' intent).[116] What should be noted is that the difficulties extant in determining which Supreme Court decisions should be accorded respect and which decisions should be derided does not necessarily mean that each branch of government should have equal abilities to determine the constitutionality of legislation and government action. For the same caustic acidity by which this coordinate construction argument eats away at the legitimacy of Supreme Court decisions[117] renders all Supreme Court decisions suspect and contestable.

While it makes a good deal of sense to recognize the fallibility of the Supreme Court, as it can sometimes simply muscle through five votes, there is a good case to be made for strong deference to at least a subset of Court decisions. This subset includes at a minimum Court decisions that guard against the self-serving or self-dealing agreements discussed above in relation to affirmative action and legislative vetoes, where individuals have been fenced out of the process. This is in some way derivative of Ely's "representation reinforcement" idea.[118] This subset should also include the cases of flag burning and hate speech, as the coordinate construction argument, at least in these cases, seems to conflate rights and laws. Laws can be changed by simple majorities, or in a Dahlian perspective by an active minority.[119] But rights are very different. Not only do we traditionally hold these rights as a practical matter until a supermajority intercedes, the very nature of rights is, according to Jefferson, "inalienable." One cannot consent to give up the right to speech, for such a right preexists the Constitution. Thus, instead of having to accept the "judicial supremacy" notion heralded by Larry Alexander and Frederick Schauer,[120] one could simply recognize, as Pickerill has done, that our system should embrace "judicial primacy."[121]

Judicial primacy recognizes the necessity of guarding against constitutional monologue from either the courts or the elected branches, and suggests that dialogue as a normative matter is preferable to both judicial supremacy and to a cycling judicial dialogue. Yet as an empirical matter, we have seen what could have been an elected branch check on judicial monopolization turned into elected branch monopolization of constitutional interpretation. The continued maintenance of affirmative action contracting programs in Portland, speech codes on American college campuses, school prayer statutes, flag burning statutes, and legislative vetoes is much more reflective of elected branch monopolization than of judicial supremacy. Only in the instances of Philadelphia's and Miami's affirmative action programs, with the long-term back and forth between the elected branches and the courts in Philadelphia and with the bureaucratic gutting of Miami's program, do we see examples of (and certainly a less than perfect example, in the case of Miami) a constitutional dialogue taking place.

Coordinate construction scholars, however, could argue that the cases of Philadelphia and Miami simply demonstrate the differences between dialogue and monologue, without ever privileging Supreme Court constitutional decision making. Yet in looking at all of these cases together, one is struck by several facts that urge toward accepting a somewhat greater primacy for the courts in constitutional decision making. In the cases of affirmative action, speech codes, school prayer, flag burning, and legislative vetoes, the courts speak with a nearly uniform voice. Yet the variation among the elected branches' response in cases of cities that opted to maintain a full-bore affirmative action plan in the face of *Croson*, colleges that continued to operate speech codes after *R.A.V.*, public schools that utilized prayer since the long line of establishment clause cases, police who continued to arrest people for burning a flag after *Texas v. Johnson*, and agencies subject to legislative vetoes after *Chadha* suggests that constitutional rights are exceptionally contingent. While contested law is not particularly problematic for some scholars, the notion that rights are no more firmly entrenched than "mere" laws threatens to undermine the entire premise of rights. One does not abdicate one's right to equal treatment under the law because one lives in Portland, Oregon, or one's right to free speech because one attends the University of Wisconsin, or one's right to not have an established religion because one attends high school in Odessa, Texas.

Typically, the remedy for constitutional violation is the lawsuit. Yet the elected branches are not static and they are not stupid. They have figured out that by derailing the litigation process, they can attack the nexus between constitutional violation and constitutional remedy. By employing checkmate moves, not only do governments steel in place unconstitutional laws, they also attack the Court's role as the primary arbiter of the meaning of the Constitution. Such meaning is necessarily affected by the role of politics on the ground, but the attack renders both constitutional rights and mere laws only in the realm of politics. While certainly law itself is often the by-product of politics, law is not only politics.

The Supreme Court, and the lower courts as faithful agents of the principal, stands as a singular arbiter of the Constitution among many arbiters of the Constitution. Its decisions are neither self-evident nor self-enforcing. Yet in the view of judicial primacy, without a deferential view toward the Court, if only in the area of constitutional rights, the Court's voice is diminished, as are the substantive rights protected by the Court. For the endless cycling provides the elected branches with the continual opportunity to dodge, evade, and trump the Supreme Court's rulings, either via outright nullification or via opportunities for fashioning checkmate moves. These checkmate moves, no matter whether they take the form of interest group co-option, bureaucratic nonimplementa-tion, or something else, threaten to become monopolistic centers of power that threaten both what constitutional supremacy and constitutional dialogue scholars hold dear. Hamilton was certainly correct that the judiciary is the least dangerous branch, "having neither force nor will, but merely judgment." Checkmate imperils the entire premise by which our rights are protected.

CONCLUSION

It is emphatically the duty and province of the judiciary to say what the law is.
Chief Justice Marshall, *Marbury v. Madison* (1803)

In the preceding pages I have explained what can happen after the Supreme Court exercises its power of judicial review, striking down laws as unconstitutional. With all the attention focused on who the Supreme Court justices are, how each justice views the Constitution, and how each justice might vote on the next big case, it is surprising how relatively little attention is paid to the actual consequences of constitutional decision making. It is particularly curious that we do not always understand what happens after the Court decides, because who the justices are, how each justice views the Constitution, and how each justice might vote on the next big case are important only if Supreme Court decisions matter. Most individuals take it for granted that these decisions matter, but political scientists have been much more skeptical of the Court's power to transform society.

When the Supreme Court declares laws unconstitutional, most people assume that similar laws around the country are also unconstitutional. When the Supreme Court decided *City of Richmond v. Croson,* the decision implicated the other 200 or so minority business enterprise (MBE) programs around the country. When the Supreme Court decided *R.A.V. v. City of St. Paul,* the decision implicated hundreds of speech codes around the country. When the Supreme Court decided *Engel v. Vitale* and *Abington Township v. Schempp,* the decisions implicated all public schools around the country that used prayer in the school. When the Supreme Court decided *Texas v. Johnson,* the decision implicated flag burning statutes in forty-eight other states. And when the Supreme Court decided *INS v. Chadha,* the decision implicated more than 200 other legislative vetoes embedded in federal legislation. Yet in each of these cases, unconstitutional laws have largely persisted.

Responses to Supreme Court decisions are quite varied. Some cities and other governments did dismantle their unconstitutional affirmative action programs in response to *Croson.* Some universities did repeal their unconstitutional speech codes after *R.A.V.* In light of *Engel* and *Abington Township,* some public schools stopped offering Christian benedictions to start the school day. No state entirely repealed its flag burning statute in response to *Johnson,* though some states have now limited the kinds of actions that might be prosecuted. And after *Chadha,* Congress has in some instances modified the form of legislative vetoes.

But quite surprisingly to many, following *Croson,* at least 150 cities established new unconstitutional affirmative action programs; after *R.A.V.,* more than 100 colleges and universities enacted new unconstitutional speech codes; and despite a series of Supreme Court decisions striking down improper mixtures of church and state, to this day approximately half the public schools in the South routinely violate the establishment clause of the Constitution. While states have not established new flag burning statutes, most states have simply left their questionable statutes on the books unchanged or have modified their statutes in line with an unconstitutional federal flag burning statute overruled in *Eichman.* And despite the Court's clear rules in *Chadha,* Congress has continued to pass statutes containing legislative veto provisions.

Many of these unconstitutional laws have attracted litigation. Courts have repeatedly struck down challenged affirmative action programs, speech codes, school prayer, flag burning statutes, and legislative vetoes. This has been true whether the affirmative action programs have been called "quotas" or "goals," whether the speech codes have been called "harassment policies" or "Fundamental Standard Interpretation: Free Expression and Discriminatory Harassment." This has been true whether the prayer came in the form of commencement prayers or moments of silence. This has been true whether riots result from the flag burning or someone defecates on a flag. And this has been true whether Congress calls legislative vetoes "committee vetoes" or "congressional recommendations." The lower courts are not a major obstacle to ending the persistence of unconstitutional laws.

Yet despite the litigation directed toward these unconstitutional laws, legislatures and executives at all levels of government have been able to maintain and in some cases increase their supply of unconstitutional laws. They have done so by capitalizing on the social, legal, and political barriers to litigation. Litigation is not cost-free, and when the elected branches can increase these costs they are able to thwart the judiciary from ever ruling against these unconstitutional programs. By crafting checkmate moves or stopping a lawsuit before it ever reaches the courthouse doors, the elected branches derail the litigation process before it can run its course and allow unconstitutional laws to persist.

The maintenance of unconstitutional legislations and acts goes beyond merely having obnoxious words imprinted on our nation's legislative codes. As Jon Gould wrote, "Don't mistake symbolism for impotence. [An unconstitutional law on the books] provides cues to the community about the range of acceptable behavior."[1] These laws result in individuals being treated differently by the government because of their race without sufficient justification, subjected to arbitrary rulings by subsets of our government, and harassed by government officials. These actions are accomplished by virtue of the long-term structural advantages adherent to the elected branches and the creation or maintenance of social, legal, or political barriers to litigation. The dominance of the elected branches over the judiciary casts doubt on the coordinate construction thesis, as the constitutional dialogue typically resembles more an elected branch monologue than a conversation over the meaning of the Constitution. When one considers the empirical reality of widespread elected branch evasion of Supreme Court doctrine and the concept of constitutional dialogue, one finds a constitutional monopoly coming from the elected branches—whereas the authors of the U.S. Constitution feared a judicial constitutional monopoly. A concept of judicial primacy, allowing for more constitutional dialogue than judicial supremacy but recognizing the judicial role in the protection of constitutional rights more than the constitutional dialogue scholars do, is one way to avert this dangerous convergence. In this concluding chapter, I briefly summarize the major findings of the book and then discuss the social, legal, and political components of checkmate moves and how the concept of judicial primacy strengthens the judiciary's hand to compete effectively with the elected branches and ensure the meaningful protection of our constitutional rights.

The Persistence of Unconstitutional Laws

SOCIAL BARRIERS TO LITIGATION

Despite the lore of the lawsuit in the American psyche, this study has found that there are too few lawsuits to effectively end the persistence of unconstitutional laws. This lack of lawsuits stems in part from the dearth of social conditions conducive to litigation. These factors include knowledge of the underlying events, knowledge of rights, and the backlash or perceived backlash against instituting litigation.

Individuals are not always aware of unconstitutional government action. A firm owner may not know the government let a black-only bid, a college student may not know the particulars of a university "student conduct policy," a high school student may not know that school officials lead the football team in prayers before each game, a resident of a state may not know that her state criminalizes the burning of a U.S. flag, a hospital administrator may not know that a federal provision of the law appropriated funds to the hospital prior to the exercise of a committee veto. In each of these cases the government is likely violating the Constitution but the potential plaintiffs are not aware of the underlying facts, and a lawsuit is stymied.

Even when one does know of an offending unconstitutional government action, one may not know that such action is actually unconstitutional. This lack of knowledge could stem from unfamiliarity with the Constitution, from a belief that the ubiquity of the practice demonstrates its constitutionality, or even from policy advocates who are familiar with Supreme Court doctrine and inappropriately focus only on the elements of a case that seem supportive to their position. The doctrine in *Croson, R.A.V.,* and most constitutional decisions typically contains language that seems as if affirmative action, hate speech, school prayer, flag burning, or legislative veto regulations could pass constitutional muster, but the reality is something else. Justice Marshall was correct in his lament that the Court's promise of future constitutionality is often illusory.

When one knows of the events giving rise to a constitutional violation and understands the law sufficiently to think it reasonable to pursue a lawsuit in pursuit of vindication, the fear of a lawsuit backlash may also be inhibitive. Our constitutional landscape, in the words of Donald Downs, has been "built on the backs of scoundrels." Lawsuits are often associated with greedy individualists rather than virtuous community-minded individuals. And while reputational harm may be enough to sway some people from instigating a lawsuit, others have been physically harmed as a result of filing a lawsuit. Taken together, all these factors limit the number of lawsuits challenging the constitutionality of laws and aid in the persistence of unconstitutional laws.

LEGAL BARRIERS TO LITIGATION

Once the social barriers to litigation are overcome, a potential plaintiff must still be able to hurdle legal barriers to litigation as well. Not only must legal claims fulfill the requisite elements of a claim, they are also subject to formal filing prerequisites, including the proper filing of pleadings, the payment of relevant fees, adherence to jurisdictional requirements, and meeting justiciability standards. There also must be an incentive for a lawsuit, both for the plaintiff to instigate the lawsuit and for the defendant to risk something by continuing the unconstitutional actions.

Although doctrinally, the Supreme Court has wide latitude in determining the standards by which constitutional claims will be adjudged, the elected branches can still influence the level of difficulty aggrieved individuals may face in seeking redress in court.[2] This is readily apparent in filing fees, cost-shifting statutes, and proposals to strip the courts of jurisdiction. Other, less formal legal mechanisms exist that increase the cost of litigation and thus decrease the likelihood of litigation. In the affirmative action context, hundreds of jurisdictions have engaged in the disparity study process, yet not once has a program been upheld on the merits of a case because of a disparity study. What these disparity studies do accomplish, however, is force the opponent to spend money and time to rebut the statistical analysis done in the studies. Governments defend their MBE programs by pointing out that there is a statistically significant difference between the utilization and the availability of minority contractors, typically categorized according to racial or ethnic group and by industry type. But these studies are nearly always deemed insufficient to control for a litany of other explanatory factors (e.g., availability of working capital, experience, quality of past performance) associated with a racial disparity in contracting. Thus, even when these jurisdictions are armed with a report, it has not provided the sought-after constitutional bulwark to justify a program but instead has caused plaintiffs to hire their own expert witnesses to rebut such evidence. Although expert witnesses do not cost the same $500,000 that the disparity studies cost, the time needed to review such evidence can quickly ratchet up the expenses necessary to challenge it.

The doctrine of standing is an important component of the legal barriers to litigation. Without a long exegesis of the origins and development of standing (as already provided by others),[3] the basic idea is that plaintiffs to a lawsuit must have a sufficient stake in the litigation for it to be a "case" or a "controversy" under Article III of the Constitution. Standing, unlike the other elements of justiciability—mootness, ripeness, advisory opinions, and the political question doctrine—does not focus on the what but rather on the who. The Court wants to ensure that people or entities that bring a lawsuit have a sufficient stake in the determination of the issue.

Standing has both a constitutional and a prudential component.[4] For a case to go forward, "a plaintiff must . . . demonstrate that he/she has suffered 'injury in fact,' that the injury is 'fairly traceable' to the actions of the defendant, and that the injury will likely be redressed by a favorable decision."[5] In essence, this is the constitutional equivalent of the "no harm, no foul" rule in pickup basketball. It also helps protect the courts against an onslaught of lawsuits, and encourages other methods of democratic participation. If a complainant is merely upset about a particular public policy rather than an aggrieved victim, the doctrine of standing generally forecloses a lawsuit. Even if a party has constitutional standing, the Court may nevertheless deny standing and limit access to the courts where individual rights would not be vindicated via litigation. Access would instead be reserved for those litigants best suited to assert a particular claim. Congress can, and often does, eliminate the prudential concerns by providing in legislation for individuals to sue to protect the public interest.

There are, however, limits to what Congress can provide in legislation regarding standing. It is not seriously held that an act of Congress could do away with the "case" and "controversy" requirement. *Lujan* more or less ruled that a simple act of Congress attempted to challenge this basic constitutional guarantee, and the Supreme Court struck such a provision down. For Congress to do away with a constitutional requirement is similar to the situation in *Marbury,* where, at least according to Chief Justice Marshall, Congress unconstitutionally enlarged the original jurisdiction of the Court to include writs of mandamus. If Congress can decide that the Court can hear a matter where there is not a case or controversy, Congress is either above the Constitution or at least seriously challenging the separation of powers embodied in our constitutional system.

In the typical case, it has been Congress that has attempted to enlarge the sphere of cognizable plaintiffs for a lawsuit and the courts that have stopped Congress in its tracks. Yet as this book has demonstrated, the elected branches have been able to capitalize on the judicial limitations surrounding standing; the elected branches have been able to employ the concept of standing as a checkmate move. Miami's bureaucratic nonimplementation of its MBE program banked on denying standing to everyone; colleges and universities that hold speech codes over a compliant student body while rarely ever pulling the trigger on their use count on no one being able to sue; and police who threaten individuals who abuse the American flag with arrest but refrain from doing so rely on the concept of standing to maintain unconstitutional legislation. These government actors depend on the specific injury requirement, interpreted from Article III of the Constitution, to preserve unconstitutional laws. And even the Supreme Court itself has cautioned the judiciary to be vigilant in its application of the standing doctrine—especially in the arena of judicial review. Chief Justice Rehnquist wrote for the Court, "Our standing inquiry has been especially rigorous when reaching the merits of the dispute would force us to decide whether an action taken by one of the other two branches of the Federal Government was unconstitutional."[6]

POLITICAL BARRIERS TO LITIGATION

Once the social and legal barriers to litigation have been surmounted, governments may still employ political barriers to litigation. Portland's affirmative action program has remained free of litigation chiefly because the city has neutralized the leading anti–affirmative action interest group with labor assistance programming. The interest group Associated General Contractors is, all else held constant, better off with the affirmative action encompassing program than it would be if it challenged the unconstitutional law. Congress's legislative vetoes have remained litigation-free chiefly because they have neutralized the agencies with the need for recurrent funding decisions. The executive agencies are, all else held constant, better off with the legislative vetoes than they would be if they challenged the unconstitutional law. These side agreements, either in terms of an explicit quid pro quo or with an implicit threat of future retaliation, allow these unconstitutional laws to persist.

While the parties to these particular agreements may be better off with unconstitutional laws in place, there still may be aggrieved persons, who now have to navigate through their own set of social, legal, and political barriers to litigation. These unconstitutional laws may benefit some individuals, but they also hurt an untold number of other individuals. Beyond the contractor in Portland or the agency beneficiary in New York, these laws send a message to the public that rights are sacrosanct only for some—only for those anointed individuals who have the social, legal, and political moxie to negotiate with the government.

One possible reply to my suggestion that these barriers ought to be eliminated and that we ought to have more lawsuits is that there are other, perhaps more valuable means of redress.[7] Although some other means of democratic participation exist that could be utilized to thwart some of these unconstitutional laws, only a very limited segment of our government is elected, and an even smaller segment of elected officials is ever defeated in an election. Elections will not take care of constitutional wrongs levied by the director of purchasing in Portland, the dean of students at the University of Wisconsin, a high school teacher in Texas, or a police officer in Arizona.

Judicial Primacy

The Supreme Court's role in constitutional decision making, by virtue of the checkmate actions of legislatures and executives around the country, has in essence been rendered subservient to the elected branches of government. While a diminished role for the courts is not necessarily problematic when ruling on issues related to run-of-the-mill laws, in the realm of constitutional rights, the lack of equality threatens to undermine not only the basic coequality of the branches of government but also the very foundation of rights. The constitutional conversation favored by coordinate construction scholars places the judiciary in the repeated position of being thwarted by checkmate moves, rather than tending toward consensus. The adoption of what scholars term "judicial primacy" would better position the courts to maintain a proper balance of power among the co-equal branches of government and protect our constitutional rights.

Views about which branch of government, or group, if any, should maintain the authoritative view of constitutional meaning are split. These views range from those expressed by adherents of judicial supremacy, who posit a strong and centralized role for the Supreme Court, issuing commands to be followed down to the legislatures and executives, to those of believers in popular constitutionalism, who advocate for a populist-based determination of the constitution,[8] to those of scholars who hold that rather than a single authoritative view of the Constitution, constitutional decision making is best described as a constitutional dialogue among the branches of government.[9] This conversation oscillates back and forth between the judiciary and the elected branches and continues ostensibly ad infinitum unless and until a consensus emerges between the judiciary and the elected branches.

This book makes clear as an empirical matter that the Court-centered views of judicial supremacy are lacking. Despite the Court's issuing strong, clear commands in a series of relatively high-profile civil rights and civil liberties cases and creating a bright line for Congress for textbook legislative procedure, in the real world of politics, the law as crafted by the Court is subservient to the laws favored by the elected branches; the pervasiveness of checkmate moves renders the coordinate construction notion largely devoid of empirical veracity. Rather than a constitutional conversation, the interaction between the branches of government regarding constitutional decision making is more akin to a monologue than the dialogue envisioned by the theory. Whether the locus of constitutional decision making functionally resides with the legislature (as the cases of legislative vetoes, affirmative action, and speech codes seem to indicate) or with the people (as the cases of school prayer and flag burning seem to indicate), practically speaking, the views of the Constitution put forth by Congress, city councils, school administrators, and police officers have more to do with the everyday lives of Americans than does the view of the Constitution put forth by the Supreme Court.

As a normative matter, I have suggested throughout this book that the Court's pronouncements over the Constitution should play a more primary role in constitutional decision making. Court views of the Constitution ought to be accorded a higher place in a hierarchy of constitutional visions and discussions. This is not to say that the judiciary should play the *only* role in authoritatively declaring the meaning of the Constitution. Rather, this concept of judicial primacy envisions the relationship between the branches of government much as constitutional dialogue scholars do but suggests that the endless cycling that takes place in the dialogue functionally blocks the courts from authoritative constitutional decision making. The existence of checkmate moves limits the judiciary from ever substantively disagreeing with the elected branches. The delay, stalling, and avoidance machinations of the elected branches keep the judiciary in such a deferential role as to make the concept of co-equal branches of government positively Orwellian. If we were able to rid our constitutional system of the checkmate moves, the Court's role in judicial dialogue could be enhanced without the result being a monopolistic view of the Constitution. The dialogue would continue, but without the nefarious machinations that currently serve to shut the judiciary out of the constitutional dialogue.

The current situation, which is characterized by an asymmetrical power dynamic of checkmate, may be cheered by those scholars who wish to "take the Constitution away from the courts" or "leave constitutionalism to the people." A closer examination of the resultant balance of power illustrates that judicial primacy ought to inform our understanding of judicial review.

Let us consider the balance of powers between the federal elected branches. As long as the interests of Congress and those of the president coincide with one another, there are many reasons to believe that limiting the power of the judiciary is rational. When both democratically elected branches of government share a constitutional vision with the people, it seems reasonable to believe we would live within a scheme at least resembling "consent of the governed." Yet it is a mistake to believe that the elected branches are necessarily more democratic than the courts, especially if one considers social choice theory, the two-party system, and the power of incumbency. But it is also more normal in the last forty years for the interests of Congress and those of the president to be misaligned; since 1969, majority control of at least one house of Congress and the president have been from different political parties 75 percent of the time. As such, both Congress and the executive branch have it in their collective interests to empower the Court as a check against the other institution. This concept of judicial primacy is not based on the particular training of members of the Court best positioning the Supreme Court for constitutional decision making but instead is predicated on maintaining competing power centers. Maintaining judicial power serves as a bulwark against runaway governments, in which Congress and the president act in concert, but also effectively as a tie-breaking force in the case of divided government. Judicial primacy, therefore, serves as a moderating influence on the sometimes factionalized influences of government.

When the Supreme Court strikes down an affirmative action program or a hate speech regulation yet maintains that the practices could be constitutional, Cass Sunstein argues that the Court is engaging in a form of "judicial minimalism," or a "one-case-at-a-time" approach. Sunstein suggests that the Court's limited approach is not only sound but desirable for avoiding judicial tyranny by "[stimulating] public processes and directing the citizenry toward more open discussion of underlying questions of policy and principle."[10] Sunstein suggests that the Court in effect has three options open to it in receiving cases: to uphold the challenged law, to strike down the challenged law, or to "remand" the issue by an avoidance technique. He argues that we ought to conceive of a fourth option: a judicial minimalist approach, "one that resolves little beyond the single case, but that operates as a catalyst for public discussion." This fourth technique operates more or less as a remand not back to the lower courts but instead to the public.

Thus, Sunstein defends the particularized nature of the Court's affirmative action jurisprudence as leaving open questions of public policy, and as such to encourage democratic participation. As Justice Stephen Breyer has written, an engaged citizenry and self-government are the cornerstones of our American constitutional system.[11] And it is this participation in the creation of public policy that can serve as a check against governmental—including judicial—abuses of power. Thus, Breyer argues that "active liberty" as a guiding form of judicial decision making is more in line with judicial restraint than with judicial activism. The justices' practice of considering which of several outcomes increases democratic participation—and using that determination in Court rulings—is part of the Madisonian tradition of checks on governmental actions. Justice Breyer argues in his discussion of affirmative action that the Court should use the effect of the decision on democratic participation as a guide to finding an outcome.

One could well imagine, then, that both Justice Breyer and Professor Sunstein would laud the massive legislative efforts post-*Croson*, the further rounds of litigation, and the popular referendum efforts post-*Grutter*. These are all examples of some form of democratic participation following the Court's ruling. Yet while it is difficult to argue against the abstract notion of democratic participation, there are some problems with the Sunstein and Breyer argument in relation to some very familiar cases of judicial review.

As an empirical matter, whether the Court issues a minimalist or maximalist opinion, it is hard to argue that such an opinion is related to democratic participation. To take some examples from Sunstein, we may consider *Roe v. Wade* or *Miranda v. Arizona,* both maximalist opinions invalidating statutes ("the greatest foreclosure of political deliberation"). Since the time of *Roe* there have been almost forty additional cases decided at the Supreme Court level implicating abortion.[12] There have been constitutional amendments proposed, single-issue political campaigns waged, and an untold number of protests against the protection of the right.[13] It is hard to see how this opinion has challenged democratic participation. Similarly, with regard to *Miranda,* one would be hard-pressed to find the specific text of a Supreme Court opinion as well known as the text from this particular case. Of course, this owes more to television than to Chief Justice Warren's inherent appeal to the people, but calling out this particular opinion as somehow limiting democracy seems inapropos. The notion that the policy space has been limited by the Court is a very time-bound and judicial-centric idea that seems to neglect what politics is really about.

Court decisions, no matter in which direction and how clear or convoluted, are part of the policy process. Whether one rules that affirmative action violates the rights of white students or is constitutionally permissible, there will be political reactions. And to those decisions there will also be reactions. Following *Grutter,* we have seen a political mobilization effort across Michigan in an attempt to ban race-based admissions in the law school.[14] Based on what we witnessed in California, Texas, and Florida after their attempts to ban affirmative action via referenda or executive order, it is less than clear that a court decision in this area, no matter how it is crafted, shuts off debate.[15]

Judicial primacy, on the other hand, is not a simple judicial monopoly on the Constitution. Instead, judicial primacy suggests, in contravention to the opinion of judicial supremacy scholars, that many voices are necessary for a constitutional dialogue. The courts should not simply replicate what is being complained about here; judicial primacy does not provide for a constitutional monopoly. It is the problem of checkmate moves that threatens the notion of constitutional dialogue, rendering the courts subservient to the elected branches. To ensure that the judiciary is able to proffer its side of the constitutional conversation, more deference must be given to the courts, and the era of checkmate moves must come to an end.

Restoring the Balance of Powers

When the Supreme Court strikes down legislation under the Constitution, engaging in judicial review, with few exceptions lower courts readily comply with the Court's ruling in similar cases. There has been a near uniform response from both federal and state courts in finding similar programs unconstitutional. Despite the outcome-determinative nature of the litigation, however, unconstitutional laws around the country have continued to flourish. These unconstitutional laws have been able to persist in part because of actions taken by the elected branches to derail the litigation process—to keep the courts from ever sitting in judgment of these laws. This frustration of the nexus between constitutional wrong and constitutional vindication, or the erection of social, legal, or political barriers to litigation, diminishes the Court's role in protecting constitutional rights. I refer to actions toward this end as checkmate moves.

This pattern from the affirmative action realm of judicial pronouncement—a smattering of litigation resulting in lower court rulings in line with the Supreme Court, followed by elected branch checkmate moves—is also present in the cases of hate speech, school prayer, and legislative vetoes. Courts can also be weakened by their own opinions, as has occurred in the matter of flag burning. These checkmate moves, when considered in light of the motivation to create unconstitutional legislation and acts—which are sometimes willful and at other times merely negligent—and in light of the systematized relationship between the elected branches and the courts, help explain the persistence of unconstitutional laws and acts. Despite the judiciary's willingness to strike down unconstitutional legislation and acts, the necessary social, legal, and political conditions for litigation are not always present, and their absence can thwart the ability of citizens to seek protection for their constitutional rights and steel in place these offending government actions.

The ability of the elected branches to fashion a checkmate move threatens the judiciary's legitimacy as the arbiter of what the law is. If the elected institutions remain free to ignore the Court's rulings, the judicial check on legislative abuses is significantly impinged upon. Just as the key to establishing checkmate was to erect legal, social, and political barriers to litigation, restoration of the Court's power stems from legal, social, and political reforms.

The case studies utilized in this book demonstrate that the law itself can be an obstacle to ending the persistence of unconstitutional laws. The Court sometimes rules that laws are unconstitutional "as applied" as opposed to facially (as occurred with the flag burning statutes), sometimes insincerely promises constitutionality (as occurred with affirmative action and hate speech), and runs up against problems with standing (as occurred with Miami's affirmative action program and flag burning laws). Governments are therefore comfortable either maintaining or creating new unconstitutional laws in the face of Supreme Court precedent, and because of the government's ability to fashion checkmate moves, these unconstitutional laws remain free from litigation. One possible avenue for the Supreme Court is to modify some of its jurisprudence in a way that would allow the judiciary an expanded access to evaluating problematic laws. To do so, however, the Court must be careful not to aggrandize its own power but rather must follow historical precedent for increasing the Court's legitimacy: the justices must craft their opinions to give power away to legislative institutions.

In the introduction I brought forward the concept of impact studies. These studies are in general "gap studies," in which scholars compare what should have happened following a Supreme Court decision with what actually occurred.For example, such studies might include what happened following judicial decisions concerning school desegregation, abortion, pay equity, hate speech, police searches and seizures, children's rights, and prison reform.[16] The majority of these studies suggest what we have seen in this book: there is a yawning gap between the pronouncements of the courts and the results on the ground. This is not to say that the rulings lack all impact and that the Court cannot and does not accomplish changes in behavior. Rather, as just about all of these scholars have maintained, impact is not impossible but is highly contingent and subject to contest.

The judiciary, as Hamilton famously penned in *Federalist* 81, is "the least dangerous branch." That, however, should not be confused with being a non-dangerous branch of government. That is to say, the judiciary can exert considerable influence on a wide range of institutions and actors, just comparatively less than the elected branches do. Court decisions can mobilize interest groups, spur the creation of new economic activities, prompt legislative activity, and encourage executive branch officials to act. As McCann and Rosenberg both suggest, however, the Supreme Court does not act as a club, striking down laws and commanding action from the elected branches. Thus, schools did not effectively desegregate in response to *Brown*,[17] and the gender wage gap did not end in response to *County of Washington v. Gunther*.[18] In the case of *Croson*, minority employment did not weaken following the "end" of affirmative action.[19]

While courts may not be agents of massive social change, their decisions can and do result in a very different world. As a result of *Croson*, not only were MBE activists mobilized but the decision seemingly created an entire cottage industry of disparity study consultants. Legislative and executive branch officials undertook actions they would not have *but for* the Court's decision. And though the world did not fundamentally change for MBE contractors, the intersection of law and public policy seems to indicate that the Court may have this capacity in some circumstances. Had the policy of affirmative action resulted in more concrete gains for minority contractors, and had the *Croson* decision vitiated the coping mechanisms put into play by the elected branch, there could have been substantial impact, even in terms more compatible with traditional impact studies.

This book has not demonstrated, nor was it intended to demonstrate, that Rosenberg or McCann was wrong. In fact, this study confirms the existence of another case in which (1) there was not nationwide important positive social change following a Supreme Court decision and (2) activists were mobilized to act following the Court ruling. The study has also demonstrated two distinct types of cases following Court decisions: those in which plaintiffs brought lawsuits and won, and those in which locales managed to avoid litigation for the better part of two decades. What separates those thirty jurisdictions where programs fell by the wayside from the jurisdictions where unconstitutional legislation and acts persisted? The difference lay in the ability of a government to derail the litigation process. Because the lawsuits themselves would nearly always be successful, the key operation was to stop the lawsuits.

What the court must do in response to this imbalance is to focus on the continuing relationship it has with the elected branches, and how that iterative relationship is stymied by the checkmate moves. Certainly the Court could go down the road of absolutes, as it did in ousting racially restrictive housing covenants in *Shelley v. Kramer*[20] or anti-miscegenation statutes in *Loving v. Virginia*,[21] and it could *possibly* prevent the elected branches from acting in response. This approach, however, would not be foolproof, nor would it have to be. Rather, the key for the judiciary is to be cognizant of the range of choices available to the elected branches to pursue after a court decision. Instilling some levels of absolutes is one possible method by which the judiciary could narrow that range of choices, but there are more fruitful possibilities.

The Court's focus during litigation over the Fourteenth Amendment, such as in *Croson,* and during constitutional litigation in general, is on whether what the government did was justified *at the time.* For affirmative action, the Court is concerned to discern whether the government had a compelling state interest when it passed the legislation and whether the resulting legislation was narrowly drawn to that interest. The idea behind using the strict scrutiny test is that it allows the Court to ferret out an unseemly (and unconstitutional) motivation on the part of the government.[22] The Court in *Croson* explained that

> The purpose of strict scrutiny is to "smoke out" illegitimate uses of race by assuring that the legislative body is pursuing a goal important enough to warrant use of a highly suspect tool. The test also ensures that the means chosen "fit" this compelling goal so closely that there is little or no possibility that the motive for the classification was illegitimate racial prejudice or stereotype.[23]

Thus, the Supreme Court in *Croson* specified that for legislation to survive strict scrutiny, it must be "narrowly tailored to achieving a compelling state interest."

These eight words, however, were then transformed into two separate tests: a compelling state interest and a narrowly tailored test. What the judiciary left out of its analysis is the strict scrutiny nexus—what links the compelling state interest component of strict scrutiny to the narrowly drawn component of strict scrutiny. The Court should have realized that the word "achieving" links the "compelling state interest" and "narrowly tailored" components. To pass constitutional muster, governments should be required to prove that they are, in fact, achieving their compelling state interest. There is not a much better view of a government's actual purpose than discovering the actual impact of the legislation. If governments maintain legislation that does not achieve its stated original purpose, then continuing maintenance of the program necessarily serves other goals. By the Court's failing to require jurisdictions to show that they are in fact really addressing the underlying rationale for having the legislation, the Court does little to address the illegitimate use of race or other suspect classifications in legislation.

As the national arbiter of what amounts to local policy or even university policy, the Court is in a unique and powerful position to see that its policies are implemented and its own legitimacy increased. But the Court must be careful not to aggrandize the judiciary in the process. The Court lacks the capacity to micromanage policy effectively, and subjects itself to criticism over its handling of long-standing disputes—as has happened in the area of school desegregation orders.[24]

The key is rather to look back into history to a time when the Court navigated out of a challenge to its legitimacy and to emulate how the Court did so. In the early 1800s, the Supreme Court was faced with the very real possibility of being ignored by the executive and becoming not just the least dangerous branch but possibly also a non-dangerous branch of government. Justice John Marshall, in *Marbury v. Madison*,[25] avoided marginalizing the Court by refusing to order the Jefferson administration to rectify *Marbury*'s wrong. By ruling that the Supreme Court did not have jurisdiction to issue a writ of mandamus in Marbury's case on original jurisdiction, Marshall's short-term restraint provided a long-term buttressing of the Court's power. To be sure, the Judiciary Act of 1789 likely contemplated the Supreme Court's use of judicial review, and I do not intend to assert that *Marbury* "established" judicial review, but what is important is that the Court's restraint was of long-term benefit for the institution. In the same vein, today's Supreme Court has the ability to increase its long-term legitimacy, and hence power, by delegating power to legislatures around the country. By giving away power to a competing institution, its long-term interests may be better served.

What I propose is that strict scrutiny, and other rule signals used by the Court, incorporate a form of legislation evaluation as part of the legal standard. That is to say, legislation that does not achieve its constitutionally permissible interest should be judged unconstitutional. The strict scrutiny test ought not to fictionalize the political process but instead judge legislation by the purposes actually served as opposed to possibly served. In *Croson,* the Court assigned the compelling state interest standard behind MBE programs as "assuring that public dollars, drawn from the tax contributions of all citizens, do not serve to finance the evil of private prejudice." This is well and fine and good, and if a race-based program ensured that tax dollars did not bankroll a racially discriminatory system, that ought to survive constitutional muster. But in a situation such as obtains in Miami, where the program does not come close to divesting tax dollars from a discriminatory system but instead serves as a political shield against constituents angry about race relations in the city and demanding government responsiveness, one would be hard-pressed to make a straight-faced argument that the program ought to survive.

This forward thinking about policy effects should not be entirely foreign to the judiciary. In the *Croson* formulation of what counts as narrowly tailored, the Court informs that legislation must, among other things, (1) contain a sunset provision and (2) not overly burden excluded groups. The ending date requirement is an acknowledgment of the time-bound nature of affirmative action, and the burden shouldered by excluded groups cries out for an empirical assessment. What better way is there to know of the burden on excluded groups than an actual evaluation?

While the prospective look at the outcome of judicial policymaking is not completely unfamiliar to the Court, the Court should not be the institution charged with making such an evaluation. Instead of miring the judiciary in the unenviable position of formally serving as a local policy evaluator, the Court should place the legislative institution responsible for passing the adjudicated legislation in the position of evaluating the impact of the legislation. The Court should charge the legislative institutions that craft these policies with evaluating them on a set schedule. Whether the Court would use a twenty-five-year time span, as Justice O'Connor wrote about in the Michigan affirmative action cases, or a more reasonable five-year program is not crucial at this stage. Rather, what is important is placing the onus on the legislature to revisit the issue and demonstrate that it is working, or have an automatic rescission of the statute. If a legislature could not demonstrate that its program was fundamentally on the road toward achieving its purpose, such legislation would be null and void.

This choice to refrain from aggrandizing the role of the judiciary in the policy process serves several purposes, including (1) increasing the long-term legitimacy of the Court, (2) increasing compliance among jurisdictions by decreasing the need for checkmate moves, and (3) placing democratically accountable representatives in their proper roles. Though there is some risk in having the same institution responsible for both policy innovation and evaluation, the danger is minimized by this provision of a new legal hook for prospective plaintiffs in seeking to overturn government legislation. Thus the ultimate result empowers the people in terms of keeping the government accountable for performance, and also binds together each branch of government in a way that limits instances of power aggrandizement, while substantively protecting our constitutional rights.

The protection of our constitutional rights is often not taken seriously. Checkmate allows for the easy maintenance of unconstitutional legislation, which insulates officials from taking unpopular actions. Rather than having to take an anti–affirmative action, pro–hate speech, or anti–flag desecration position, these elected officials and street-level bureaucrats can appease active minorities (in the Dahlian sense of the word) who feel championed by feckless leaders. What would perhaps be more virtuous in a democratic sense is for these same leaders to take courageous stands by standing up for our constitutional rights. Instead of championing policies contrary to the values of our American system, leaders could push for a culture of rights, not only helping to inform citizens of their rights but also helping Americans cherish these bulwarks of liberty. What we have now is a distinct difference between law as written and law as practiced. The lack of enforcement of some of these unconstitutional written laws is obviously preferable to their enforcement. Yet both choices are obnoxious. And it is the persistence of unconstitutional laws, both unenforced and enforced, that challenges the Court's role in our system of government, and the concept of equality. To rectify these wrongs, we ought to push for their eradication.

NOTES

INTRODUCTION

1. Nelson Lund, "Illusions of Antidiscrimination Law," in *Beyond the Color Line: New Perspectives on Race and Ethnicity in America,* ed. Abigail Thernstrom and Stephan Thernstrom (New York: Hoover Institute Press, 2002), 319–39.

2. *City of Richmond v. J.A. Croson Co.,* 488 U.S. 469 (1989).

3. Avon W. Drake and Robert D. Holsworth, *Affirmative Action and the Stalled Quest for Black Progress* (Urbana: University of Illinois Press, 1996); Julia B. Anderson, "The Administrative and Fiscal Impacts of the Supreme Court Decision in *City of Richmond v. J.A. Croson Co.* on Minority Business Enterprise Programs in Baltimore, Maryland and Richmond, Virginia" (PhD diss., University of Maryland–Baltimore County, 1995).

4. Anderson, "Administrative and Fiscal Impacts."

5. See especially chapter 1 and the discussion of *Adarand Constructors, Inc. v. Peña,* 515 U.S. 200 (1995).

6. Gerald Gunther, "Foreword: In Search of Evolving Doctrine on a Changing Court: A Model for a Newer Equal Protection," *Harvard Law Review* 86 (1972): 1.

7. The U.S. Supreme Court has on rare occasion upheld legislation with analysis like strict scrutiny in relation to free speech, for example, in *Buckley v. Valeo,* 424 U.S. 1, 24 (1976), *Frisby v. Schultz,* 487 U.S. 474 (1988), *Hill v. Colorado,* 530 U.S. 703 (2000), and *Burson v. Freeman,* 504 U.S. 191 (1992), but a full majority of the Court has not upheld race-based legislation under strict scrutiny since *Korematsu v. United States,* 323 U.S. 214 (1944), and *Hirabayashi v. United States,* 320 U.S. 81 (1943).

8. Al Kamen, "High Court Voids Minority Contract Set-Aside Program;

Richmond Policy Ruled to Be Bias in Reverse," *Washington Post,* January 24, 1989, A1.

9. Edward I. Koch, "Equal Opportunity—Without Minority Set-Asides," *New York Times,* February 20, 1989, A19.

10. Charles Fried, "Affirmative Action after *City of Richmond v. J.A. Croson Co.:* A Response to the Scholars' Statement," *Yale Law Journal* 99 (1989): 155.

11. Tom Ichniowski and Mary Powers, "*Croson's* Impact Widens," *Engineering News-Record,* December 14, 1989, 17.

12. Avon W. Drake and Robert D. Holsworth, *Affirmative Action and the Stalled Quest for Black Progress* (Urbana: University of Illinois Press, 1996).

13. What is also noteworthy is that the 1990s also ushered in an era of conservative retrenchment on the Court. See Thomas M. Keck, *The Most Activist Supreme Court in History: The Road to Modern Judicial Conservatism* (Chicago: University of Chicago Press, 2004).

14. Technically, judicial review involving the Constitution could also apply to entirely private action, but only in the realm of slavery in contravention of the Thirteenth Amendment. With this one exception, judicial review is entirely related to the actions of governments in what is called the "state action" doctrine. To be sure, what counts as state action can sometimes be unclear, but nevertheless the Constitution is largely directed toward empowering and limiting governments, not private individuals. See, e.g., Laurence C. Tribe, *American Constitutional Law,* 3rd ed., § 3-14–§ 3-22 (Mineola, NY: Foundation Press, 2000).

15. By elected branches, I refer to Congress and the president, as do most scholars, but I also include federal office holders who are largely though not exclusively in the domain of the executive branch, and the corresponding state officials. This broader sense of the elected branches also captures lower-level civil servants, such as police officers and teachers. In many ways, then, "elected branches" can be understood as referring to nonjudicial government employees.

16. Quoted in Helen Hershkoff, "State Courts and the 'Passive Virtues': Rethinking the Judicial Function," *Harvard Law Review* 114 (2001): 1833.

17. William Haltom and Michael McCann, *Distorting the Law: Politics, Media, and the Litigation Crisis* (Chicago: University of Chicago Press, 2004) (media coverage is much more likely to focus on seemingly unreasonable cases resulting in jury awards than on reasonable cases resulting in cases not pursued). See also Thomas Burke, "Judicial Implementation of Statutes: Three Stories about the Americans with Disabilities Act," in *Making Policy, Making Law: An Interbranch Perspective,* ed. Mark C. Miller and Jeb Barnes (Washington, DC: Georgetown University Press, 2004).

18. See Thomas M. Keck, "From *Bakke* to *Grutter:* The Rise of Rights-Based Conservatism," in *The Supreme Court and American Political Development: The Interplay of the Internal and External in Supreme Court Decision-making,* ed. Ronald Kahn and Ken I. Kersch (Lawrence: University Press of Kansas,

2006), 414–42; Kevin R. den Dulk, "In Legal Culture, But Not of It: The Role of Cause Lawyers in Evangelical Legal Mobilization," in *Cause Lawyering and Social Movements,* ed. Austin Sarat and Stuart Scheingold (Palo Alto: Stanford University Press, 2006); and Jeffrey R. Dudas, "Rights and Regulation in Bush's America: Or, How the New Right Learned to Stop Worrying and Love Equal Rights," in *The Intersection of Rights and Regulation,* ed. Bronwen Morgan (Aldershot, Hampshire, UK: Ashgate Press, 2007).

19. One possibility is that the elected branch response is more akin to a stalemate, in which the judiciary is not mortally wounded, as checkmate implies, but instead simply lacks a response to the elected branch move. Stalemate, however, implies more of a détente situation, in which neither side has an effective move to unleash. I suggest in this book that the elected branches can and do pierce the core function of the courts as the primary arbiters of constitutional decision making. Thus, "checkmate" more accurately expresses the hierarchical relationship that has developed in our system instead of the professed co-equality.

20. J. Mitchell Pickerill, *Constitutional Deliberation in Congress: The Impact of Judicial Review in a Separated System* (Durham, NC: Duke University Press, 2004); Charles O. Jones, *The Presidency in a Separated System* (Washington, DC: Brookings Institution Press, 1994).

21. Alexander Bickel, *The Least Dangerous Branch: The Supreme Court at the Bar of Politics,* 2nd ed. (New Haven: Yale University Press, 1962).

22. Neal Devins and Louis Fisher, "Judicial Exclusivity and Political Instability," *Virginia Law Review* 84, no. 1 (1998): 83–106; Barry Friedman, "Dialogue and Judicial Review," *Michigan Law Review* 91 (1993): 577; John Agresto, *The Supreme Court and Constitutional Democracy* (Ithaca, NY: Cornell University Press, 1984); Mark Galanter, "Why the 'Haves' Come Out Ahead: Speculations on the Limits of Legal Change," *Law and Society Review* 9 (1974): 95–160.

23. Bob Woodward and Scott Armstrong, *The Brethren: Inside the Supreme Court* (New York: Simon and Schuster, 1979) ("Its decisions ultimately affect the rights and freedom of every citizen—poor, rich, blacks, Indians, pregnant women, those accused of crime, those on death row, newspaper publishers, pornographers, environmentalists, businessmen, baseball players, prisoners and Presidents"); Edward P. Lazarus, *Closed Chambers: The First Eyewitness Account of the Epic Struggles Inside the Supreme Court* (New York: Random House, 1998) ("Whether the issue is abortion, race discrimination, sexual harassment, the environment, criminal justice, religious liberty, freedom of speech, or almost any other aspect of how we live and even how we die, Americans have come almost routinely to expect the courts, especially the Supreme Court, to take sides on every issue of national urgency and help resolve our most vexing social problems"); Robert H. Bork, *The Tempting of America: The Political Seduction of the Law* (New York: Free Press, 1990) ("the Constitution provides judges with the

ultimate coercive power known to our political arrangements. In the hands of judges, words become action: commands are issued by courts, obeyed by legislatures, and enforced by executives. The reading of the words becomes freedoms and restrictions for us; the course of the nation is confirmed or altered; the way we live and the ways we think and feel are affected"); William J. Brennan, "The Constitution of the United States: Contemporary Ratification," in *Interpreting the Constitution*, ed. Jack N. Rakove (Boston: Northeastern University Press, 1990) ("Consequences flow from a Justice's interpretation in a direct and immediate way. A judicial decision respecting the incompatibility of Jim Crow with a constitutional guarantee of equality is not simply a contemplative exercise in defining the shape of a just society. It is an order—supported by the full coercive power of the State—that the present society changes in a fundamental aspect. Under such circumstances the process of deciding can be a lonely, troubling experience for fallible human beings conscious that their best may not be adequate to the challenge. We Justices are certainly aware that we are not final because we are infallible; we know that we are infallible only because we are final. One does not forget how much may depend on the decision. More than the litigants may be affected. The course of vital social, economic and political currents may be directed").

24. Gerald H. Rosenberg, *Hollow Hope: Can Courts Bring About Social Change?* (Chicago: University of Chicago Press, 1991); Bradley C. Cannon and Charles A. Johnson, *Judicial Policies: Implementation and Impact*, 2nd ed. (Washington, DC: CQ Press, 1999).

25. *Roe v. Wade*, 410 U.S. 113 (1973).

26. Robert A. Carp and Ronald Stidham, *Judicial Process in America*, 4th ed. (Washington, DC: CQ Press, 1998); Rosenberg, *Hollow Hope*.

27. Rosenberg, *Hollow Hope*.

28. Cannon and Johnson, *Judicial Policies*.

29. Mark Graber, *Rethinking Abortion: Equal Choice, the Constitution, and Reproductive Politics* (Princeton, NJ: Princeton University Press, 1996).

30. *Brown v. Board of Education*, 347 U.S. 483 (1954).

31. Rosenberg, *Hollow Hope* (finding only about 2 percent of all black children attended an integrated public school in the South, defining "integrated" as a school with at least one white child, more than ten years following *Brown*); Gary Orfield, *Public School Desegregation in the United States, 1968–1980* (Washington, DC: Joint Center for Political Studies, 1983).

32. *Engel v. Vitale*, 370 U.S. 421 (1962); *Abington Township School District v. Schempp*, 374 U.S. 203 (1963).

33. Kevin McGuire, "Public Schools, Religious Establishments, and the U.S. Supreme Court: An Examination of Policy Compliance," *American Politics Research* 37 (2009): 50–74; Alison Gash, "In Due Time: The Courts and Backlash," paper presented at the annual meeting of the Southern Political Science Association, New Orleans, January 6–8, 2005; William K. Muir,

Prayer in the Public Schools: Law and Attitude Change (Chicago: University of Chicago Press, 1967). See also Neela Banjeree, "School Board to Pay in Jesus Prayer Lawsuit." *New York Times,* February 28, 2008, A15.

34. Louis Fisher, "The Legislative Veto: Invalidated, It Survives," Symposium: Elected Branch Influences in Constitutional Decisionmaking, *Law and Contemporary Problems* 65, no. 4 (1993): 273–92.

35. Vastine Davis Platte, "Flag Desecration and Flag Misuse Laws in the United States," Congressional Research Service Report 95-182 (Washington, DC: Congressional Research Service, March 29, 1005). See also *Wisconsin v. Jansen,* 580 N.W.2d 260 (Wis. 1998).

36. *R.A.V. v. City of St. Paul,* 505 U.S. 377 (1992).

37. Jon B. Gould, *Speak No Evil: The Triumph of Hate Speech Regulation* (Chicago: University of Chicago Press, 2005). See also Donald A. Downs, *Restoring Free Speech and Liberty on Campus* (Cambridge: Cambridge University Press, 2005).

38. Alexander Hamilton, "Federalist no. 78," in *The Federalist Papers,* ed. Clinton Rossiter (New York: Penguin Books, 1961).

39. Thomas Jefferson, *The Writings of Thomas Jefferson,* ed. Paul Leicester Ford, 10 vols. (New York: G.P. Putnam's Sons, 1892–99), 10:141, quoted in Keith E. Whittington, "Presidential Challenges to Judicial Supremacy and the Politics of Constitutional Meaning," *Polity* 33, no. 3 (2001): 365–95, 368.

40. Keith E. Whittington, *Political Foundations of Judicial Supremacy: The Presidency, the Supreme Court, and Constitutional Leadership in U.S. History* (Princeton, NJ: Princeton University Press, 2007), 247.

41. Whittington, "Presidential Challenges," 368–69.

42. James Meernik and Joseph Ignagni, "Judicial Review and Coordinate Construction of the Constitution," *American Journal of Political Science* 41, no. 2 (1997): 447–67.

43. Larry Alexander and Frederick Schauer, "On Extrajudicial Constitutional Interpretation," *Harvard Law Review* 110 (1997): 1359–87.

44. Ronald Dworkin, *Freedom's Law* (Cambridge, MA: Harvard University Press, 1996), 35, quoted in Whittington, *Political Foundations of Judicial Supremacy,* 91.

45. Friedman, "Dialogue and Judicial Review," 580.

46. Bruce Ackerman, *We the People: Vol. 1, Foundations* (Cambridge, MA: Harvard University Press, 1991); Louis Fisher, "Judicial Finality or Ongoing Colloquy?," in *Making Policy, Making Law: An Interbranch Perspective,* ed. Mark C. Miller and Jeb Barnes (Washington, DC: Georgetown University Press, 2004); Friedman, "Dialogue and Judicial Review"; Mark Tushnet, *Weak Courts, Strong Rights: Judicial Review and Social Welfare Rights in Comparative Constitutional Law* (Princeton, NJ: Princeton University Press, 2008); Whittington, "Presidential Challenges"; see also John Ferejohn, "A Positive Theory of Statutory Interpretation," *International Review of Law and Economics* 12 (1992): 263–79.

47. Ackerman, *We the People*, 5n14; Tushnet, *Weak Courts, Strong Rights* ("Dialogic accounts of constitutional law treat the people, legislatures, executives, and the courts in conversation"); Robert A. Burt, *The Constitution in Conflict* (Cambridge, MA: Harvard University Press, 1992); Friedman, "Dialogue and Judicial Review"; Alexander Bickel, *The Least Dangerous Branch: The Supreme Court at the Bar of Politics,* 2nd ed. (New Haven: Yale University Press, 1962); Abram Chayes, "The Role of Judges in Public Law Litigation," *Harvard Law Review* 89 (1976): 1281, 1316.

48. Friedman, "Dialogue and Judicial Review," 654.

49. See, e.g., Mark Tushnet, *Taking the Constitution Away from the Courts* (Princeton, NJ: Princeton University Press, 1999) (titling his first chapter "Against Judicial Supremacy").

50. Larry Alexander and Frederick Schauer, "Extrajudicial Constitutional Interpretation," *Harvard Law Review* 110, no. 7 (March 1997): 1379.

51. The one exception would be Mark Tushnet, who argues that we ought to abolish judicial review. Tushnet suggests that judicial review (1) is not particularly important and (2) may cause Congress to act irresponsibly. This argument is probably more rhetorical than serious. Tushnet claims his wife believes nothing of it, and he says even he doesn't always believe it.

52. Jeb Barnes and Mark C. Miller, "Putting the Pieces Together: American Lawmaking from an Interbranch Perspective," in *Making Policy, Making Law: An Interbranch Perspective,* ed. Mark C. Miller and Jeb Barnes (Washington, DC: Georgetown University Press, 2004).

53. J. Mitchell Pickerill, *Constitutional Deliberation in Congress: The Impact of Judicial Review in a Separated System* (Durham, NC: Duke University Press, 2004), 152.

54. Thomas M. Keck, "From *Bakke* to *Grutter:* The Rise of Rights-Based Conservatism," in *The Supreme Court and American Political Development,* ed. Ronald Kahn and Ken I. Kersch (Lawrence: University Press of Kansas, 2006), 435.

55. For a slightly different categorization and a more comprehensive literature review, see Canon and Johnson, *Judicial Policies.*

56. On Supreme Court decisions helping to focus public opinion, see Roy B. Flemming, John Bohte, and B. Dan Wood, "One Voice Among Many: The Supreme Court's Influence on Attentiveness to Issues in the United States, 1947–1992," *American Journal of Political Science* 41 (October 1927): 1224–50. On decisions helping to polarize public opinion, see Charles H. Franklin and Liane C. Kosaki, "Republican Schoolmaster: The U.S. Supreme Court, Public Opinion and Abortion," *American Political Science Review* 83 (September 1989): 751–71, 753.

57. Timothy R. Johnson and Andrew D. Martin, "The Public's Conditional Response to Supreme Court Decisions," *American Political Science Review* 92 (June 1998): 299–309.

58. Johnson and Martin, "The Public's Conditional Response to Supreme

Court Decisions"; Flemming, Bohte, and Wood, "One Voice Among Many"; Franklin and Kosaki, "Republican Schoolmaster"; Gregory A. Caldeira, "Public Opinion and the U.S. Supreme Court: FDR's Court-Packing Plan," *American Political Science Review* 81, no. 4 (1987): 1139–53.

59. Mathew D. McCubbins and Jeffrey Lax, "Courts, Congress and Public Policy, Part I: The FDA, the Courts and the Regulation of Tobacco," *Journal of Contemporary Legal Issues* 15 (2006): 165–98; Mathew D. McCubbins and Jeffrey Lax, "Courts, Congress and Public Policy, Part II: The Impact of the Reapportionment Revolution on Urban and Rural Interests," *Journal of Contemporary Legal Issues* 15 (2006): 199–218; L. Timothy Perrin et al., "If It's Broken, Fix It: Moving Beyond the Exclusionary Rule," *Iowa Law Review* 83 (1998): 669; Michael W. McCann, *Rights at Work: Pay Equity Reform and the Politics of Legal Mobilization* (Chicago: University of Chicago Press, 1994); Rosenberg, *Hollow Hope;* Myron W. Orfield Jr., "The Exclusionary Rule and Deterrence: An Empirical Study of Chicago," *University of Chicago Law Review* 54 (1987): 1016; Donald Horowitz, *The Courts and Social Policy* (Washington, DC: Brookings Institution Press, 1977).

60. Rosenberg, *Hollow Hope;* Perrin, "If It's Broken, Fix It"; Orfield, "The Exclusionary Rule and Deterrence"; McCann, *Rights at Work;* Horowitz, *Courts and Social Policy.*

61. Rosenberg, *Hollow Hope.*

62. Perrin, "If It's Broken, Fix It," 669 (citing Nagel). The expected effect of the adoption of the exclusionary rule should be to increase crime, as ceteris paribus the likelihood of conviction of a crime should decrease if evidence obtained unconstitutionally is inadmissible in court.

63. Ibid., 669 (citing Comment, "Effect of *Mapp v. Ohio* on Police Search-and-Seizure Practices in Narcotics Cases," *Columbia Journal of Law and Social Problems* 87, no. 102 [1968]: 4).

64. Ibid., 660 (citing Pallin Oaks, "Studying the Exclusionary Rule in Search and Seizure," *University of Chicago Law Review* 37:665–757).

65. Ibid., 734.

66. Drake and Holsworth, *Affirmative Action;* Keck, *Most Activist.*

67. McCann, *Rights at Work.*

68. Gould, *Speak No Evil;* Malcolm M. Rubin and Edward L. Rubin, *Judicial Policy Making and the Modern State: How the Courts Reformed America's Prisons* (Cambridge: Cambridge University Press, 1998); David A. Schultz and Stephen E. Gottlieb, "Legal Functionalism and Social Change: A Reassessment of Rosenberg's 'The Hollow Hope,'" in *Leveraging the Law: Using the Courts to Achieve Social Change,* ed. David A. Schultz (New York: Peter Lang Publishing, 1998; Mathew D. McCubbins, Roger G. Noll, and Barry R. Weingast, "Politics and the Courts: A Positive Theory of Judicial Doctrine and the Rule of Law," *Southern California Law Review* 68 (1995): 1631, 1683; William N. Eskridge Jr. and Phillip P. Frickey, "The Supreme

Court, 1993 Term Forward: Law as Equilibrium," *Harvard Law Review* 108 (1994): 27–96; Kenneth M. Dolbeare and Phillip E. Hammond, *The School Prayer Decisions: From Court Policy to Local Practice* (Chicago: University of Chicago Press, 1971); Robert A. Dahl, "Decisionmaking in a Democracy: The Supreme Court as a National Policymaker," *Journal of Public Law* 6 (1957): 279–95.

69. Gould, *Speak No Evil.* See also Downs, *Restoring Free Speech.*

70. Malcom Feeley and Edward L. Rubin, *Judicial Policy Making and the Modern State* (Cambridge: Cambridge University Press, 2000).

71. Ibid., 167.

72. Researchers may select cases to study on the dependent variable, or in other words because there has been little to no impact. This may overestimate the extent of noncompliance. The three case studies in this book are in-depth explorations of the post-*Croson* reactions in Philadelphia; Portland, Oregon; and Miami, Florida. In addition, I explore nationwide judicial, legislative, and executive reactions to the case in these three chapters respectively. Philadelphia, Portland, and Miami provide a high-quality collection of cases with which to analyze affirmative action in action. According to the 2000 census, Philadelphia's population is approximately 45 percent black and 45 percent white, Portland's population is almost 80 percent white, and Miami's population is approximately half Latino. In addition to the varied geographic diversity, it was largely for this type of racial and ethnic diversity that I selected these three cities for my study.

73. Bradley C. Canon and Charles A. Johnson, *Judicial Policies: Implementation and Impact,* 2nd ed. (Washington, DC: CQ Press, 1998).

74. McCann, *Rights at Work,* 181.

75. Keith Bybee argues exactly the opposite here—that *Croson* is exceptionally ambiguous. I tackle this argument later in this book and simply state here that the routinized responses to *Croson* militate against the suggestion of ambiguity. See Keith J. Bybee, "The Political Significance of Legal Ambiguity: The Case of Affirmative Action," *Law and Society Review* 34, no. 2 (2000): 263–90.

76. The same is true of the other cases examined here as well. See, e.g., Gould, *Speak No Evil,* 125 ("there may remain questions about R.A.V.'s clarity. . . . These constructions, however are overly narrow").

77. Walter F. Murphy, C. Herman Pritchett, Lee Epstein, and Jack Knight, *Courts, Judges, and Politics: An Introduction to Judicial Process,* 6th ed. (Boston: McGraw Hill, 2006).

78. Sean Farhang, "Partisanship, Trial Lawyers, and the Legislative Use of Litigation to Enforce the Law," paper presented at the American Political Science Association annual meeting, Philadelphia, August 31–September 3, 2006.

79. Ibid.

80. Murphy et al., *Courts, Judges, and Politics;* Herbert M. Kritzer et al., "To

Confront or Not to Confront: Measuring Claiming Rates in Discrimination Grievances," *Law and Society Review* 25 (1991): 883; Richard E. Miller and Austin Sarat, "Grievances, Claims, and Disputes: Assessing the Adversary Culture," *Law and Society Review* 15 (1981): 544.

81. Dana Priest, "CIA Holds Terror Suspects in Secret Prisons: Debate Is Growing Within Agency about Legality and Morality of Overseas System Set up after 9/11," *Washington Post,* November 2, 2005, A1; Carol D. Leonnig, "Secret Court's Judges Were Warned about NSA Spy Data: Program May Have Led Improperly to Warrants," *Washington Post,* February 9, 2006, A1.

82. Christopher Lee, "Noted with Interest," *Washington Post,* March 3, 2006, A15.

83. See, e.g., John W. Strong, ed., McCormick on Evidence, 4th ed., § 55 (St. Paul, MN: West Publishing, 1992).

84. See, e.g., *Francis v. Henderson,* 425 U.S. 536 (1976); *Wainwright v. Sykes,* 433 U.S. 72 (1977).

85. Michael J. Saks, "Do We Really Know Anything about the Behavior of the Tort Litigation System—And Why Not?" *University of Pennsylvania Law Review* 140 (1992): 1147–1292.

86. Haltom and McCann, *Distorting the Law;* Saks, "Do We Really Know Anything about the Behavior of the Tort Litigation System?"

87. Research, however, has also demonstrated that unpopular causes can limit the efficacy of extrajudicial politics and force groups into a litigation strategy. See Emily Zackin, "Popular Constitutionalism's Hard When You're Not Very Popular: Why the ACLU Turned to Courts," *Law and Society Review* 42, no. 2 (2008): 367–96.

88. While this logic sets up instances of success and failure, and in this book I present examples of success and failure, in everyday political life it is probably more accurate to describe a continuum of success, ranging from the problematic unilateral to more idealized multilateral constitutional decision making.

89. As I discuss in chapter 5, there are many reasons to still be concerned about Miami's maintenance of the hollowed-out unconstitutional affirmative action program. Yet that concern does not by itself lend one to easily categorize the Miami case as a failure or a success.

90. *City of Richmond v. J.A. Croson Co.,* 488 U.S. 469 (1989).

ONE   Supreme Policymaking

1. *Brown v. Board of Education,* 347 U.S. 483 (1954).

2. Tamar Jacoby, *Someone Else's House: America's Unfinished Struggle for Integration* (New York: Free Press, 1998). Other scholars trace the origins of the actual words "affirmative action" back to the Taft-Hartley Act, albeit with a different connotation. See Ira Katznelson, *When Affirmative Action Was White: An Untold History of Racial Inequality in Twentieth-Century America*

(New York: W. W. Norton, 2005); note, "Back Pay Awards for Unfair Labor Practices under the Taft-Hartley Act," *Yale Law Journal* 62, no. 3 (1953): 488–96.

3. Charles Murray, *Losing Ground* (New York: Basic Books, 1984).

4. Thomas Byrne Edsall and Mary D. Edsall, *Chain Reaction: The Impact of Race, Rights, and Taxes on American Politics* (New York: W. W. Norton, 1991).

5. Jacoby, *Someone Else's House.*

6. Timothy Bates and Darrell Williams, "Do Preferential Procurement Programs Benefit Minority Business?" *American Economic Review* 86 (1996): 294–97.

7. George R. La Noue, "The Impact of *Croson* on Equal Protection Law and Policy," *Albany Law Review* 61 (1997): 1–41.

8. Steven Thernstrom and Abigail Thernstrom, *America in Black and White: One Nation, Indivisible* (New York: Simon and Schuster, 1997).

9. Maria E. Enchautegui et al., *Do Minority-Owned Businesses Get a Fair Share of Government Contracts?* (Washington, DC: Urban Institute, 1997).

10. Arguments against affirmative action are presented by Lino Graglia, "Affirmative Action Promotes Discrimination," in *Affirmative Action,* ed. Bryan Grapes (San Diego: Greenhaven Press, 2000); Thomas Sowell, "Affirmative Action Harms Minority Students," ibid.; Linda Chavez, "Promoting Racial Harmony," in *The Affirmative Action Debate,* ed. George E. Curry (Reading, MA: Addison-Wesley, 1996); Lee Epstein et al., "Do Political Preferences Change? A Longitudinal Study of U.S. Supreme Court Justices?" *Journal of Politics* 60 (1993): 3; Dinesh D'Souza, *Illiberal Education: The Politics of Race and Sex on Campus* (New York: Free Press, 1991); and Shelby Steele, *The Content of Our Character* (New York: St. Martin's Press, 1990). Arguments for affirmative action are presented by Ronald Dworkin, "Affirming Affirmative Action," *New York Review of Books* 45 (1998): 16, 91–102; Charles R. Lawrence III and Mari Matsuda, *We Won't Go Back: Making the Case for Affirmative Action* (Boston: Houghton Mifflin, 1997); Kweisi Mfume, "Why America Needs Set-Aside Programs," in Curry, *The Affirmative Action Debate;* Christopher F. Edley, *Not All Black and White: Affirmative Action, Race, and American Values* (New York: Hill and Wang, 1996); and Michael Rosenfeld, *Affirmative Action and Justice: A Philosophical and Constitutional Inquiry* (New Haven: Yale University Press, 1991).

11. Both arguments are from Daniel A. Farber, "Missing the 'Play of Intelligence,'" *William and Mary Law Review* 36 (1994): 147.

12. John F. Witte, "The Efficiency of Equality," paper presented at the Association of Public Policy Analysis and Management annual meeting, Seattle, November 2, 2000; Richard D. Kahlenberg, *The Remedy: Class, Race, and Affirmative Action* (New York: Basic Books, 1996); Nathan Glazer, "The Case for Racial Preferences," *Public Interest* 135 (1999): 45–63; Chang-Lin Tien, "Affirmative Action Promotes Diversity," in Grapes, *Affirmative*

Action, 23–28; Cornell West, "Affirmative Action in Context," in Curry, *The Affirmative Action Debate,* 31–35; Orlando Patterson, 2000. "Affirmative Action Should Be Reformed," in Grapes, *Affirmative Action,* 54–58.

13. Adolph Reed, "The Black Urban Regime: Structural Origins and Constraints," *Comparative Urban and Community Research,* 1987, 1–72; Derrick Bell, *And We Are Not Saved: The Elusive Quest For Racial Justice* (New York: Basic Books, 1987); Richard Delgado, "The Imperial Scholar: Reflections on a Review of Civil Rights Literature," *University of Pennsylvania Law Review* 132 (1984): 561.

14. Jed Rubenfeld, "Affirmative Action," *Yale Law Journal* 107 (1997): 427–72.

15. Louis Fisher and Neal Devins, *Political Dynamics of Constitutional Law* (St. Paul, MN: West Publishing, 1992).

16. Samuel Issacharoff, "When Substance Mandates Procedure: *Martin v. Wilks* and the Rights of Vested Incumbents in Civil Rights Consent Decrees," *Cornell Law Review* 77 (1992): 189.

17. Daniel A. Farber, "The Outmoded Debate over Affirmative Action," *California Law Review* 82 (1994): 893–934.

18. Jim Chen, "Is Affirmative Action Fair? Diversity in a Different Dimension: Evolutionary Theory and Affirmative Action's Destiny," *Ohio State Law Journal* 59 (1998): 811.

19. This literature, spanning more than 200 works, has been neatly summarized in Harry J. Holzer and David Neumark, "Assessing Affirmative Action," *Journal of Economic Literature* 38, no. 3 (2000): 483–568. For an updated review, see Martin J. Sweet, "Minority Business Enterprise Programmes in the United States of America: An Empirical Investigation," Affirmative Action Symposium, *Journal of Law and Society* 33, no. 1 (2006): 160–80.

20. Laurence C. Tribe, *American Constitutional Law* (Mineola, NY: Foundation Press, 1988).

21. *Zobel v. Williams,* 457 U.S. 55, 60 (1982).

22. *Northeast Bancorp, Inc. v. Governors of the Federal Reserve Sys.,* 472 U.S. 159 (1985).

23. *Kotch v. Board of River Port Pilots Comm'rs,* 330 U.S. 552 (1947).

24. See *Romer v. Evans,* 517 U.S. 620 (1996); *City of Cleburne v. Cleburne Living Center,* 473 U.S. 432 (1985); *USDA v. Moreno,* 413 U.S. 528 (1973).

25. *Craig v. Boren,* 429 U.S. 190, 197 (1976).

26. *Miller v. Johnson,* 515 U.S. 900, 904 (1995).

27. *Regents of the University of California v. Bakke,* 438 U.S. 265 (1978).

28. *Wygant v. Jackson Board of Education,* 476 U.S. 267 (1986).

29. *Croson,* 779 F.2d 181 (1985).

30. *Fullilove v. Klutznick,* 448 U.S. 448 (1980).

31. *City of Richmond v. J.A. Croson Co.,* 488 U.S. 469, 476–77 (1989). Justice O'Connor announced the judgment of the Court and delivered the opinion of the Court with respect to Parts I, III-B, and IV. She also delivered

an opinion with respect to Part II, in which Chief Justice Rehnquist and Justice White joined, and an opinion with respect to Parts III-A and V, in which Chief Justice Rehnquist, Justice White, and Justice Kennedy joined. Justice Stevens concurred in the judgment and concurred with respect to Parts I, III-B, and IV. Justice Kennedy concurred in the judgment and offered a concurrence for Part II of the opinion. Justice Scalia concurred in the judgment. Justice Marshall dissented, joined by Justices Brennan and Blackmun. And Justice Blackmun dissented, joined by Justice Brennan.

32. Appellant brief in *City of Richmond v. J.A. Croson Co.*, 488 U.S. 469 (1989), 1988 WL 1025698.

33. Appellant brief in *City of Richmond v. J.A. Croson Co.*, 488 U.S. 469 (1989), 1988 WL 1025698.

34. Virvus Jones, "What the Supreme Court Said in the Richmond Case," *St. Louis Post Dispatch,* February 13, 1990, 2B.

35. Richard Kindleberger, "Lawyers: Don't Abandon Set-Asides," *Boston Globe,* March 31, 1989, 21.

36. Judith C. Areen et al., "Constitutional Scholars' Statement on Affirmative Action after *City of Richmond v. J.A. Croson Co.,*" *Yale Law Journal* 98 (1989): 1712.

37. Gunther, "Foreword."

38. *City of Richmond v. J.A. Croson Co.,* 488 U.S. 469, 492 (1989).

39. *City of Richmond v. J.A. Croson Co.,* 488 U.S. 469, 510 (1989).

40. *City of Richmond v. J.A. Croson Co.,* 488 U.S. 469, 509 (1989).

41. *Contractors Ass'n of E. Penn. v. City of Philadelphia,* 6 F.3d 990, 1010 (3rd Cir. 1993).

42. *City of Richmond v. J.A. Croson Co.,* 488 U.S. 469, 509–510 (1989) (*citing* Sheet Metal Workers v. EEOC, 1986).

43. Drake and Holsworth, *Affirmative Action.*

44. *City of Richmond v. J.A. Croson Co.,* 488 U.S. 469, 507 (1989).

45. *City of Richmond v. J.A. Croson Co.,* 488 U.S. 469, 510–11 (1989).

46. *City of Richmond v. J.A. Croson Co.,* 488 U.S. 469, 507 (1989).

47. *City of Richmond v. J.A. Croson Co.,* 488 U.S. 469, 498 (1989).

48. Keith J. Bybee, "The Political Significance of Legal Ambiguity: The Case of Affirmative Action," *Law and Society Review* 34, no. 2 (2000): 263–90.

49. Cass Sunstein, *One Case at a Time: Judicial Minimalism on the Supreme Court* (Cambridge, MA: Harvard University Press, 2001).

50. *Metro Broadcasting, Inc. v. FCC,* 497 U.S. 547 (1990).

51. *Metro Broadcasting, Inc. v. FCC,* 497 U.S. 547, 564–65 (1990).

52. *Adarand Constructors, Inc. v. Peña,* 515 U.S. 200 (1995).

53. Ibid. ("The contractor shall presume that socially and economically disadvantaged individuals include Black Americans, Hispanic Americans, Native Americans, Asian Pacific Americans, and other minorities, or any other individual found to be disadvantaged by the [Small Business] Administration pursuant to section 8(a) of the Small Business Act").

54. Ibid., 224.

55. *Grutter v. Bollinger,* 539 U.S. 306 (2003).

56. *Gratz v. Bollinger,* 539 U.S. 244 (2003).

57. While President Bush nominated Judge John Roberts to replace Justice O'Connor, the subsequent death of Chief Justice Rehnquist led Bush to cast aside the initial plan. After Rehnquist's death, Bush withdrew his nomination of Roberts to replace Justice O'Connor and instead nominated Roberts to fill the chief justice position on the Court. It was only after this switch that Bush nominated Judge Alito to replace Justice O'Connor.

58. *Parents Involved in Community Schools v. Seattle School District No. 1,* 551 U.S. 701 (2007), joined with *Meredith, Custodial Parent and Next Friend of McDonald v. Jefferson County Bd. of Ed. et al.*

59. James C. Brent, "An Agent and Two Principals: U.S. Court of Appeals Responses to *Employment Division, Department of Human Resources v. Smith* and the Religious Freedom Restoration Act," *American Politics Quarterly* 27, no. 2 (1999): 236–68; Donald R. Songer, Jeffrey A. Segal, and Charles M. Cameron, "The Hierarchy of Justice: Testing a Principal-Agent Model of Supreme Court-Circuit Court Interactions," *American Journal of Political Science* 38 (1994): 673–96; Jeffrey R. Lax, "Certiorari and Compliance in the Judicial Hierarchy: Discretion, Reputation, and the Rule of Four," paper presented at the American Political Science Association annual meeting, Boston, August 28, 2002; Mathew D. McCubbins, Roger G. Noll, and Barry R. Weingast, "Politics and the Courts: A Positive Theory of Judicial Doctrine and the Rule of Law," *Southern California Law Review* 68 (1995): 1631–83. For principal-agent theory applied to legislative-bureaucratic relations, see Mathew D. McCubbins and Thomas Schwartz, "Congressional Oversight Overlooked: Police Patrols Versus Fire Alarms," *American Journal of Political Science* 28 (1984): 165–79.

60. *H.K. Porter Co., Inc. v. Metropolitan Dade County,* 489 U.S. 1062 (1989), *cert. granted, lower court ruling vacated and remanded* (held unconstitutional in 975 F.2d 762 [11th Cir. 1992]).

61. *American Subcontractors Association v. City of Atlanta,* 376 S.E.2d 662 (Ga. 1989).

62. See, e.g., *Coral Const. Co. v. King County,* 729 F. Supp. 734 (W.D. Wash., 1989).

63. See, e.g., *Coral Const. Co. v. King County,* 941 F.2d 910 (9th Cir. 1991).

64. *United Fence & Guard Rail Corp. v. Cuomo,* 1991 WL 197675 (N.D. N.Y. 1991); *Harrison and Burrowes Bridge Constructors, Inc. v. Cuomo,* 1992 WL 75049 (N.D. N.Y. 1992); *Associated General Contractors of Connecticut v. City of New Haven,* 791 F. Supp. 941 (D. Conn. 1992); *Maryland Highways Contractors Ass'n, Inc. v. State of Md.,* 933 F.2d 1246 (4th Cir. 1991); *Feriozzi Co., Inc. v. City of Atlantic City,* 266 N.J. Super. 124, 628 A.2d 821 (N.J. Super.L. 1993); *Dickerson Carolina, Inc. v. Harrelson,* 443 S.E.2d 127 (N.C. App. 1994).

65. Ichniowski and Powers, "*Croson's* Impact Widens."

66. *See Sierra Club v. Morton*, 405 U.S. 727 (1972).

67. *Cone Corp. v. Florida Dept. of Transp.*, 921 F.2d 1190 (11th Cir. 1991); *Capeletti Bros., Inc. v. Metropolitan Dade County*, 776 F. Supp. 1561 (S.D. Fla. 1991); *Michigan Road Builders Ass'n, Inc. v. Blanchard*, 761 F. Supp. 1303 (W.D. Mich. 1991); *Cone Corp. v. Hillsborough County*, 1994 WL 371386 (M.D. Fla. 1994).

68. The fourth case involved a group representing black contractors contending that Asians and other "minorities" should not qualify for the MBE program. *Maryland Minority Contractor's Ass'n, Inc. v. Maryland Stadium Authority*, 70 F. Supp. 2d 580 (D. Md. 1998). The court, in this case, applied standing from *Northeastern Florida* faithfully.

69. *Ohio Contractors Ass'n v. City of Columbus, Ohio*, 733 F. Supp. 1156 (S.D. Ohio 1990); *General Bldg. Contractors Ass'n, Inc. v. City of Philadelphia*, 762 F. Supp. 1195 (E.D. Pa. 1991); *First Capital Insulation, Inc. v. Jannetta*, 768 F. Supp. 121 (M.D. Pa. 1991); *Martin Associates, Inc. v. New York City Health and Hospitals Corp.*, 607 N.Y.S.2d 841 (N.Y. Sup. 1993).

70. *L.K. Comstock & Co., Inc. and Luis Elec. Corp., a Joint Venture v. New York Convention Center Development Corp.*, 179 A.D.2d 322 (N.Y. A.D. 1 Dept., 1992).

71. Docia Rudley and Donna Hubbard, "What a Difference a Decade Makes: Judicial Response to State and Local Minority Business Set-Asides Ten Years After *City of Richmond v. J. A. Croson*," *Southern Illinois University Law Journal* 25 (2000): 1–39.

72. *Hi-Voltage Wire Works, Inc. v. City of San Jose*, 12 P.3d 1068 (Cal. 2000).

73. *Cornelius v. Los Angeles County etc. Authority*, 49 Cal. App. 4th 1761 (Cal. App. 2 Dist. 1996); *Maryland Minority Contractor's Ass'n, Inc. v. Maryland Stadium Authority*, 70 F. Supp. 2d 580 (D. Md. 1998); *Hillside Drilling, Inc. v. City of Berkeley*, 2002 WL 413371 (N.D. Cal. 2002).

74. *Converse Const. Co., Inc. v. Massachusetts Bay Transp. Authority*, 899 F. Supp. 753 (D. Mass. 1995).

75. *Indianapolis Minority Contractions Association, Inc. v. Wiley*, 1998 WL 1988826 (S.D. Ind. 1998).

76. *Domar Electric, Inc. v. City of Los Angeles*, 41 Cal. App. 4th 810 (Cal. App. 2 Dist. 1995).

77. *Ritchey Produce Co., Inc. v. Ohio Dept. of Adm. Serv.*, 707 N.E.2d 871 (Ohio 1999).

78. *Adarand Constructors, Inc. v. Slater*, 228 F.3d 1147 (10th Cir. 2000).

79. *Concrete Works of Colorado v. City and County of Denver*, 321 F.3d 950 (10th Cir. 2003).

80. *Associated General Contractors of Ohio, Inc. v. Drabik*, 214 F.3d 730 (6th Cir. 2000).

81. *Adarand Constructors, Inc. v. Mineta*, 534 U.S. 103 (2001) (dismissing certiorari as improvidently granted).

82. *Sherbrooke Turf v. Minnesota Department of Transportation,* 345 F.3d 964 (8th Cir. 2003).

83. *Northern Contracting v. State of Illinois,* 2005 WL 2230195 (N.D. Ill.).

84. I have excluded cases analyzing federal programs occurring before the Supreme Court extended the Croson analysis of state and local affirmative action programs to federal programs in 1995 in *Adarand v. Peña.* I also exclude five Comptroller General Administrative decisions—not decided by Article III judges. Interestingly, of these five cases, the administrative law judge (ALJ) upheld the federal government's use of an MBE program, despite the ruling in *Adarand.* In each instance the ALJ declared there was "a lack of a clear controlling precedent." Why *Adarand* was not used as a clear controlling precedent was not explained. Since there is no record of appeal of these decisions, it may be that these cases were settled by the government following the ALJ decisions.

85. Chay and Fairlie, "Set-Asides and Black Self-Employment."

86. George R. La Noue, "Who Counts? Determining the Availability of Minority Contractors for Public Contracting after *Croson," Harvard Journal of Law and Public Policy* 21, no. 3 (1998): 797; Leslie A. Nay and James E. Jones Jr., "Equal Employment and Affirmative Action in Local Governments: A Profile," *Law and Inequality: A Journal of Theory and Practice* 8:1 (1989): 103–49.

87. E. Mabry Rogers and Rodney Moss, "M/WBE Subcontracting: Is It Working/Workable?" in *Public Bonding and Construction Through The Year 2000* (Chicago: American Bar Association, 1994) (neither lawyer returned any of my several phone calls or emails asking for jurisdiction-specific citations).

88. Martin J. Sweet, "Affirmative Action in Action: The Impact of Minority Business Enterprise Programs in Miami, 1972–1997," paper presented at the American Political Science Association annual meeting, San Francisco, August 30–September 2, 2001.

89. Loan Le and Jack Citrin, "Affirmative Action," in *Public Opinion and Constitutional Controversy,* ed. Nathaniel Persily et al. (New York: Oxford University Press, 2008).

90. Ibid.

91. This finding, however, may be due to the particular time in which the question was asked, as in 1986 income was not significantly related to affirmative action support in any setting. Le and Citrin, "Affirmative Action."

92. Ibid.

93. Sweet, "Minority Business Enterprise Programmes."

94. Thomas D. Boston, *Affirmative Action and Black Entrepreneurship* (New York: Routledge, 1999), 16; Timothy Bates and Darrell Williams, "Racial Politics: Does It Pay?" *Social Science Quarterly* 74, no. 3 (1993): 507–22.

95. Samuel L. Myers and Tsze Chan, "Who Benefits from Minority Business Set-Asides? The Case of New Jersey," *Journal of Policy Analysis and Manage-*

ment 15 (1996): 202–26; Bates and Williams, "Do Preferential Procurement Programs Benefit Minority Business?"

96. Sweet, "Minority Business Enterprise Programmes."

TWO   Philadelphia and the Ongoing Dialogue

1. Buzz Bissinger, *A Prayer for the City* (New York: Random House, 1997), 31.

2. Ibid., xii.

3. Carolyn Adams et al., *Philadelphia: Neighborhoods, Division, and Conflict in a Post Industrial City* (Philadelphia: Temple University Press, 1991); Stephanie G. Wolf, "The Bicentennial City 1968–1982," in *Philadelphia: A 300-Year History,* ed. Russell F. Weigley (New York: W. W. Norton, 1982); Judith Goode and Jo Anne Schneider, *Reshaping the Ethnic and Racial Relations and Philadelphia: Immigrants and Divided City* (Philadelphia: Temple University Press, 1994).

4. Theodore Hershberg, "A Tale of Three Cities: Blacks, Immigrants, and Opportunity in Philadelphia, 1850–1880, 1930, 1970," in *Philadelphia: Work, Space, Family, and Group Experience in the 19th Century,* ed. Theodore Hershberg (Oxford: Oxford University Press, 1981).

5. Angel L. Ortiz, "The Illusion of Inclusion: Affirmative Action in Philadelphia. A City Council Report," February 2001 (on file with author).

6. Robert A. Beauregard, "Local Politics and the Employment Relation: Construction Jobs in Philadelphia," in *Economic Restructuring and Political Response* (Newbury Park, CA: Sage Publications, 1989), 147–79, 155.

7. Charles A. Elstrom and Thomas J. Keil, "Political Attachment in Black Philadelphia: Does 'Public-Regardingness' Apply?" *Urban Affairs Quarterly* 8, no. 4 (1973): 489–506; Beauregard, "Local Politics and the Employment Relation."

8. Adams et al., *Philadelphia.*

9. Douglas Yates, *The Ungovernable City: The Politics of Urban Problems and Policy Making* (Cambridge, MA: MIT Press, 1984), 9.

10. Bissinger, *Prayer,* 81.

11. Adams et al., *Philadelphia.*

12. City Council Hearing Before the Committee on Finance, February 17, 1982, transcript (on file with author).

13. This observation was made by both a bureaucrat and an interest group official in interviews I conducted in Philadelphia in 2001. To preserve confidentiality, I characterize those who spoke with me only as bureaucrat, legislator, or interest group member and identify the date only to year.

14. City Council Hearing Before the Committee on Finance, March 23, 1982, transcript (on file with author). Harper's comments echoed city attorney Carl Singley's testimony from the first hearing: "[The percentages are] essentially ballpark figures. . . . There [were] not sufficient data available to this council that would indicate the number of minority businesses that currently exist in Philadelphia and the surrounding area that would

be capable of performing the contracts that the city lets on an annual basis."

15. Interview with bureaucrat, Philadelphia, 2001.

16. Interview with bureaucrat, Philadelphia, 2001.

17. Interview with bureaucrat, Philadelphia, 2001.

18. Adams et al., *Philadelphia,* 148.

19. Ibid.

20. Ibid.

21. Drake and Holsworth, *Affirmative Action.*

22. Ibid.; Anderson, *Administrative and Fiscal Impacts.*

23. Mark Galanter, "Why the 'Haves' Come Out Ahead: Speculations on the Limits of Legal Change," *Law and Society Review* 9 (1974): 95–160.

24. McCann, *Rights at Work;* Mark Tushnet, *The NAACP's Legal Strategy Against Segregated Education, 1925–1950* (Chapel Hill: University of North Carolina Press, 1987).

25. Drake and Holsworth, *Affirmative Action,* 190.

26. Interview with bureaucrat, Philadelphia, 2001.

27. See also Kenneth R. Mayer and David T. Canon, *The Dysfunctional Congress: The Individual Roots of an Institutional Dilemma* (Boulder, CO: Westview Press, 1991).

28. Interview with interest group official, Philadelphia, 2001.

29. *Regents of the University of California v. Bakke,* 438 U.S. 265, 307 (1978) (Powell, J. concurring).

THREE   Portland and Unsuccessful Court–Elected Branch Interactions

1. Mason Tillman Associates, "City of Portland," in *Oregon Regional Consortium Disparity Study,* May 1996, 2:6-6 (on file with author).

2. *The Portland Oregonian,* February 8, 2001, E14.

3. State of Oregon Commission on Black Affairs, "Public Hearing Summary and Key Findings: *Croson vs. Richmond, Mattson vs. Multnomah County:* Impact on African American Businesses and Contractors" (Salem: State of Oregon Commission on Black Affairs, 1992), 12 (on file with author).

4. City of Portland's Office of Management and Finance, Bureau of Purchases, Contractor Development Division, *Fair Contracting and Employment Strategy: Three Year Review* (Portland, OR: Office of Management and Finance, 2001), 6 (on file with author).

5. State of Oregon Commission on Black Affairs, "Public Hearing Summary," 12.

6. Interview with legislator, Portland, OR, 2002. To preserve confidentiality, I characterize those who spoke with me only as bureaucrat, legislator, or interest group member and identify the date of the interview only to year.

7. Interview with bureaucrat, Portland, OR, 2002.

8. State of Oregon Commission on Black Affairs, "Public Hearing Summary," 12.

9. Interview with bureaucrat, Portland, OR, 2002.

10. Mason Tillman Associates, "City of Portland."

11. Interview with bureaucrat, Portland, OR, 2002.

12. Interview with bureaucrat, Portland, OR, 2002.

13. Interview with bureaucrat, Portland, OR, 2002.

14. Interview with bureaucrat, Portland, OR, 2002.

15. Interview with legislator, Portland, OR, 2002.

16. George La Noue, "The Disparity Study Shield: Baltimore and San Francisco," in *Racial Preferences in Public Contracting*, ed. Roger Clegg and Walter H. Ryland (Washington, DC: National Legal Center for the Public Interest, 1993).

17. Interview with legislator, Portland, OR, 2002.

18. Interview with bureaucrat, Portland, OR, 2002.

19. City of Portland, *Three Year Review*, 4.

20. Interview with bureaucrat, Portland, OR, 2002.

21. Interview with bureaucrat, Portland, OR, 2002.

22. Interview with bureaucrat, Portland, OR, 2002.

23. Interview with contractor, Portland, OR, 2002.

24. Interview with bureaucrat, Portland, OR, 2002.

25. Mason Tillman Associates, "City of Portland," 2:1-6.

26. City of Portland, *Three Year Review*, 74.

27. Interview with legislator, Portland, OR, 2002.

28. Interview with interest group, Portland, OR, 2002.

29. Interview with contractor, Portland, OR, 2002.

30. Interview with bureaucrat, Portland, OR, 2002.

31. City of Portland, *Three Year Review.*

32. Interview with bureaucrat, Portland, OR, 2002.

33. Interview with legislator, Miami, FL, 2002.

34. Mason Tillman Associates, "City of Portland," 2:1-2–1-3.

35. Interview with legislator, Portland, OR, 2002.

36. City of Portland, *Three Year Review*, 75.

37. Drake and Holsworth, *Affirmative Action.*

38. *L.D. Mattson, Inc. v. Multnomah County*, 703 F. Supp. 66 (OR D. Ct., 1988).

39. Interview with interest group, Portland, OR, 2002.

40. Byron E. Shafer, *The Two Majorities and the Puzzle of Modern American Politics* (Lawrence: University Press of Kansas, 2003); Alexander P. Lamis, *The Two-Party South* (New York: Oxford University Press, 1988); Earl Black and Merle Black, *Politics and Society in the South* (Cambridge, MA: Harvard University Press, 1987).

41. Interview with bureaucrat, Portland, OR, 2002.

42. Interview with bureaucrat, Portland, OR, 2002.

43. Interview with interest group, Portland, OR, 2002.

44. Interview with bureaucrat, Portland, OR, 2002.

45. Interview with interest group, Portland, OR, 2002.
46. Interview with bureaucrat, Portland, OR, 2002.

FOUR   Miami and Executive Checkmate

1. Interview with bureaucrat, Miami, FL, 2001. To preserve confidentiality, I characterize those who spoke with me only as bureaucrat, legislator, or interest group member and identify the date only to year.
2. Marvin Dunn, *Black Miami in the Twentieth Century* (Gainesville: University of Florida Press, 1997).
3. Interview with legislator, Miami, FL, 2001.
4. Interview with bureaucrat, Miami, FL, 2001.
5. Interview with bureaucrat, Miami, FL, 2001.
6. Interview with bureaucrat, Miami, FL, 2001.
7. This also accords with how many universities in the United States took cues from other universities in their response to a Supreme Court ruling against hate speech regulations. See Jon B. Gould, "The Precedent That Wasn't: College Hate Speech Codes and the Two Faces of Legal Compliance," *Law and Society Review* 35 (2001): 345–92.
8. *South Florida Chapter of the Associated General Contractors v. Metropolitan Dade County, Florida,* 723 F.2d 846, 848 (11th Cir. 1984).
9. Interview with interest group, Miami, FL, 2001.
10. The other components of the program had not been challenged in *Engineering Contractors Association of South Florida v. Metropolitan Dade County,* 122 F.3d 895 (11th Cir. 1997), and thus remained free for the county to administer.
11. *Hershell Gill Consulting Engineers v. Miami-Dade County,* 333 F. Supp. 2d 1305, 1310 (S.D. Fla. 2004).
12. Dorothy J. Gaiter, "Racial Reviews: Court Ruling Makes Discrimination Studies a Hot New Industry," *Wall Street Journal,* August 13, 1993, A1.
13. Office of the City Attorney, Miami, FL, Legal Opinion Letter, March 30, 2005. In fact, the city's Purchasing Department also notes that the program, despite no legislative amendments, is "not a mandatory program"; http://www.ci.miami.fl.us/Procurement/pages/MWBE/default.asp.
14. Interview with bureaucrat, Miami, FL, 2001.
15. Interview with bureaucrat, Miami, FL, 2001.
16. Interview with bureaucrat, Miami, FL, 2001.
17. Interview with legislator, Miami, FL, 2001.
18. Interview with bureaucrat, Miami, FL, 2001.
19. Interview with legislator, Miami, FL, 2001.
20. Interview with legislator, Miami, FL, 2001.
21. Interview with bureaucrat, Miami, FL, 2001.
22. U.S. Bureau of the Census, *General Population and Housing Characteristics 2000* (Washington, DC: U.S. Department of Commerce, Bureau of the Census, 2000), http://factfinder.census.gov.

23. Interview with bureaucrat, Miami, FL, 2001.

24. Interview with contractor, Miami, FL, 2001.

25. Interview with legislator, Miami, FL, 2001.

26. Interview with interest group, Miami, FL, 2001.

27. Interview with legislator, Miami, FL, 2001.

28. Interview with bureaucrat, Miami, FL, 2001.

29. Martin J. Sweet, "The Supreme Court, Affirmative Action, and the Evidence: 1973–1996," paper presented at the American Political Science Association annual meeting, Atlanta, GA, September 2–5, 1999. There is some overlap among these categories, and thus the apparent total number of firms, 273, is more than the 242 businesses certified on the lists. For example, civil engineers who are involved in construction are listed under both "Professional Services" and "Construction," and construction firms that also rent or sell equipment may be listed under "Construction" and "Goods" or "Other Services."

30. Interview with bureaucrat, Miami, FL, 2001; interview with interest group, Miami, FL, 2001.

31. George R. La Noue, "Who Counts? Determining the Availability of Minority Contractors for Public Contracting after *Croson*," *Harvard Journal of Law and Public Policy* 21, no. 3 (1998): 797.

32. Interview with bureaucrat, Miami, FL, 2001.

33. U.S. Bureau of the Census, *Finances of County Governments, 1997 Census of Governments,* Vol. IV; *Finances of Municipal and Township Governments, 1997 Census of Governments,* Vol. IV (Washington, DC: U.S. Department of Commerce, Bureau of the Census, 2000).

34. Interview with legislator, Miami, FL, 2001.

35. Interview with legislator, Miami, FL, 2001.

36. Interview with legislator, Miami, FL, 2001.

37. Interview with legislator, Miami, FL, 2001.

38. Interview with bureaucrat, Miami, FL, 2001.

39. Interview with legislator, Miami, FL, 2001.

40. Interview with legislator, Miami, FL, 2001.

41. Interview with legislator, Miami, FL, 2001.

42. Interview with bureaucrat, Miami, FL, 2001.

43. Interview with bureaucrat, Miami, FL, 2001.

44. Interview with legislator, Miami, FL, 2001.

45. Interview with legislator, Miami, FL, 2001.

46. Interview with legislator, Miami, FL, 2001.

47. Interview with contractor, Miami, FL, 2001.

48. Interview with contractor, Miami, FL, 2001.

49. Interview with legislator, Miami, FL, 2001.

50. Dario Moreno, "Cuban Americans in Miami Politics: Understanding the Miami Model," in *The Politics of Minority Coalitions: Race, Ethnicity, and Shared Uncertainties,* ed. Wilbur C. Rich (Westport, CT: Praeger, 1996).

51. Interview with contractor, Miami, FL, 2001.

52. Interview with contractor, Miami, FL, 2001.

53. Interview with legislator, Miami, FL, 2001.

54. Robert A. Dahl, *Who Governs? Democracy and Power in an American City* (New Haven: Yale University Press, 1961).

55. Interview with bureaucrat, Miami, FL, 2001.

56. Interview with contractor, Miami, FL, 2001.

57. Jonathan Skrentny, "Affirmative Action: Some Advice for the Pundits," *American Behavioral Scientist* 41, no. 7 (1998): 877–85.

58. Malcolm Feeley and Edward L. Rubin, *Judicial Policy Making and the Modern State* (Cambridge: Cambridge University Press, 2000); David Schultz and Stephen E. Gottlieb, "Legal Functionalism and Social Change: A Reassessment of Gerald Rosenberg, *The Hollow Hope: Can Courts Bring About Social Change?" Journal of Law and Policy* 12 (1996): 63; Michael W. McCann, *Rights at Work: Pay Equity Reform and the Politics of Legal Mobilization* (Chicago: University of Chicago Press, 1994); Peter H. Schuck, "Public Law Litigation and Social Reform: Review of *The Hollow Hope: Can Courts Bring About Social Change?*, by Gerald N. Rosenberg and *Rebellious Lawyering: One Chicano's Vision of Progressive Law Practice,* by Gerald P. Lopez," *Yale Law Journal* 102 (1993): 1763–86.

59. Interview with legislator, Miami, FL, 2001.

60. Interview with legislator, Miami, FL, 2001.

61. Douglas S. Massey and Nancy A. Denton, *American Apartheid: Segregation and the Making of the Underclass* (Cambridge, MA: Harvard University Press, 1993).

62. Ibid.

63. Daniel A. Lipson, 2001. "Policy Evolution: The Rise Of 'Affirmative Action as We Don't Know It' in Undergraduate Admissions at UC-Berkeley and UT-Austin," paper presented at the American Political Science Association annual meeting, San Francisco, August 31, 2001.

64. Kirk Nilesen, "Teele's (Or)deal: A Nightmarish Chapter in the Annals of Miami Government Ends. Or Does It?" *Miami New Times,* August 15, 2002.

65. Kevin Hill, Dario Moreno, and Lourdes Cue, "Racial and Partisan Voting in a Tri-Ethnic City: The 1996 Dade County Mayoral Election," *Journal of Urban Affairs* 23 (2001): 291–307.

66. Nielsen, "Teele's (Or)deal."

67. Francisco Alvarado, "Tales of Teele: Sleaze Stories," *Miami New Times,* July 28, 2005.

68. Interview with legislator, Miami, FL, 2001.

69. Francisco Alvarado, "The Teele Conspiracy," *Miami New Times,* September 2, 2004.

70. Fronts are one of the well-known and well-documented problems with contracting affirmative action programs. Tamar Jacoby, *Someone Else's*

House: America's Unfinished Struggle for Integration (New York: Free Press, 1998).

71. Ihosvani Rodriguez, "Ex-Commissioner Indicted on Charges of Money Laundering," *South Florida Sun-Sentinel,* July 15, 2005, 1B.

72. Jacoby, *Someone Else's House.*

73. Samuel L. Myers and Tsze Chan, "Who Benefits from Minority Business Set-Asides? The Case of New Jersey," *Journal of Policy Analysis and Management* 15 (1996): 202–26.

74. Thomas D. Boston, *Affirmative Action and Black Entrepreneurship* (New York: Routledge, 1999).

75. Martin J. Sweet, "Minority Business Enterprise Programmes in the United States of America: An Empirical Investigation," Affirmative Action Symposium, *Journal of Law and Society* 33, no. 1 (2006): 160–80.

76. Bates and Williams, "Do Preferential Procurement Programs Benefit Minority Business?" 294.

77. Kenneth Y. Chay and Robert W. Fairlie, "Minority Business Set-Asides and Black Self-Employment," University of California Working Paper, 1998, http://econ.ucsc.edu/~fairlie/ (accessed August 15, 2000).

FIVE   Beyond Affirmative Action

1. *INS v. Chadha,* 462 U.S. 919 (1983).

2. *Texas v. Johnson,* 491 U.S. 397 (1989).

3. *U.S. v. Eichman,* 496 U.S. 310 (1990).

4. *Engel v. Vitale,* 379 U.S. 421 (1962); *Abington Township v. Schempp,* 374 U.S. 203 (1962).

5. *R.A.V. v. City of St. Paul,* 505 U.S. 377 (1992).

6. *Gitlow v. New York,* 268 U.S. 652 (1925).

7. *West Virginia v. Barnette,* 319 U.S. 624 (1943).

8. *Brandenburg v. Ohio,* 395 U.S. 444 (1969).

9. *Chaplinsky v. New Hampshire,* 315 U.S. 568 (1942).

10. *New York Times v. Sullivan,* 376 U.S. 254 (1964); *Time v. Hill,* 385 U.S. 374 (1967); *Gertz v. Robert Welch,* 418 U.S. 323 (1974).

11. *Miller v. California,* 389 U.S. 968 (1967).

12. Thomas C. Grey, "How to Write a Speech Code Without Really Trying: Reflections on the Stanford Experience," Symposium: Developments in Free Speech Doctrine: Charting the Nexus Between Speech and Religion, Abortion, and Equality, *University of California Davis Law Review* 29 (1996): 891–956.

13. Jon B. Gould, *Speak No Evil: The Triumph of Hate Speech Regulation* (Chicago: University of Chicago Press, 2005).

14. *R.A.V. v. City of St. Paul,* 505 U.S. 377 (1992).

15. *Minn. Legis. Code* § 292.02 (1990).

16. *Chaplinsky v. New Hampshire,* 315 U.S. 568 (1942).

17. *R.A.V. v. City of St. Paul,* 505 U.S. at 388 (1992); *Kucharek v Hanaway,* 902 F.2d 513, 517 (1990).

18. Timothy A. Shiell, *Campus Hate Speech on Trial* (Lawrence: University Press of Kansas, 1998).

19. David E. Bernstein, *You Can't Say That: The Growing Threat to Civil Liberties from Antidiscrimination Laws* (Washington, DC: Cato Institute, 2003).

20. Donald A. Downs, *Restoring Free Speech and Liberty on Campus* (Cambridge: Cambridge University Press, 2005).

21. *Doe v. Michigan,* 721 F. Supp. 852 (E.D. Mich. 1989).

22. *UWM Post v. Board of Regents of the University of Wisconsin,* 774 F. Supp. 1163 (E.D. Wis. 1991).

23. *Iota Xi Chapter of Sigma Chi Fraternity v. George Mason University,* 773 F. Supp. 792 (E.D. Va. 1991).

24. *Dambrot v. CMU,* 55 F.3d 1177 (6th Cir. 1995).

25. *Corry v. Stanford Univ.,* No. 1-94-CV-740309 (Cal. Super. Ct. Feb. 27, 1995).

26. Gould, *Speak No Evil.*

27. Ibid., 153.

28. A federal judge issued a preliminary injunction against Shippensburg, and in response the university rescinded its program, agreed to pay attorney fees for the plaintiff, and announced that its code "is an unenforceable university statement of values and does not bind student conduct or expression in any way."

29. *Roberts v. Haragan,* 346 F. Supp. 2d 853 (N.D. Tex, 2004).

30. Downs, *Restoring Free Speech.*

31. Donald A. Downs, "Review of *Speak No Evil: The Triumph of Hate Speech Regulation,* by Jon B. Gould, 2005, Chicago: University of Chicago Press," *Perspectives on Politics* 4, no. 2 (2006): 386–87.

32. *West Virginia v. Barnette,* 319 U.S. 624 (1943).

33. *Engel v. Vitale,* 370 U.S. 421 (1962).

34. *Abington Township School District v. Schempp,* 374 U.S. 203 (1963).

35. Robert H. Birkby, "The Supreme Court and the Bible Belt: Tennessee Reaction to the *Schempp* Decision," *Midwest Journal of Political Science* 10 (1966): 305; William K. Muir, *Prayer in the Public Schools* (Chicago: University of Chicago Press, 1967); Kenneth M. Dolbeare and Phillip E. Hammond, *School Prayer Decisions from Court Policy to Local Practice* (Chicago: University of Chicago Press, 1971).

36. Birkby, "The Supreme Court and Bible Belt."

37. William M. Beaney and Edward N. Beiser, "Prayer and Politics: The Impact of *Engel* and *Schempp* on the Political Process," *Journal of Public Law* 13 (1964): 475–503. See also Kenneth M. Dolbeare and Phillip E. Hammond, *School Prayer Decisions from Court Policy to Local Practice* (Chicago: University of Chicago Press, 1971).

38. *Wallace v. Jaffree,* 472 U.S. 38 (1985).

39. Ibid.

40. *Lee v. Weisman,* 505 U.S. 577 (1992) (striking down prayers offered during high school graduation); *Sante Fe Independent School District v. Doe,* 530 U.S. 271 (2000) (striking down inter alia the delivery of Christian prayers over the public address system at home football games).

41. Kevin McGuire, "Public Schools, Religious Establishments, and the U.S. Supreme Court: An Examination of Policy Compliance," *American Politics Research* 37 (2009): 50–74.

42. *Coles v. Cleveland Board of Education,* 171 F.3d 369 (1999).

43. *Chandler v. Siegelman,* 230 F.3d 1313 (11th Cir. 2000); *Doe v. Ouachita Parish Schools,* 274 F.3d 289 (5th Cir. 2001).

44. *Adler et al. v. Duval County School Board,* 206 F.3d 1070 (11th Cir. 2001); *Appenheimer v. Washington High School* (D. Ill. 2001).

45. *Selman v. Cobb County School District,* 390 F. Supp. 2d 1286 (D. Ga. 2005); *Kitzmiller v. Dover Area School District,* 400 F. Supp. 2d 707 (M.D. Pa. 2005).

46. Associated Press, "Kanawha Won't Encourage, Deny Student-Led Prayer Under New Policy," *Associated Press State and Local Wire,* March 7, 2003.

47. American Civil Liberties Union, "Louisiana School Board Repeatedly Defied Federal Court Order, Charges ACLU," press release, April 5, 2005.

48. Associated Press, "Tangipahoa Board Won't Be Held in Contempt for Pre-Game Prayer," *Associated Press State and Local Wire,* April 14, 2005.

49. "Roy Moore's Big Rock," editorial, *St. Louis Post-Dispatch,* November 17, 2003.

50. Torsten Ove, "ACLU Files Suit Over Clarion Schools' Prayers," *Pittsburgh Post-Gazette,* May 27, 2005, www.post-gazette.com/pg/05147/511342-85 .htm (suit brought on behalf of Doe 1 and Doe 2, "because passions are high enough in the district that they could be in danger"); American Civil Liberties Union, "ACLU of Nebraska Files Complaint Against School Official Who Lead Prayers at Assembly," press release, March 21, 2001 (student requested anonymity fearing retribution); American Civil Liberties Union, "ACLU of Nebraska Sues Over Graduation Prayer; Family That Complained Fears Retaliation," press release, November 29, 2001.

51. Seth Jackson, "Atheists as a Minority: Strategies to Overcome Societal Prejudice." *SSA Quarterly* 1, no. 2 (2004): 4.

52. *Pledge Protection Act of 2005,* 109th Cong., 1st sess., 2006, HR 2389.

53. See, e.g., *Frazier v. Alexandre,* CS-05-81142-CIV (S.D. Fla. 2006).

54. *Public Expression of Religion Act of 2005,* HR 2679, and *Veterans' Memorials, Boy Scouts, Public Seals, and Other Public Expressions of Religion Protection Act of 2006,* S 3696, both 109th Cong., 1st sess., 2006.

55. Robert J. Goldstein, *Flag Burning and Free Speech: The Case of* Texas v. Johnson (Lawrence: University Press of Kansas, 2000).

56. *Texas v. Johnson,* 491 U.S. 397 (1989).

57. See generally Henry Cohen, "Freedom of Speech and Press: Exceptions to the First Amendment," Congressional Research Service, 2003; William W.

Van Alstyne, *The American First Amendment in the Twenty-First Century: Cases and Materials,* 3rd ed. (New York: Foundation Press, 2002); Rodney A. Smolla, *The First Amendment: Freedom of Expression, Regulation of Mass Media, Freedom of Religion* (Durham, NC: Carolina Academic Press, 2002).

58. *Texas v. Johnson,* 491 U.S. 397 (1989).

59. *U.S. v. Eichman,* 496 U.S. 310 (1990).

60. John R. Luckey, "Flag Protection: A Brief History and Summary of Recent Supreme Court Decisions and Proposed Constitutional Amendment," CRS Report 7-5700, January 7, 2009.

61. *U.S. v. Haggerty,* 731 F. Supp. 415 (W.D. Wash. 1990); *U.S. v. Eichman,* 731 F. Supp. 1123 (1990).

62. Robert Corn-Revere, "Implementing a Flag-Desecration Amendment to the U.S. Constitution: An End to the Controversy or a New Beginning?" *First Reports* 6, no.1 (July 2005): 1–61.

63. Ibid.

64. Vastine Davis Platte, "Flag Desecration and Flag Misuse Laws in the United States," Congressional Research Service, 1995.

65. Ibid. Texas did not rescind the statute following *Eichman.*

66. Ibid.

67. *Iowa Code* 718A.1 (1993).

68. *State of Wisconsin v. Janssen,* 580 N.W. 2d 260 (Wis. 1998).

69. Goldstein, *Flag Burning and Free Speech,* 245.

70. Ibid., 249.

71. *Winsness v. Yocum,* 433 F.3d 727 (10th Cir. 2006).

72. *Winsness v. Campell,* 2006 WL 463529 (D. Utah 2006).

73. Peter Wallenstein, *Tell the Court I Love My Wife: Race, Marriage, and Law—An American History* (New York: Palgrave/Macmillan, 2002); Julie Novkov, *Racial Union: Law, Intimacy, and the White State in Alabama, 1865–1954* (Ann Arbor: University of Michigan Press, 2008).

74. Gabriel Chin et al., "Still on the Books: Jim Crow and Segregation Law Fifty Years after *Brown v. Board of Education,*" *Michigan State Law Review,* 2006, 457.

75. *Loving v. Virginia,* 388 U.S. 1 (1967).

76. *U.S. v. Brittain,* 319 F. Supp. 1058 (E.D. Ala. 1970).

77. *Lamont v. Postmaster General,* 381 U.S. 301 (1965).

78. See J. Mitchell Pickerill, "Congressional Responses to Judicial Review," in *Congress and the Constitution,* ed. Neal Devins and Keith E. Whittington (Durham, NC: Duke University Press, 2005) (suggesting that many scholars overlook the distinction between "as applied" and "facial" rulings).

79. Brief of the U.S. Senate in *Immigration and Naturalization Service v. Chadha,* 1981 WL 388494 (1981), 2–3.

80. See generally Laurence H. Tribe, *American Constitutional Law,* 3rd ed., vol. 1, § 2-6 (New York: Foundation Press, 2000).

81. *Immigration and Naturalization Service v. Chadha,* 462 U.S. 919, 967 (1983) (White, J. dissenting). See also James Abourez, "The Congressional Veto: A Contemporary Response to Executive Encroachments on Legislative Prerogative," *Indiana Law Journal* 52 (1977): 323–43.

82. Louis Fisher, "The Legislative Veto: Invalidated, It Survives," in Symposium: Elected Branch Influences in Constitutional Decisionmaking, *Law and Contemporary Problems* 65, no. 4 (1993): 273–92.

83. See also Elizabeth M. Martin, "An Informational Theory of the Legislative Veto," *Journal of Law, Economics, and Organization* 13, no. 2 (1977): 319–43.

84. Fisher, "The Legislative Veto."

85. Louis B. Fisher, "Legislative Vetoes After *Chadha,*" Congressional Research Service Report (on file with author).

86. *U.S. Senate v. Federal Trade Commission,* 463 U.S. 1216 (1983).

87. *Process Gas Consumers Group v. Consumer Energy Council,* 463 U.S. 1215 (1983), *summarily aff'g* 691 F.2d 575 (D.C. Cir., 1982) (en banc), and 673 F.2d 425 (D.C. Cir. 1982).

88. In fact, presidents have since the time of *Chadha* often used "signing statements" when approving legislative vetoes. See Fisher, "The Legislative Veto," 288 (citing President Bush's executive signing statement that the questionable provisions in a bill "constitute legislative vetoes similar to those declared unconstitutional by the Supreme Court in *Chadha.* Accordingly, I will treat them as having no legal force or effect in this or any other legislation in which they appear"). See also Louis Fisher, "Committee Controls of Agency Decisions," Congressional Research Service Report for Congress, 21 (on file with author).

89. Fisher, "The Legislative Veto," 287.

90. Fisher, "Committee Controls," 21.

91. *AFGE v. Pierce,* 697 F.2d 303 (D.C. Cir. 1982) (panel composed of now Justice Ginsburg and Judges Bork and Bazelon).

92. *Hechinger v. Metropolitan Washington Airports Authority,* 36 F.3d 97 (D.C. Cir. 1994).

93. *Metropolitan Washington Airports Authority v. Citizens for the Abatement of Aircraft Noise,* 501 U.S. 252 (1991).

94. *City of Alexandria v. U.S.,* 3 Ct. Cl. 667 (1983).

95. *City of Alexandria v. U.S.,* 737 F.2d 1022 (Fed. Cir. 1984).

96. Fisher, "Committee Controls," 19; Fisher, "After *Chadha,*" 3.

97. Fisher, "Committee Controls," 31.

98. See Martha L. Gibson, "Managing Conflict: The Role of the Legislative Veto in American Foreign Policy," *Polity* 26, no. 3 (1994): 441–72.

99. Michael J. Glennon, "The Good Friday Accords: Legislative Veto by Another Name?" *American Journal of International Law* 83, no. 3 (1989): 544–46.

100. *Burton v. Baker,* 723 F. Supp. 1550 (DDC 1989). See also Cranston v. Rea-

gan, 611 F. Supp. 247 (D.C. D. Ct. 1985) (finding a committee referral provision nonjusticiable).

101. Edward Walsh, "OMB Objection Raises House Panel's Hackles; Administration May Lose Foreign-Aid Option," *Washington Post,* August 13, 1987, A13.

102. Fisher, "After *Chadha."*

103. Abner J. Mikva, "How Well Does Congress Support and Defend the Constitution?" *North Carolina Law Review* 61 (1983): 587.

104. Fisher, "Committee Controls," 19.

105. Seth F. Kreimer, "Exploring the Dark Matter of Judicial Review: A Constitutional Census of the 1990s," *William and Mary Bill of Rights Journal* 5 (1997): 427.

106. Matthew D. Adler, "Judicial Restraint in the Administrative State: Beyond the Countermajoritarian Difficulty," *University of Pennsylvania Law Review* 145 (1997): 759.

107. Ibid.

108. Compare *Clinton v. City of New York,* 524 U.S. 417 (1998), and *Raines v. Byrd,* 521 U.S. 811 (1997).

109. David Glick of Princeton University first recognized that these particular bargains are emblematic of the Coase theorem. See Ronald Coase, "The Problem of Social Cost," *Journal of Law and Economics* 3 (1960): 1.

110. Novkov, *Racial Union.*

111. Paul M. Sniderman and Edward G. Carmines, *Reaching Beyond Race* (Cambridge, MA: Harvard University Press, 1997); Christopher Slobogin and Joseph Schumacher, "Reasonable Expectations of Privacy and Autonomy in Fourth Amendment Cases: An Empirical Look at 'Understandings Recognized and Permitted by Society,'" *Duke Law Journal* 42 (1993): 727–75.

112. Keith E. Whittington, *Constitutional Construction: Divided Powers and Constitutional Meaning* (Cambridge, MA: Harvard University Press, 1999); Tushnet, *Taking the Constitution Away;* Mark A. Graber, "Establishing Judicial Review?" *Political Research Quarterly* 51 (1999): 221–39.

113. See, e.g., Bernard Schwartz, *A Book of Legal Lists: The Best and Worst in American Law, with 150 Court and Judge Trivia Questions* (Oxford: Oxford University Press, 1997); "Top 10 Supreme Court Decisions That Should Be Reversed," *Human Events,* January 17, 2006.

114. *Kelo v. City of New London,* 545 U.S. 469 (2005).

115. *Hawaii Housing Authority v. Midkiff,* 467 U.S. 229 (1984).

116. Mark A. Graber, *Dred Scott and the Problem of Constitutional Evil* (Cambridge: Cambridge University Press, 2006).

117. Compare Daniel A. Farber and Suzanna Sherry, "200,000 Cards of Dimitri Yrasov: Further Reflections on Scholarship and Truth," *Stanford Law Review* 46 (1994): 647.

118. John Hart Ely, *Democracy and Distrust: A Theory of Judicial Review* (Cambridge, MA: Harvard University Press, 1980).

119. Robert A. Dahl, *Preface to Democratic Theory* (New Haven: Yale University Press, 1963).
120. Alexander and Schauer, "Extrajudicial Constitutional Interpretation."
121. J. Mitchell Pickerill, *Constitutional Deliberation in Congress: The Impact of Judicial Review in a Separated System* (Durham, NC: Duke University Press, 2004).

CONCLUSION

1. Jon B. Gould, *Speak No Evil: The Triumph of Hate Speech Regulation* (Chicago: University of Chicago Press, 2005), 175.
2. Some level of blame must also be leveled at the judiciary, for the decisions of the judiciary can sometimes hamper the opportunities for future judicial review. The Court's use of "as applied" rulings rather than "facial" rulings can prevent the judiciary from being able to strike down unconstitutional laws.
3. See Laurence H. Tribe, *American Constitutional Law,* 3rd ed., § 3-14–§ 3-21 (New York: Foundation Press, 2000), 385–464.
4. *Valley Forge College v. Americans United for Separation of Church and State,* 454 U.S. 464 (1982).
5. *Lujan v. Defenders of Wildlife,* 504 U.S. 555, 560–61 (1992).
6. *Raines v. Byrd,* 521 U.S. 811, 819–20 (1997).
7. Gerald H. Rosenberg, *Hollow Hope: Can Courts Bring About Social Change?* (Chicago: University of Chicago Press, 1991).
8. Larry D. Kramer, *The People Themselves: Popular Constitutionalism and Judicial Review* (New York: Oxford University Press, 2004).
9. Louis Fisher, "Judicial Finality or Ongoing Colloquy?" in *Making Policy, Making Law: An Interbranch Perspective,* ed. Mark C. Miller and Jeb Barnes (Washington, DC: Georgetown University Press, 2004); Barry Friedman, "Dialogue and Judicial Review," *Michigan Law Review* 91 (1993): 577; Keith E. Whittington, "Presidential Challenges to Judicial Supremacy and the Politics of Constitutional Meaning," *Polity* 33, no. 3 (2001): 365–95.
10. Cass Sunstein, *One Case at a Time: Judicial Minimalism on the Supreme Court* (Cambridge, MA: Harvard University Press, 2001), 118.
11. Stephen Breyer, *Active Liberty: Interpreting Our Democratic Constitution* (New York: Knopf, 2005).
12. "Transcript: Sen. Specter Discusses Alito Nomination," *Washington Post,* October 31, 2005.
13. See Rosenberg, *Hollow Hope.*
14. Peter Slevin, "Court Battle Likely on Affirmative Action: Michigan Voters Approved Ban, But Opponents of the Measure Persist," *Washington Post,* November 18, 2006, A2.
15. Daniel Lipson, "Embracing Diversity: The Institutionalization of Affirmative Action as Diversity Management at UC-Berkeley, UT-Austin, and UW-Madison," *Law and Social Inquiry* 32, no. 4 (2007): 985–1026.

16. Rosenberg, *Hollow Hope* (school desegregation and abortion); Michael W. McCann, *Rights at Work: Pay Equity Reform and the Politics of Legal Mobilization* (Chicago: University of Chicago Press, 1994) (pay equity); Gould, *Speak No Evil* (hate speech; see also Donald A. Downs, *Restoring Free Speech and Liberty on Campus* [Cambridge: Cambridge University Press, 2005]); L. Timothy Perrin et al., "If It's Broken, Fix It: Moving Beyond the Exclusionary Rule," *Iowa Law Review* 83 (1998): 669, and Myron W. Orfield Jr., "The Exclusionary Rule and Deterrence: An Empirical Study of Chicago," *University of Chicago Law Review* 54 (1987): 1016 (police searches and seizures); Donald Horowitz, *The Courts and Social Policy* (Washington, DC: Brookings Institution Press, 1977) (children's rights); Malcolm Feeley and Edward L. Rubin, *Judicial Policy Making and the Modern State* (Cambridge: Cambridge University Press, 2000) (prison reform).

17. Rosenberg, *Hollow Hope.*

18. McCann, *Rights at Work.*

19. Martin J. Sweet, "Minority Business Enterprise Programmes in the United States of America: An Empirical Investigation," Affirmative Action Symposium, *Journal of Law and Society* 33, no. 1 (2006): 160–80.

20. *Shelley v. Kramer,* 334 U.S. 1 (1948).

21. *Loving v. Virginia,* 388 U.S. 1 (1967).

22. See also Evan Gerstmann, *The Constitutional Underclass: Gays, Lesbians, and the Failure of Class-Based Equal Protection* (Chicago: University of Chicago Press, 1999).

23. *City of Richmond v. J.A. Croson Co.,* 488 U.S. 469, 493 (1989).

24. Horowitz, *The Courts and Social Policy.*

25. *Marbury v. Madison,* 5 U.S. 137 (Cranch 1803).

INDEX

compelling state interest, 34; in *Croson*, 37, 38, 39–44, 98, 171–72, 173; Dade County, Florida, MBE program fails test of, 97; in *Grutter v. Bollinger*, 45; in post-*Croson* cases, 50, 51; requiring achievement of, 172; statistical analyses of, 53. *See also* "narrowly tailored" legislation

Concrete Works of Colorado v. County of Denver (2003), 49–50

Congress: executive branch interests versus those of, 165; Flag Protection Act passed by, 137, 138; House attempts to strip jurisdiction from federal courts in Pledge of Allegiance cases, 135; responses to judicial review, 148–49; special powers under Section 5 of Fourteenth Amendment, 35, 37, 38, 50–51, 73; and standing, 161. *See also* legislative vetoes

Constitution: amending to overturn Supreme Court decisions, 138, 149; Article III, 46, 160; bicameralism and presentment provisions, 145; coordinate construction of, 9–13; dialogue in interpretation of, 23; Fifth Amendment, 45; judicial primacy as especially important in cases of rights, 5, 26, 152–54, 158, 163; knowledge of events surrounding violation of, 19–20, 158; knowledge of one's rights, 20, 158; litigation as typical remedy for violation of, 154; monopolistic interpretation of, 9, 12; persistence of unconstitutional laws, 8, 12, 18, 19, 27–28, 158–63, 168; prioritizing rights over elected branches, 5. *See also* coordinate construction (departmentalization); First Amendment; Fourteenth

Amendment; judicial primacy; judicial review; judicial supremacy

Contract Coordinating Committee (C3) (Portland), 81–83

Contractors' Association of Eastern Pennsylvania, 62

"conversation stoppers," 8, 12

Cooper v. Aaron (1958), 10

coordinate construction (departmentalization), 9–13; and barriers to litigation, 17; checkmate renders it devoid of empirical veracity, 164; on differences between dialogue and monologue, 153; elected branch dominance casts doubt on, 157; reactions to *Croson* lumped together by, 25

Coral Construction Company v. King County (1991), 87

costs: as barrier to litigation, 18, 19, 159–60; courts effectively raise, 52; litigation as not cost-free, 157; of litigation in school prayer cases, 135

County of Washington v. Gunther (1981), 14–15, 170

courts. *See* judiciary

Cubans, 95, 112, 113

Dade County (Florida): black population of, 103; black suburbanization in, 118; general expenditure budget of, 109–10; MBE program in, 96–98, 119; and types of work contracted by City of Miami, 105

Dahl, Robert A., 114

democratic participation, 166–67

desegregation of schools. *See* school desegregation

Deveny, Tyler, 134–35

dialogue literature, 6, 8

direct costs, as barrier to litigation, 18

Gitlow v. New York (1925), 126
Good Friday Accords, 146
Gould, Jon, 125, 128–29, 157
Graber, Mark, 152
Gratz v. Bollinger (2003), 45, 50, 55
Gray, William H., III, 62
Green, William, 61–62, 65
Grutter v. Bollinger (2003), 45–46, 50, 55, 166, 167
Gunther, Gerald, 39

Hamilton, Alexander, 1, 9, 17, 154, 170
Harper, Beverly, 63–64, 192n14
Harvard University, 35
hate speech, 125–31; blocking litigation regarding, 4; as elected branch monologue, 17; standing in cases of, 19; after Supreme Court rulings on, 8, 13, 15, 125. *See also* speech codes
Hawaii Housing Authority v. Midkiff (1984), 152
Hirabayashi v. United States (1943), 36, 177n7
Hispanics: in Dade County, Florida, MBE program, 97; in Miami MBE program, 95, 99, 101, 103–8, 112, 113, 114, 118; in Philadelphia, 62
Humphrey, Hubert, 30

Immigration and Nationality Act, 143–44
impact (gap) studies, 6, 17, 169
INS v. Chadha (1983), 125, 143–45, 147, 153, 156
interest groups: in anti-affirmative action legislation, 3; governmental co-optation of, 22, 23, 24, 54, 77, 88, 150; Philadelphia affirmative action program challenged by, 60; policy advances sought via legislation by, 5; in speech-code litigation, 129–30.

See also Associated General Contractors (AGC)
intermediate scrutiny, 33, 34, 35, 37, 38, 44

Jackson, Andrew, 93
Jackson, Robert H., 4, 126
Jefferson, Thomas, 9, 17, 152–53, 172
Johnson, Lyndon B., 30, 59, 60, 111
Johnson, Texas v. (1989), 125, 136–38, 139, 141–42, 153, 156
Joint Center for Political and Economic Studies, 52
Jones, Virvus, 39
judicial primacy, 23–27, 163–68; for averting elected branch monopoly, 158; as especially important in individual rights, 5, 26, 152–54, 158, 163; on judicial interpretation as omnipresent in constitutional interpretation, 25–26; judicial supremacy contrasted with, 158, 163; for maintaining balance of power, 163, 165; on many voices needed in constitutional dialogue, 167; Miami situation highlights need for, 93; as moderating influence, 165; new concept required, 2; on policymaking as "interactive, sequential, and alternative," 12–13; Portland's unconstitutional affirmative action program as threat to, 91–92; reactions to *Croson* show need for, 25
judicial process scholars, 18, 19
judicial review: barriers to litigation eviscerate, 22; checkmate moves as response to, 4, 9, 23, 26; congressional response to, 148–49; coordinate construction opposed to, 9–13; *Marbury v. Madison* in, 172–73; public law scholars on finality of, 10; some

Marshall, John, 22, 93, 155, 161, 172

Marshall, Thurgood, 35, 39, 44, 51, 159, 188n31

Maryland Minority Contractor's Ass'n, Inc. v. Maryland Stadium Authority (1998), 190n68

Matson v. Multnomah County (1988), 78, 88, 89

MBE. *See* minority business enterprise (MBE) programs

MBEC (Minority Business Enterprise Council) (Philadelphia), 66, 72, 75

McCann, Michael, 16, 170

McConnell, Michael, 140, 141, 142

McCormick Tribune Freedom Museum, 20

McGuire, Kevin, 125, 133

Metro Broadcasting, Inc. v. FCC (1990), 44, 45

Miami, 93–123; airport theft and fraud scheme, 121–22; Community Redevelopment Agency, 120–21; demographics, 57; ethnic make-up, 184n72; governmental system, 57; low volume of city contracts, 109–10; as majority-minority city, 94; minority construction employment, 56; origins of affirmative action in, 94–95; population of Primary Metropolitan Statistical Area, 105; racial segregation in, 117; Teele case, 119–22; white males as percentage of population, 116. *See also* Miami MBE program

Miami-Dade County (Florida). *See* Dade County (Florida)

Miami MBE program: availability of minority contractors, 98, 99, 102–10; avoids litigation, 23, 93–94, 98, 99–100, 109–10, 116–17, 124, 161; certification of businesses,

104; as constitutionally suspect, 98–99, 116; court–elected branch interaction in, 24–25, 116, 118–19, 153; disparity study, 53, 98–99; as effectively abandoned, 100; geography as alternative to race, 117–18; interests served by, 110–16; kinds of work contracted, 104, 105–9; lack of implementation, 23, 24–25, 53, 93–94, 99–100, 101, 109, 110, 116–17, 118, 119; large minority businesses excluded, 95; mixed response to *Croson,* 23, 24–25, 53, 93, 94, 99–102, 109, 118–19; multiple goals of, 109, 111–16; Overtown Franchise program, 117–18; passage, 95; placed under Purchasing Department, 100, 109; sheltered market program, 95, 100; specifics, 95; staff cuts, 101, 109; standing limits judicial review, 25, 94, 169; as too small to challenge, 109–10; why city hasn't dismantled it, 110, 116

Midkiff, Hawaii Housing Authority v. (1984), 152

Minority Business Enterprise Council (MBEC) (Philadelphia), 66, 72, 75

Minority Business Enterprise Legal Defense and Education Fund, 52, 64

minority business enterprise (MBE) programs, 31–32; barriers to entry for minority contractors, 37; cities with, 66; courts as hostile to after *Croson,* 57; *Croson* implicates, 1–3, 16, 155, 184n72; in Dade County, Florida, 96–98, 119; effects of *Croson* decision, 55–57, 170; federal, 30–31; fraud, 67, 122; goals, 111–15; judicial responses to *Croson,* 46–52; legislative responses to *Croson,*

race-based measures (*continued*)
  federal, 45; strict scrutiny for, 45,
  177n7; Supreme Court specifies
  how to establish legal and legitimate, 39–44; tension with equal
  protection guarantee, 36. *See also*
  minority business enterprise (MBE)
  programs
race-neutral measures: in evaluation
  of race-based legislation, 41, 43,
  98; Miami attempts to implement,
  117–18
rational basis review, 33–34
R.A.V. v. City of St. Paul (1992), 8, 15,
  125, 127–28, 153, 156
*Regents of the University of California v.
  Bakke* (1978), 35, 36, 37, 39, 45
Rehnquist, William H.: *Concrete
  Works of Colorado v. County of
  Denver*, 50; *Croson*, 188n31; Roberts
  replaces, 189n57; on standing, 162;
  University of Michigan affirmative
  action cases, 46; *Wygant v. Jackson
  Board of Education*, 35
religious freedom: First Amendment
  on, 131. *See also* school prayer
Rendell, Ed, 68
"representation reinforcement," 152
Richmond (Virginia): African American population, 37; discrimination in construction contracts, 37;
  minority business enterprise (MBE)
  programs, 37, 42. See also *City of
  Richmond v. J.A. Croson Co.* (1989)
rights: as contingent, 153–54; culture of,
  175; judicial primacy as especially important for individual, 5, 26, 152–54,
  158, 163; knowledge of one's, 20, 158
ripeness, as barrier to litigation, 18, 160
*Ritchey Produce Co., Inc. v. Ohio Dept.
  of Adm. Serv.* (1999), 49

Roberts, John, 46, 189n57
Roe v. Wade (1973), 6–7, 13, 16, 57, 167
Rosenberg, Gerald H., 170

saluting the flag, 126, 135
*Santa Fe Independent School District v.
  Doe* (2000), 200n40
Scalia, Antonin, 46, 50, 127, 128,
  188n31
Schauer, Frederick, 11, 153
school desegregation: *Brown v. Board
  of Education*, 7, 14, 15–16, 29–30, 57,
  170; as elected branch monologue,
  17; *Parents Involved in Community
  Schools v. Seattle School District
  No. 1*, 46; segregation remains after
  Supreme Court ruling, 7, 14, 57,
  170, 180n31; Warren Court refuses
  to set specific time frames for, 22
school prayer, 131–35; *Abington Township School District v. Schempp*, 125,
  132, 156; barriers to litigation, 4,
  18, 131, 134–35, 158; continues after
  Supreme Court ban, 7, 13, 125,
  132–33, 156; courts repeatedly strike
  down, 156–57; courts speak with
  uniform voice on, 153; as elected
  branch monologue, 17; *Engel v. Vitale*, 125, 132, 156; litigation, 133–34;
  social costs of litigation, 21, 130, 131,
  134–35; *Wallace v. Jaffree*, 132
scrutiny: degrees of, 33–34, 37; intermediate, 33, 34, 35, 37, 38, 44. *See
  also* strict scrutiny
"separate but equal" doctrine, 7, 29–30
Shelley v. Kramer (1948), 171
sheltered market programs, 31; in
  Miami, 95, 100; in Portland, 84–87,
  90, 91
*Sherbrooke Turf v. Minnesota Depart-
  ment of Transportation* (2003), 50

Constitutionalism
and Democracy

CHRISTINE L. NEMACHECK
Strategic Selection: Presidential Nomination of Supreme Court Justices from Herbert Hoover through George W. Bush

BARRY ALAN SHAIN, ED.
The Nature of Rights at the American Founding and Beyond

MARK C. MILLER
The View of the Courts from the Hill: Interactions between Congress and the Federal Judiciary

AMY STEIGERWALT
Battle over the Bench: Senators, Interest Groups, and Lower Court Confirmations

MARTIN J. SWEET
Merely Judgment: Ignoring, Evading, and Trumping the Supreme Court